LOVE IS;

THE WORLD
OF
STAR TREK

LOVE IS. YOU

BOOKS BY DAVID GERROLD

Non-Fiction

The World of Star Trek

The Trouble With Tribbles

Fiction

Deathbeast

The Flying Sorcerers (with Larry Niven)

The Galactic Whirlpool

The Man Who Folded Himself

Moonstar Odyssey

Space Skimmer

When Harlie Was One

The War Against the Chtorr:
Book I: A Matter for Men
Book II: A Day for Damnation

THE WORLD
OF
STAR TREK™

REVISED EDITION

Written by
David Gerrold
in association with *Starlog* magazine

BLUEJAY BOOKS INC.

Library of Congress Cataloging in Publication Data

Gerrold, David, 1944–
  The World of Star Trek.

1. Star trek (Television program) 2. Star trek (Motion picture) 3. Star trek II, the wrath of Khan (Motion picture) I. Title.
PN1992.77.S73G47 1984   791.45′72   84-9205
ISBN 0-312-94463-2

For Henry and Gail Morrison,
with love

THANK YOU

Dennis Ahrens
Betty Ballantine
Harve Bennett
Stan Burns
William Campbell
Gene L. Coon
James Doohan
Diane Duane
John Dwyer
Irving Feinberg
Dorothy Fontana
Matt Jefferies
DeForest Kelley
Walter Koenig
David McDonnell
Nichelle Nichols
Leonard Nimoy
Fred Phillips
Rita Ratcliffe
Ruth Rigel
Susan Sackett
Tony Sauber
William Shatner
George Takei
Bjo Trimble
Teresa Victor
Linda Wright
Howard Zimmerman

and of course,
Gene Roddenberry

The opinions expressed in this book are the author's and
do not necessarily reflect those of the universe.

THE WORLD
OF
STAR TREK

INTRODUCTION TO THE 1984 EDITION

THE first edition of this book was published in May 1973. Eleven years and ten printing later, I have finally gotten the chance to *finish* this book.

Let me explain that.

The original STAR TREK television series premiered at 8:30, Thursday evening, September 8, 1966, on NBC television.*

At the end of its first two years on NBC, the show was in danger of being cancelled. Its followers—already a growing phenomenon—initiated a letter campaign to the network to persuade them to continue the series. Eventually over a million letters were sent in to NBC, and the series was saved for another year.

Unfortunately the network stuck it into what was probably the worst possible time slot for it: ten P.M., Friday night. At the end of its third year, in spring 1969, STAR TREK was finally cancelled. The network said the ratings were "weak." A total of seventy-nine episodes had been produced.

A few months later, in the fall of that same year, those same seventy-nine hours of STAR TREK were made available by Paramount Studios—through the process of syndication—for rerun on local TV stations across the country. Over a hundred and fifty separate markets purchased the show and scheduled it for airing between the hours of four and seven P.M.—

—where it was discovered by a whole new audience.

---

* I submitted my first outline to the show on the following Monday. Producer Gene L. Coon was impressed enough with that outline to invite me to submit stories for the series' second season. One of those outlines became the episode, "The Trouble with Tribbles." I have been *involved* with STAR TREK ever since. If I had known then. . . .

In fall 1969, the original seventy-nine episodes of the STAR TREK TV-series demonstrated a power to pull ratings that was amazing then—and continues to amaze even today. The show has become one of those *perpetual* TV shows—like "Twilight Zone" and "I Love Lucy." You can always find it somewhere in the *TV Guide*.

That was when the STAR TREK Phenomenon truly began. Like Topsy, it wasn't created, it just grew—often wildly and out of control. It was all the separate pieces—the letter campaigns, the fanzines, the film clips, the conventions—all coming together at once to become something *more*. It was one of the most unusual occurrences in American television history. Never before had a TV series become even more popular *after* its cancellation. And its popularity has *continued* to grow ever since!

STAR TREK's fans have created a vast network of communication. There are countless clubs, newsletters, fanzines—even computer bulletin boards. STAR TREK conventions continue to be held every year—not only in the United States, but in England and Japan and Australia as well.

The first edition of this book was an (admittedly) incomplete attempt to chronicle the birth of the STAR TREK Phenomenon. Not surprisingly, the book became a part of that phenomenon itself, even helping to fuel its growth. Many hundreds of thousands of copies of *The World of Star Trek* have been sold over the past eleven years, because STAR TREK's fans want to get as close to the show as they can.

Even more than that, they want to *be a part* of STAR TREK.

A history of STAR TREK's fans would be a list of enterprising (pun intended) individuals who have built bridge sets, designed blueprints, sewn their own uniforms, written songs and plays, put on conventions, made STAR TREK home-movies or written their own STAR TREK novels. They've published STAR TREK fanzines, drawn cartoons, painted pictures (sometimes wall-size murals), built models, designed new costumes and makeup for convention masquerades, collected filmclips and videotapes and props from the original TV series—not to mention all those who have studied STAR TREK and analyzed it from this position or that.

This then is the essence of the STAR TREK Phenomenon: the fans have claimed the show as their own. They are its caretakers. They are the keepers of the dream.

And that was as much as I had to write about in 1973. The first edition of *The World of Star Trek* was annoyingly incomplete because we still didn't know how it was all going to turn out.

Throughout the seventies, STAR TREK's fans kept the dream alive. They kept asking, "Please, Paramount, can we have some more STAR TREK? A new TV series perhaps? Or even a movie?'' The mail sent to the studio was *unceasing*. Fans circulated the names and addresses of the studio heads and wrote hundreds of letters a month *for years*.

I admit it. Those of us who thought we knew how the film industry worked didn't believe it was possible. After all—nobody had ever revived a cancelled TV series before; not as a series, not as a film. Certainly, it was nice to think about—the *return* of STAR TREK—but those of us who thought we knew, admitted privately that it was probably never going to happen.

Boy, were we wrong!

The journey back has been a peripatetic one, but the faith of the fans has been amply rewarded. STAR TREK has come back, bigger than ever—as *Star Trek: The Motion Picture, Star Trek: The Wrath of Khan,* and *Star Trek: The Search For Spock.* *

So, now—eleven years and ten printings later, I finally get to finish this book. This new updated edition of *The World of Star Trek* allows me to tell you how the STAR TREK Phenomenon *finally* worked out.

I just love a happy ending.

—DAVID GERROLD

---

*At the time of this writing It is still possible that the name of the third STAR TREK movie could be changed before its release.

INTRODUCTION

The World of STAR TREK—

Or should that be the Universe of STAR TREK?

No. World is correct. *World* in the sense of a self-contained reality, an alternate to *this* reality. A universe to match is implied.

Actually, there are three worlds of STAR TREK. First, there's the STAR TREK that Gene Roddenberry conceived—the original dream of a television series about an interstellar starship. Then there's the STAR TREK behind the scenes, how the cast and crew made Gene Roddenberry's ideas come true, how they were realized and sometimes altered in the realization. And finally, there's the STAR TREK Phenomenon, the world that the fans of the show created, the reality that they built in response.

All three of these worlds are fascinating, and all three of them are dealt with in this book. Each of the worlds of STAR TREK created the next; and like interlocking rings, each had its effects on the others. The show created the stars, the stars engendered a fandom, and the fans kept the show on the air.

I've already written one STAR TREK book—it's called *The Trouble With Tribbles*, and it's the story of how I made my first sale to television, and how "The Trouble with Tribbles" episode of STAR TREK was written. This is the second part of that story, *this is the book to place it in context*.

This book is about the STAR TREK myth, what it was and how it happened—the truth behind it. The fascinating part about the myth is that even after you strip away the flackery, the studio puffery and ballyhoo—STAR TREK is *still* a piece of magic. The *Enterprise* and her crew have become a new set of gods in the science fiction pantheon.

xix

So the reason for this book is to try to preserve some of that magic so that years from now some yet unborn "Trekkie*" may open it up and be able to recapture at least a hint of STAR TREK's magic seasons.

---

*Yes, I know. There are some STAR TREK fans who object to the word "Trekkie," preferring instead to call themselves "Trekkers." I've heard the arguments on both sides—the best I can tell you is that both terms are used to describe people who like STAR TREK a lot. (Of course, STAR TREK fans don't just *like* STAR TREK—they *love* STAR TREK. I'm reminded of the lady who loved pancakes: "You must come visit sometime, I've got closets full!")

PART ONE

The First World
of STAR TREK—
Gene Roddenberry's Dream

FIRST, there was Gene Roddenberry's dream, a television show called "STAR TREK."

The idea was described as "Wagon Train to the Stars," or "Hornblower in Space"—the adventures of a far-traveling starship and her crew.

Perhaps the best description of the show is in the lines spoken at the beginning of every episode:

"Space—the final frontier. These are the voyages of the starship *Enterprise*, her five-year mission to explore strange new worlds, to seek out new life and new civilization, to boldly go where no man has gone before."

Or, more exactly, from *The Star Trek Guide**:

(Excerpted from orders to Captain James T. Kirk)
III. You are therefore posted, effective immediately, to command the following: The U.S.S. ENTERPRISE.

Cruiser Class—Gross 190,000 tons

**The Star Trek Guide* (in its earliest form) was a twenty-page mimeographed book distributed to all writers and prospective writers for the series. It contained descriptions of all the characters and sets as well as notes on the capabilities of the *Enterprise* and what kind of stories the series could use.

It was revised twice as the show progressed. New material was added and old material was updated. In the third edition, for instance, the *Enterprise* was upgraded from Cruiser Class to Starship Class—the feeling being that a "starship" was a special kind of vessel with greater range, speed, power and other capabilities than other vessels in space. Much of this material was reprinted in Stephen Whitfield and Gene Roddenberry's *The Making of Star Trek*.

Crew Complement—430 persons
Drive—space-warp
Range—18 years at light-year velocity
Registry—Earth, United Space Ship

IV. Nature and duration of mission:

Galaxy exploration and investigation:
    5 years

V. Where possible, you will confine your landings and contacts to Class
"M" planets approximating Earth-Mars conditions.

VI. You will conduct this patrol to accomplish primarily:
(a) Earth security, via explorations of intelligence and social sys-
    temscapable of galaxial threat, and
(b) Scientific investigation to add to the Earth's body of knowl-
    edge of alien life forms and social systems, and
(c) Any required assistance to the several Earth colonies in your
    quadrant, and the enforcement of appropriate statues affecting
    such Federated commerce vessels and traders as you may
    contact in the course of your mission.

In sum—"Hornblower in Space." Just as Captain Horatio Hornblower was
the highest representative of English law in the far waters in which he sailed,
so would Captain James T. Kirk of the *Enterprise* be the highest legal representative of Starfleet Command in the far reaches of the galaxy.

He would be explorer, ambassador, soldier, and peacekeeper. He would
be the sole arbiter of Federation law wherever he traveled—he would be a
law unto himself.

The implication here is that *there are no other channels of interstellar
communication*. At least, none as fast as the *Enterprise*.

Let's examine this for a moment, because it's essential to understanding
the STAR TREK format. Captain Kirk is an autonomous power. Purely from a
television point of view, he *must* be an autonomous power—otherwise the
series lacks drama and he lacks interest. If Kirk could check back with Starfleet
Command every time he was in trouble, he would never have any conflicts
at all. He would simply be a crewman following orders. He wouldn't be an
explorer or an ambassador at all—just the Captain of the local gunboat on
the scene.

For Kirk to be a dramatic and interesting human being, he must be wholly responsible for his own actions as a representative of the Federation. As such, every decision he has to make becomes an important one.

Fortunately, the exigencies of space travel—especially faster-than-light travel—support this kind of dramatic concept.

We must make one assumption, though—that faster-than-light travel is possible. This is the basic assumption of STAR TREK: that man *can* reach the stars. It is the only assumption we need to make, but it is the hook on which the whole series (and much of science fiction, in general) hangs. Without faster-than-light travel, we are stuck in our own solar system—and that's too much of a limitation for our storytellers. Why should we deny ourselves a background as broad and irresistible as a whole galaxy—or a universe?

Science fiction is the contemporary fairy tale, it's the twentieth-century morality play. At its worst, it's merely romantic escapism; but at its best, it is the postulation of an alternate reality with which to contemplate this one. Strictly from a dramatic point of view, we *need* the assumption of faster-than-light velocities. It is as necessary to the genre as the assumption that miracles can happen is necessary to the artistic success of a medieval religious pageant. (In either case, the implication is optimism about the workings of the universe.)

Despite the fact that almost everything we know about the workings of the universe suggests that it is impossible to achieve the speed of light or velocities faster than that, we can still make the assumption. We are violating Einstein's Theory of Relativity, as well as the vast body of scientific knowledge that backs it up, but we *can* make the assumption. Not just for dramatic reasons, but for scientific ones as well.

You see, if it *is* possible to travel faster than light, the method will not be discovered by anyone who has already decided that it is impossible. Rather, the discovery will require a man who assumes that it *is* possible, and who will speculate at length on the conditions necessary to achieve such. In fact, this is how the hypothesis of the tachyon was arrived at—a tachyon, *if it exists,* is a particle that cannot travel at leass than the speed of light, only faster. If tachyons can now be proven to exist, then we will know that faster-than-light travel *is* possible. So, the assumption is not so outrageous as some science purists might insist.

STAR TREK postulates an alternate reality where faster-than-light travel is an established fact. Granted this one assumption, we can then proceed to establish the nature of an interstellar society. One of the things we must know is the nature and quality of that society's communications.

Given the STAR TREK format, given the workings of the universe derived from the one basic assumption that we have to make, we can establish that there are only four possible channels of communication between the planets of different stars.

Three of them are impractical.

If we examine them all, we'll see why they're impractical. And also, we'll see why Captain James T. Kirk can't help but be an autonomous power.

The first method of communication, of course, is radio. Or television. Or modulated laser beams. Or any kind of wave modulation that travels exactly at the speed of light. Obviously, if the speed of light limits our spaceships, it also limits our radios.

The nearest star to our own sun, Sol, is Proxima Centauri. It's 4.3 light-years away—that means that light, traveling at slightly more than 186,000 miles *per second*, will still take four and one third years to get there. *Any* quantity traveling at the speed of light will take that long. And that's assuming the signal was still strong enough to be detected when it arrived. (Even a pencil-thin laser beam will spread, when projected from the Earth to the moon, to cover an area more than a half-mile in diameter. And that's only to the moon. How far is it to Proxima Centauri?)

No, the reason why we can't use radio or light waves is that they're self-limiting. The key word is *limit*. Hang on a minute and you'll see.

STAR TREK *almost* got around this. The TV series postulated a "subspace radio." While this was never explained in detail, the implication was that this was a method of communication much faster than light, *but still not instantaneous*.

A message to Starfleet Command sent by subspace radio might take several hours or days. Beyond that, either the time lag was too great or the *Enterprise* was out of range. The answer was too slow in coming.

This is the same limitation as with radio waves—only the scale is different.

When you are thinking in terms of interstellar distances, there is no such thing as a small number. Even the small numbers are big ones. If your subspace radio is not instantaneous, if it functions at a measurable speed, *then that speed is its limit*. And no matter how fast it is, the distances of the galaxy are still vast enough to make that speed seem insignificant. The point can be reached where, even if your ship is not yet out of range, a dialogue still becomes impossible. Given enough distance, even the smallest time lag will magnify eventually.

Let's try another.

The third method of interstellar communication involves the use of robot-torpedoes; that is, unmanned faster-than-light ships, guided by inboard computers. They would be launched from one planet to deliver a message to another, light-years away. The torpedoes would not be spaceships per se; rather, they would be propulsion units, guidance system and payload only. There would be no life-support capabilities at all.

As couriers, these torpedoes would be as fast as their propulsion systems would allow; at least as fast, probably faster, than comparable manned ships.

This particular channel of communication was never used or shown on STAR TREK—but given the technology that could design and build a starship *Enterprise*, the capability to build robot-torpedoes as well also had to be there.

The use of such torpedoes would be highly practical for planet-to-planet communication. A robot can deliver mail just as easily as a manned ship.

On the other hand, the torpedo would be almost completely *im*practical for ship-to-planet or planet-to-ship communications. (How does a preprogrammed torpedo find an unprogrammed ship?) From the dramatic standpoint alone, the faster-than-light torpedo is as impractical as the radio and the subspace radio. There is still a time lag.

The torpedo is just an interstellar carrier pigeon. Like the other two methods, it can deliver a message or it can send one—but it cannot serve as the vehicle for a dialogue. And a dialogue is *precisely* the kind of interstellar communication that we are looking for. A *dramatic* story requires it.

If there were an instantaneous communication channel available, then a ship like the *Enterprise* would be unnecessary and her mission redundant. Obviously, there is no such instantaneous channel—at least, not in the STAR TREK universe. The existence of the *Enterprise* proves it.

You see, the *Enterprise* is the fourth method of interstellar communication. It is the only practical vehicle of interstellar *dialogue* between two far removed existences—and as such, it is the one we are primarily interested in as a basis for stories about divergent planetary cultures clashing with one another.

The situation of this interstellar society is almost exactly analogous to the Earth of the eighteenth century. Then too, communications over vast distances were slow and uncertain. The arrival of a courier was always an event. Even if the news he was carrying was several weeks, months, or years old, it was still the most recent news available.

When one government had to deal with another, they used diplomatic notes and couriers—and in matters of highest policy, they depended upon their ambassadors. Because communications were so slow, an ambassador could be a particularly important individual. He was the arm and authority of his government. He was its voice. He was the man who determined and enacted the policies of his nation with regard to his specific area of authority.

Likewise, the Captain of the *Enterprise* must be just such an ambassador. He will be a minister with a portfolio of his own making. Carefully briefed as to Starfleet's goals and policies, it will be his responsibility to interpret them and act in the wide variety of situations he will confront. He is a piece of Starfleet itself. He is the piece entrusted with the mission of conducting the "interstellar dialogue."

Now, let's translate that into television.

A successful dramatic television series needs (a) a broad-based format about (b) an interesting individual or group of individuals whose responsibilities force them into (c) unusual situations and confrontations, requiring (d) decisive and positive action on the part of the protagonist and his cohorts.

Any successful dramatic series will fulfill these requirements. The *better* it fulfils them, the more likely it is to be a success.

Let's define our terms here:

Dramatic: synonymous with conflict. A confrontation is implied. The story is man against _____. (Fill in the blank.) Man against man, man against nature, man against himself. The protagonist, or hero, is prevented from reaching his goal by an obstacle or series of obstacles. The more difficult these obstacles are, the more heroic he has to be in order to overcome them. How he overcomes them tells us what kind of a person he is.

The story is told as a series of climaxes rising in intensity, each more exciting than the one before. Every climax involves a confrontation with an obstacle, until the final climax when either the obstacle or the hero is defeated.

In drama *other* than series television—say, a play or a movie—the event that is being told is the most important event in the hero's life. It is the whole reason for the existence of a story about this person. We are not interested in Robinson Crusoe *after* he's rescued; we don't care about Dr. Frankenstein after the monster has been killed; we are through with Robert Armstrong after *King Kong* topples from the Empire State Building. Only the final confrontation is important—and what the hero learns from it.

What the hero learns from the event is what makes it the most important event in his life. The hero *must learn something*. (Or *fail* to learn something, but in that case, the audience has to recognize that he has failed.) Scarlett O'Hara learns that she really does love Rhett Butler. Dorothy learns that you need brains, a heart, and courage, and that it's inside you all the time or you never had it at all. Ryan O'Neal learns that Being in Love Means Never Having to Say You're Sorry.

The story is about the lesson that this person has to learn—and these are the events that teach it to him. Hamlet learns how to make a decision. Oedipus learns humility.

This is the point of *all* drama. It is the sole justification for any play——except on series television.

Or for that matter, in any kind of a series. Whether it be Doc Savage, Tarzan, Sherlock Holmes, or James Bond.

In a series the form has to be turned upside down—the events depicted must *not* be the most important events in the hero's life. Otherwise, there's no point in going on with the series. Everything after that would be anticlimactic.

This is the dilemma of series television. On the one hand, the producer must present dramatic stories week after week—on the other, he must not be *too* dramatic. Otherwise, he damages the series as a whole, ending up with a cumulative body of work that is essentially *melodramatic*. And then the ho-hum reaction sets in. Thus, the television producer's problem becomes one of how to tell exciting stories week after week without descending into melodrama.

The single dramatic element which provokes excitement in a play is this: *your identity is in danger*. All others are merely variations: your life is in danger, your country is in danger, your girl friend might leave you, your wife might find out, your brother might die, the police might catch you. Something threatens to prevent you from being the person you already are or want to be. This is the hero's problem and we identify with him. He copes with it and learns something about his identity and why it's so precious to him. The audience identifies with him and his problem and learns something too.

But if you endanger the hero's identity week after week on a TV series, not only do you run the risk of melodrama—you also run the risk of falling into a formula kind of storytelling. This week Kirk is menaced by the jello monster, he kills it by freezing it to death; next week Kirk is menaced by the slime monster and kills it by drying it out; the week after that he is threatened by the mud monster and defeats it by watering it down; the following week Kirk meets the mucous monster . . . Again, the ho-hum reaction. Or even the ha-ha reaction.

Fortunately for the dramatic arts, the number of possible identities and the number of ways of endangering them is unlimited. And therein lies part of the answer to the TV producer's problem.

You don't have to endanger *the hero* every week. You can endanger someone else, someone around him—and it is his responsibility to come to that person's aid. If he incidentally has to endanger himself in the process, so much the better. The result is a semi-anthology format, and it is the only way possible in which to avoid falling into the trap of doing formula stories.

Thus, a good series format should be one which allows its hero to be primarily a decision-maker, especially as concerns other people's lives. Of course, the decisions can *and should* hurt. (That makes them *tough* decisions.) The requirements of television also necessitate a certain amount of excitement and danger—so that if there is not true drama (i.e., identity-danger) there is at least a passable imitation of same.

This is the reason why there are so many doctors, cops, cowboys, and private eyes on television. Also spies and lawyers. (And variations thereof.) These are the professions that fill the needs of series television exactly. Each of them revolves around a human identity that provides services to other human identities, thus the hero *has* to be involved with other people—and due to the nature of the services he is providing, the people are generally caught in tense and dramatic situations. The hero will have to make decisions that will affect their lives. And sometimes his own life will be endangered in the process.

The number of professions that lend themselves to excitement and danger is not all that limited—but the number of *genres* that provide a broad background to play a multitude of stories against *is* limited. How many *different* stories can you tell about a fellow who puts out oil-well fires for a living?

The number of genres suitable or practical for television is small. Despite thirty years of experimentation (and sixty years of film history before that) the field remains remarkably limited: cowboys, cops, doctors, and soap operas.

Science fiction, as a genre, has had a singularly unhappy representation on American video. The few *true* science fiction TV series that have managed to have any impact at all have been primarily anthology-type series, like Rod Serling's *Twilight Zone*. A series about a set of continuing characters had never quite made it on American network television—until STAR TREK.

But STAR TREK was a genre unto itself. And it opened a whole new range of possibilities for the television series.

A galaxy is an unlimited background. In it a writer can postulate any kind of individual and any number of ways of endangering his identity. Captain Kirk, as representative-at-large for Starfleet Command, is the perfect hero. The viewer identifies with Kirk and his commitment to fulfil the duties of a Starfleet Captain. The viewer also identifies with those around him whose identities are endangered. If in helping them, Kirk is *occasionally* endangered himself, the viewer's excitement is increased. (The viewer's excitement can be increased by this trick only so many times. If Kirk *persists* in placing himself in danger, we begin to question his credibility as a Starfleet Captain.*)

Kirk is the Captain of a mighty starship. He commands a crew of 430 persons. He is the highest Starfleet authority in the quadrant.† And his responsibilities are manifold—to himself, to his ship, to his crew, to his mission, and to the government that commissioned him.

He is interesting because he is a decider. A Captain's job is *to make decisions.*

A Captain is not a scientist, not an explorer, not a soldier, not a policeman. He can easily add a specialist to his crew to handle any of those jobs—and handle them better than he could. These things are only a small part of his responsibility. His real job is to be the executive decision-maker, to decide what research is of primary importance for the scientists to consider, to decide what planets should be explored for their resources and civilizations, to decide when and where a military operation is necessary, to determine which laws should be enforced and how. And once those decisions are made, it is for his crew to implement them; their jobs are to execute the orders that are given them.

Thus, the true function of a Captain is to *lead* a team; he must know how to delegate authority to those best able to handle the specific tasks at hand. Considering Captain Kirk in particular, we must refer again to the *Star Trek Guide:*

> "With the starship out of communication with Starfleet bases for long periods of time, a starship captain has unusually broad powers over both the lives and welfare of his crew, as well as over Earth people and activities encountered during these voyages. Kirk feels this responsibility strongly *and is fully capable of letting the worry and frustration lead him into error.*"

That last sentence (the italics are *not* mine) is especially important. Obviously it was realized quite early in the conception of the series that Captain

---

*It is by a character's actions that we discover what kind of a person he is. If a person hedges in a clinch, we will think him unsure and uncertain. If he does a foolhardy action, we might consider him a decisive risk-taker; but if he makes a habit of it, we will know him for a crazy fool. If his actions are all reflexes without thought, he becomes a stereotype, a cardboard puppet that the writer is arbitrarily moving around. It is only by variation that a character comes alive; the more varied his actions, the more depth he has dramatically.

†A large big space, one-fourth of a larger, bigger space.

Kirk would have to be aware of himself and his duties—and that he would
be very much affected by the decisions he would have to make.

Otherwise, he simply would not be a very interesting human being.

And it's human beings that we're primarily interested in. Captain Kirk
should worry—that's what distinguishes him from an android. The viewers
will identify with his concern for others.

It is Captain Kirk's concern that makes the story important. If a decision
is less than crucial, it can be made by a subordinate officer. Only the crucial
decisions will be passed up to the Captain. And if it isn't important enough
to make him sweat, then it's not worth telling a story about.

Thus STAR TREK neatly fulfils all of the requirements for a good TV series:
a broad-based format allowing a wide variety of stories, an interesting hero,
an unusual set of situations and confrontations, and the requirement of decisive and positive action from a protagonist whose job and training is to do
just that.

Plus, STAR TREK has that one added virtue mentioned before—it is a genre
unto itself. And that makes it unique.

Let's consider some specifics now. We'll start with the crew of the
Enterprise.

To make good decisions, a Captain needs good advisors. Good decisions
can be made only when *all* the facts can be considered. A Captain needs
advisors who are experts in the many fields he will have to deal with.

Aboard a ship like the *Enterprise*, one of the most important officers would
be the Science Officer. If the *Enterprise* had been purely a military vessel,
this would not be so. In that case, military advisors would have outweighed
science officers.

But because the *Enterprise*'s mission is the exploration of new worlds, the
Science Officer is second in importance only to the Captain.

"His bridge position is at the library-computer station which links the
bridge to the vessel's intricate brain, a highly sophisticated and advanced
computer which connects all stations of the ship, collects information,
makes computations, and provides information. While personnel at other
posts can feed in or extract information relating to their specific duties,
the Science Officer from his central panel can tap the resources of the
entire system—including a vast micro-library on man's history, arts,
sciences, philosophy, including all known information on other solar
systems, Earth colonies, alien civilizations, a registry of all space ves-

Interstellar communication: Uhura at her console

Kirk entertains an Andorian diplomat

Captain James T. Kirk

Science Officer Spock

Dr. McCoy

The Captain and his officers: Scott, Spock, McCoy, Uhura, and Chekov

Christine Chapel with Mr. Spock

A Klingon battlecruiser

Kor, leader of the Klingon occupation force on Organia

A Klingon captain and his crew: "Day of the Dove"

"Balance of Terror"

A Romulan fleet commander

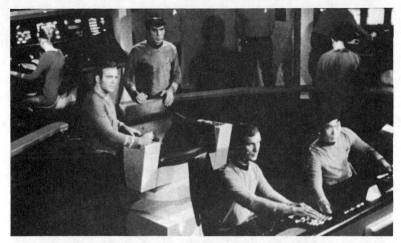

The bridge of the *Enterprise*

Everybody falls out of their chairs...

...and they all fall down again.

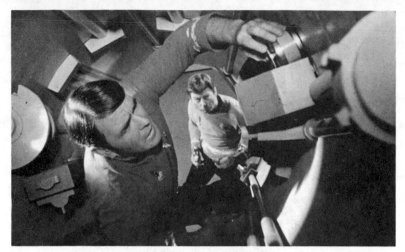

Scotty and McCoy resort to the Jefferies Tube

Wasted space: the engine room

Sick bay

sels in existence, personnel information on any member of the U.S.S. *Enterprise,* or almost anything else needed in any of our stories.''

Those are the requirements of the job—now who is the best man to fill it?

From a dramatic consideration alone, he must be an interesting person. Just as the Captain must be the man who will be most affected by his responsibilities, so must every other character in the story be an individual who is aware of the conflicts in which his job places him. (This is a series we're talking about—we don't have just one hero, we must have a set of heroes.)

The Science Officer must be able to correlate vast amounts of information presented very rapidly and synthesize accurate summaries for his Captain. This demands a being of superior mental prowess, either human or otherwise.

STAR TREK postulated an alien race called Vulcans—originally from the planet Vulcanis, but this was later shortened to Vulcan.

Physically, Vulcans resembled human beings—except that they had pointed ears and arched eyebrows. Their skin had a distinct yellowish tinge*—but that's because their blood was green, it was copper-based. (Instead of iron-based as in human beings.) They were capable of great feats of physical and mental prowess, and they had unique powers of telepathy: the Vulcan mind-meld allowed a Vulcan to enter into another being's thoughts. The Vulcan nerve-pinch could be used to momentarily stun a human being (and probably a Vulcan as well. After all, how would a culture develop such a weapon if it didn't work on its own kind?)†

Most importantly, the Vulcan culture placed a great premium on rationality. Open displays of emotion were worse than gauche—they were savage. Barbaric. An unpleasant reminder of the animal origins of every Vulcan. The bestiality of the Vulcan heart had to be stifled.

Vulcans were consciously trying to forget their past—or at least, live it down. According to STAR TREK episode ''All Our Yesterdays'' written by Jean Lissette Aroeste, Vulcan had had a long and savage history, with wars much

---

*Actually Spock started out with reddish skin, but the makeup tests on almost all colors, while okay for color broadcast, made him look as if he was wearing phony makeup on black & white TV. Therefore it was decided to use the yellowish hue. It was the local station mixers who made Spoke look green on some sets. In another color freakout, the green command level shirts never looked green on the color TV screen, but rather a kind of gold.

†The Vulcan mind-meld required the Vulcan to be in physical contact, or at most, only a short distance away from the being with whom they were in telepathic touch. The farther away, the less clear and distinct the impressions received.

more vicious and destructive than anything that has ever been experienced on Earth.*

The Vulcan culture finally rejected its savage heritage—rejected it so thoroughly that they rejected anything that smacked of it as well. Wars are emotional experiences that stem from individuals and groups of individuals and nations acting irrationally, reacting with their adrenals instead of their brains. In rejecting war and savagery, Vulcans were forced to also reject emotions.

Just as Freedom and Opportunity are the spoken goals of most Earth cultures, so did Rationality and Logic become the keystones of the Vulcan culture. Vulcans carefully bred emotionality out of themselves. They conditioned themselves and their children to be logical. They consciously altered the direction of their evolution.

The result is the supra-rational Vulcan society that produced the First Officer of the starship *Enterprise*, Mr. Spock.

Spock's father was a Vulcan who married an Earthwoman, because "it seemed the logical thing to do." It was never stated whether there were any other offspring to this union, but if so, they would also be half-human, half-Vulcan, like Spock, and prey to the same internal conflicts.†

The half-and-half nature of Spock's persona is part of what makes him such an interesting character. There is too much Earthman in him for him to be completely Vulcan, and there is much too much Vulcan in him for him to even try to be human.

Spock was raised on Vulcan, consequently he thinks like a Vulcan. More importantly, he thinks of himself *as* a Vulcan—not a human being, not even a half-breed, but a *Vulcan*. He shows pride only in his Vulcan heritage, he almost flaunts his Vulcan rationality and inherent superiority to emotional human beings. He is ashamed of his human inheritance. He tries to hide it as a weakness, as one would be ashamed of the great-uncle who was hung as a horse thief. Thus, Spock is ashamed of the fact that he has feelings. (An interesting paradox, that.) He tries to pretend he doesn't, or that he has them strictly under control, but occasionally we see that this just isn't so.

From a dramatic point of view, Spock is a beautiful character—he is the

---

*A fact that I fervently hope will remain true.

†Dorothy Fontana, story editor for STAR TREK's first two seasons, as well as author of the script "Journey to Babel" in which Spock's parents were introduced, comments thusly: "To stamp out all the obvious stories in which half a horde of Spockian brothers, sisters, half-brothers and half-sisters showed up, I arbitrarily decreed he had no other siblings. And, in my own mind, this vastly strengthened the drama in the conflict between Spock and his father in 'Journey to Babel.' "

perfect character to be the ship's Science Officer. His superior brain powers give him the ability to accurately handle the large amounts of information that are his responsibility. But the fact that he is the only Vulcan on an all-human ship sets up a host of internal pressures and conflicts. All around him are individuals flaunting their emotions—a disgusting display of fears, prejudices, loyalties, and friendships. While the human part of him wants to react to this and yearns to express itself too, the Vulcan half must keep a continual tight control.

His job as Science Officer aboard the *Enterprise* is probably one of the most difficult tasks he could be assigned. As such, it forces him to continually reexamine his own identity; but it also provides him with an unparalleled opportunity to exercise his intellectual capacities. So if Mr. Spock suffered the need to feel at home anywhere, the *Enterprise* would probably be it.

Captain Kirk's second advisor—one who is every bit as important as Mr. Spock—is Dr. McCoy, the ship's Medical Officer.

In many respects, Dr. McCoy is diametrically the opposite of Spock. Just as Spock is responsible for the ship's "mind," McCoy is responsible for its "body."

McCoy cares about the people he treats—he cares about them as individuals and he treats them as such. He is very much an emotional being—not simply that he expresses his emotions, but that he recognizes that there are fundamental biological, physical, and mental reasons for the existence of emotions. Probably he feels that Spock is somehow incomplete because the Vulcan deliberately suppresses even those feelings he does experience.

To McCoy, Spock is a bit of a neurotic—the annoying kind, the one who brags about his neurosis as a strength. To Spock, McCoy is also an annoyance because of his unscientific demeanor. McCoy not only is not logical, he doesn't even *care* about logic.

The doctor realizes that people *aren't* logical, never were meant to be, so why worry about logic at all? Because of this, he is the most outspoken officer aboard the *Enterprise*.

And, just as Captain Kirk and Mr. Spock would seem to be the perfect dramatic entities for their responsibilities, so is Dr. McCoy. Because one of the worst failings a doctor can have *is to have feelings*.

A doctor has to be callous. Really. Given the amount of suffering that he will have to deal with, he can't allow himself to care about his patients as individuals—that would mean taking on their pain and sickness as his own. Even the best of doctors will not be able to save all of his patients; many of them will die. A doctor, in order to preserve his own sanity, has to think of them as anything but human beings. How many friends can you lose—especially when it is your responsibility to save them—and still continue to function rationally?

Granted that future science and technology will provide fantastic advances in medicine. Granted that doctors will be better trained and better equipped. But planetary exploration will still be a dangerous business and men will be encountering threats and menaces that will be totally unfamiliar. A ship's doctor is going to be continually reminded that all of the people around him are mortal. For his own sake, he had better not get too close to them.

And yet, McCoy is a man with emotions—he wants to feel for other human beings. He wants to, but he must not.

Understand the contrast here: Spock prefers logic over emotions. McCoy prefers emotions over logic. But each is in a position where they must stifle part of who they are in order to fulfil their duties aboard the ship. Spock is continually reminded of his own emotionality and McCoy is continually forced to reject his.

Perhaps each of these characters recognizes the dilemma that the other is in, and more than anything else, this could be the reason for the unspoken affinity between them—the mutual shock of recognition in a topsy-turvy mirror.

They are united also by a deep-seated regard for the Captain. And make no mistake, Spock does indeed have strong feelings of loyalty and respect for Kirk. The Vulcan betrays himself in this respect time and time again. For McCoy, of course, his relationship with the Captain is one of deep affection and warmth—an old, tried friendship.

In another respect, McCoy and Spock are symbolic opposites.

Remember that Captain Kirk's job is to be a decider. These two are his chief advisors. As such, they will represent the two aspects of every decision he will have to make—especially the difficult ones that will affect other people's lives.

As advisors, each of them will express his opinions; but their opinions will not only be derived from the nature of their jobs, they will be colored by who they are as individuals. Spock represents Rationality, McCoy represents Compassion. Thus, the two of them are more than just characters aboard the *Enterprise;* they symbolize Captain Kirk's internal dilemmas. The two of them serve to verbalize the arguments that the Captain must consider. Because we cannot get into the Captain's head to hear what he is thinking, Spock and McCoy are doubly important to the series' ability to tell its stories well—*it is primarily through them that Kirk's internal conflicts can be dramatized.*

*   *   *

The symbolism can be extended into the other crew members of the *Enterprise*:

Lieutenant Uhura represents the ship's ability to communicate. Mr. Scott represents the ability to take action once a decision has been made. Mr. Sulu, as helmsman, is the tool of that action. Ensign Chekov, as a Kirk-in-training, represents the next generation of command that must be raised to understand its responsibilities.

Actually, it is not the characters themselves that represent these elements, it is their jobs as crew members. Think of the starship as a living being itself, a single entity of which her human complement is merely the equivalent of individual cells within a body. These are the pieces of the *Enterprise*'s *soma*.

Like any living creature, she needs judgment centers—a Captain; centers of rationale and emotion; organs of communication and action. It is not the personalities of the individuals that establish these symbolisms; rather these are the basic conditions of intelligent life. The people who execute these functions for the living *Enterprise* become symbols of these conditions not because of any inherent personal distinguishment, but because it is the nature of the jobs that they have assumed.

It doesn't have to be Captain Kirk at the helm, or Mr. Spock at the library-computer station. It could just as easily be Captain McGillicuddy and Mr. McGuffin. Or Captain Klutz and Mr. Cool. Anyone. It doesn't matter.

The situations they will find themselves in will remain very much the same, will call for specific patterns of response from each position, and will be precisely tailored *to test each individual the most*.

The responsibilities of Captainhood are such that whoever were to be commissioned to the helm would feel the same self-doubts in the equivalent situations. If not, then he'd be neither *human* nor interesting. And if he's not interesting, then the writers—the good ones, anyway—will tell their stories about someone else. Any writer who hacks out an adventure in which the hero *isn't emotionally involved* is not only a bad writer, he's cheating his audience.

This analysis of STAR TREK is based on the (unlikely) assumption that the full measure of creative ability can be brought to every aspect of the series' production. (We *will* deal with this later.) Purely in terms of story, however, the key word is *human*.

We are all human beings.

At the moment, we are *only* human beings. There are no other intelligences or entities with which we can establish dialogues.

As human beings, we are self-centered. It is a natural human trait, common to all of us. We like nothing more than to see ourselves in mirrors—especially the kind of mirrors that distort us, or show us the backs of our heads, or make us look prettier than we really are. And this is reflected in our arts.

Our drama is oriented to the study of man and the human experience—what it means to *be* a human being. Human beings don't come with instruction books, and we have to learn who we are every step of the way. We gaze into the mirror of drama not just because we want to be entertained, but because we want to get closer to other people by sharing a piece of their lives—and by learning about others, we hope to learn more about ourselves. We are delighted when we can gain a piece of new insight. We treasure it and cherish it as a piece of wisdom—and polish it so frequently that we reduce it to cliche. (Given enough time, all of the world's great wisdom will be expressed in cliches.) But this is the highest mark of success that an idea can achieve—to become so familiar to all men that it becomes a shorthand statement for a whole experience.

Whether a story is true drama or merely hackwork melodrama, our reasons for being interested in it remain the same—we are interested in ourselves and how *we* would react in a similar situation. Hence, we look for interesting and unusual situations in our drama, puzzles and exercises with which to test ourselves, problems against which we can measure the strength of our own identities.

We want to be as brave as our Captain Kirks, as cool as our Mr. Spocks, and as outspoken as our Dr. McCoys. We long to be as colorful and as larger-than-life as they are. But failing that—being trapped into a nine-to-five, consume or be consumed existence—we have to let our actors and writers provide these dreams for us vicariously. We will content ourselves with just *identifying* with Captain Kirk and Mr. Spock and Dr. McCoy. If we can't *be* them, well, we can still *dream* about being them.

The other characters in the series, Mr. Scott, Mr. Sulu, Mr. Chekov, Nurse Chapel and Lieutenant Uhura were not as fully developed as the three major leads.

This is not to say that they were not important to the series—they were very important—but they were never treated with the same depth of feeling. We rarely, if ever, were allowed to see if any of these individuals had any *inner* conflicts.

It was as if Kirk, Spock, and McCoy were consciously designed to be the most dramatic possible individuals for their responsibilities, while the others were merely individuals assigned to their specific jobs without much regard for any inherent dramatic conflicts. Scotty was known to love his engines, Uhura liked to sing in her off-hours, Sulu was a hobbyist, a botanist as well as a swordsman, Chekov showed great pride in being Russian, and Nurse Chapel had a crush on Spock. Period.

In *The Star Trek Guide,* each is treated with only a paragraph or two of personal description—but the descriptions are all of surface characteristics. We are not told what *drives* any of these people. We don't know what they think about, or what they fear. There simply hasn't been enough presented to let us picture these individuals as fully rounded people.

Of course, things were developed for each of these characters in the course of the series, but too often this was only the result of specific story needs. Attempts to redefine (or maybe just define in the first place) the subordinate characters *as human beings* were minimal. There were too many other things to be worried about in the hectic production schedule.

A great deal of this stems from the exigencies of television production and the basic series format. Subordinate characters are meant to be just that— *subordinate.* They are supposed to do their jobs, support the main characters, and be otherwise unnoticeable. They are not to detract from the story. They are never to be treated as if they were a main focus of an episode—there are usually only two focuses; the regular star and the guest star.

If a subordinate character starts becoming too important, the impact of the series is changed. And this is dangerous, because it's equivalent to changing the series itself into a whole new concept. A series is designed to appeal to a specific audience; if you change too much, you might lose part of that audience. If a producer does decide to make changes in his format, he has to be very careful that they are the right ones, that he is emphasizing what the audience will react well to.

An example of this is the character of Mr. Spock. As STAR TREK progressed, the role grew in importance until finally STAR TREK was no longer the adventures of Captain Kirk and the crew of the *Enterprise,* but Captain Kirk and Mr. Spock of the U.S.S. *Enterprise.* The relationships of the rest of the crew, and even the starship itself were downplayed in favor of the relationship between Kirk and Spock. It was only because the relationship between the two was so interesting that the change was justified.

None of the other subordinate characters ever commanded that kind of interest, however, and so, they remained subordinate. They remained functions of the starship rather than becoming *dramatis personae.* Lt. Uhura continued to open hailing frequencies—any robot could have done that; Mr. Scott found some trouble with the doubletalk generators—but fortunately he fixed it in time; Mr. Chekov had trouble with the helm because some superior force had overpowered the ship—he didn't know what to do about it.

As such, none of these aspects of the various STAR TREK plots required these characters to be individuals concerned about themselves and their responsibilities. They were simply there to dramatize the external conflicts of the leading characters. They were functions of the starship, not of the story.

Among the subordinate characters, the only exception to this rule was Nurse Chapel. She was the only regular character who was not a function of the starship as such. A doctor's nurse simply is not important to the overall hierarchy of command. She has no purpose except to be someone for the doctor to talk to—and anybody in a nurse's uniform could fulfil that role.

Nurse Chapel was the only subordinate character whose internal motivation was seriously developed. We were never told the trifling facts of her ancestry or her preference in music. Instead we were shown quite bluntly that Nurse Chapel loves Mr. Spock—and make no mistake, it is a tragic love because it is doomed to be unrequited. Mr. Spock could never allow himself to respond to her interest. It might be the best thing in the world for him—but he would never do it.

This is probably the primary reason for Nurse Chapel's existence aboard the *Enterprise*—to love Mr. Spock. She fulfils no other dramatic function, and no other symbolic function either. The most important continuing event in her life is her love for the ship's First Officer. She was obviously created specifically for this. The need to dramatize Spock's Vulcan aloofness requires that a woman fall in love with him and be continually rebuffed. Hence, Nurse Chapel.

This is why Nurse Chapel sometimes seems slightly out of key with all of the other subordinate roles. Hers is a basically human motivation, while the other characters are basically symbolic with human aspects superimposed upon them.*

---

*This was probably the reason why Nurse Chapel was the least popular member of the STAR TREK family. It was because of her love for Spock and his occasional moments of gentleness toward her that Christine Chapel was largely disliked among the Trekkies who adored Spock. Female fans saw her as a threat to their own fantasies and male fans saw her as a threat to Spock's Vulcan stoicism.

But those fans who have been lucky enough to meet Majel Barrett in person (now Majel Roddenberry) at science fiction or STAR TREK conventions have been surprised and delighted. The most frequently heard comment is, "But, she's beautiful!" And she is. They just couldn't see it in her as Chapel because of the relationship between her and Spock.

The characters of Uhura, Chekov, Sulu, and Scott might seem a little un-comfortable with Nurse Chapel, unable to deal with her except strictly on the most professional level. The bridge crew have minimized their inner drives, Nurse Chapel has not. Perhaps there is a mutual recognition of this, perhaps not. In any case, although there may have been trust between them, there did not seem to be a great deal of affection.

What this means to the format of the show, however, is that the characters of Uhura, Chekov, Scott, and Sulu have a great deal more dramatic versatil-ity than Chapel. She has been too thoroughly limited by her creation to a single dramatic function, while the others, having been created for no spe-cific dramatic function at all, can be assigned various dramatic responsibili-ties throughout the course of a season.

The roles of the others have been left open for development, they are blank books for the series' writers to fill as they choose. We haven't been told what drives Uhura or who Sulu loves—this can be developed later. The only flaw is that there is no guarantee than any of it *will* be developed later. We might end up with just as many questions about these people as we started with. Or maybe not. It depends on the man who sits in the producer's chair.

Fortunately, STAR TREK struck a reasonably safe middle ground with these characters. They were developed enough to be personalities, but never so much as to damage their ability to reappear the following week in the same role. If a story required a particularly violent upheaval in a character's life, generally, a character was created specifically for that upheaval. (Part of it, of course, involved keeping the lesser roles from becoming too complex to be handled by individual writers. No writer is going to know all the scripts that went before, or all the other scripts in development, hence the subordi-nate roles must be kept fairly simple and unchanging from episode to episode.)

The real strength of these roles is shown by their cumulative effect on the viewer. Although very little is presented about these characters in any spe-cific episode, the sum total feeling after viewing five or six episodes is that these *are* real people.

The involvement that results is quite deep. In a sense, the involvement is very much akin to real-life relationships. One does not meet a person and immediately find out who they are—we do not very often meet people when they are at the height of an emotional crisis. We rarely meet them even in situations which would distinctively delineate an overall set of reactions for them. Rather, we meet people as they are "maintaining"—moving from one situation to another. Or just existing between situations.

Generally, if there is a situation, it is one of "I am on my guard while I am meeting you, and you are on your guard while you are meeting me.'' It takes time and several exposures to an individual before the guard is relaxed. During that period, data is gathered and correlated. Little things, like whether one prefers peanut butter or mildew, big things, like attitudes and angers. A total picture is built up, but only gradually.

Such is the way the lesser STAR TREK characters developed in the viewer's mind. He wasn't shown much in any given week—but over a period of time, he was shown quite a bit, developing a feeling of recognition and familiarity. Enough data was eventually presented to bring the characters completely to life, and the result was that despite the hasty treatment given them in any specific script, they still seemed as real and as fully developed as the three major leads.

STAR TREK's "bad guys" however, were never fully realized as characters. As villains they were more symbolic than individual, and consisted primarily of two distinct groups—

The Klingons and the Romulans.

Klingons first:

Klingons are professional villains. They are nasty, vicious, brutal, and merciless. They don't bathe regularly, they don't use deodorants or brush their teeth. They don't even visit their dentists twice a year. They sharpen their fangs by hand because they think pain is fun. They eat Blue Meanies for breakfast.

Think of the Mongol Hordes with spaceships and ray guns. To the Klingons, Genghis Khan was a phony and Attila the Hun was a fairy. And Hitler was only a beginner. Remember Ming of Mongo from all those old Flash Gordon serials? Well, these are his descendants, selectively inbred for sheer awfulness.

A Klingon is a good person to invite to a rape—or even a murder, providing it's your own. Klingons build their battlecruisers without toilets; it makes them nastier. Klingons pick on old ladies. Klingons fart in air locks. Klingons drop litter in the streets. Klingons pick their teeth in public. And those are their good points.

Klingons do all the things that men pretend they don't—only Klingons are proud of it.

The Klingons are perfect villains.

They were introduced in an episode entitled "Errand of Mercy," by Gene L. Coon. In that episode, the neutral planet Organia is threatened by a Klingon takeover. Kirk tries to persuade the Organians to accept a Federation base on their planet for their own protection, but the Organians refuse. Although they are seemingly unprotected, they insist that they are able to cope with the Klingon threat unaided. Kirk doesn't see how, the planet is totally unarmed, and the Organians are confirmed pacifists. The Klingons are murderous butchers and Kirk fears a massacre.

When the Klingons arrive, Kirk naturally ends up getting into a fight with the Klingon captain. Excuse me, a confrontation. At which point, the Organians reveal themselves to be superior energy beings with the power to nullify the weapons of both sides. "Thou shalt not fight!" insist the Organians. At this, Kirk gets mad, "How dare you forbid us to fight with each other! It's our right!" And then he realizes that the whole purpose of his mission was to *prevent* a war. The Organians are right! The Organians have the power to enforce a peace treaty between the two empires. Grudgingly, Kirk and his Klingon counterpart, Kor, agree to a *détente*. They have no choice.

The Klingons were such delicious villains, however, that they began to crop up in other episodes: this author's own "The Trouble with Tribbles," Gene Roddenberry's "A Private Little War," Jerome Bixby's "Day of the Dove," Dorothy Fontana's "Friday's Child," and so on.

—But all of the Klingon episodes were, in one way or another, restatements of the original: Klingons and Earthmen must *not* fight.

The Organian peace treaty is a convenient limit. Otherwise any confrontation with the Klingons would immediately result in an all-out war.

From a series point of view, if the Klingons are going to appear regularly as villains in stories, then they need to be "controlled" villains. That is, the situation should be equivalent to the American-Russian cold war. Not only does this provide a good background for a wide variety of stories, both humorous and dramatic, but it is a lot more optimistic and (hopefully) believable than a space war.

After all, a race that can achieve space travel is going to have done so only through large scale programs of social cooperation, and it is hoped, in the process will have learned that there are better ways than aggression to accomplish one's goals. Perhaps they would have even forsaken goals that require aggression (in any of its forms) for their accomplishment.

Besides, if STAR TREK needs to tell a *real* war story, that's what the Romulans are for. . . .

The Romulans were precursors to the Klingons, they were developed first. They weren't quite as nasty, but they were a lot more intelligent and that made up for the missing nastiness.

Romulans first showed up in "Balance of Terror" by Paul Schneider. They also figured in "The *Enterprise* Incident."

In both of these stories, the *Enterprise* was shown in direct battle with

Romulan ships, thus implying that a state of war existed between the Earth
Federation and the Romulan Empire. As long as each government's ships
kept to their own side of the line, however, the war was limited to minor
skirmishes. If at any time it had been shown that a state of *all-out* war existed,
then STAR TREK would have had to either become a space war TV series, or
the two groups would have had to run into some more Organians. . . .

Turning to the *Enterprise* itself, the ship was designed more for its visual
impact than out of any particular sense of "this is what it will be like."

Matt Jefferies, designer for the show and the man responsible for the over-
all STAR TREK "look," submitted several designs to Gene Roddenberry.
Roddenberry winnowed, suggested and corrected, and Matt tried again.
Eventually, the familiar disc and pylons began to take shape and proportion.

One of the early forms of the *Enterprise* had the disc *below* rather than
above the central engineering pod.

The capabilities and design of the *Enterprise* as presented in *The Star Trek
Guide,* as well as seen on the show, were an incredible mixture of the clumsy
and the brilliant.

For instance, the bridge set was one of the best designed science fiction
sets in motion picture history. There are few that can equal, let alone surpass,
the bridge of the U.S.S. *Enterprise.* (Offhand, I can only think of two: the
interiors of the spaceships used in *Forbidden Planet* and *2001: A Space
Odyssey.**)

As a design for the control of a giant starship, the bridge is a model of
logic and efficiency. The Captain's eyes are before him in the form of a
giant viewscreen. So is the pilot console, which is the equivalent of his hands.
The Science Officer is to his right, ready to present whatever information is
needed. Communications and Engineering are to the rear, right and left
respectively, where they are out of the way, but convenient.

The upper walls are lined with information screens and the Captain's chair
swivels so he can survey the whole bridge easily. The lights and controls on
each panel are set in curved banks—curved to match the reach of the human
arm. Whatever operator is seated at a console, he will find all of his controls
in the most convenient possible position.

So workable is this design that the United States Navy sent a delegation
to the studio to examine the bridge set in detail. They were considering
a similar layout for a new aircraft-carrier bridge. (The new *Enterprise*
maybe. . . ?)

---

*This was written before *Star Wars*, of course.

That's the brilliant part.

The clumsy part is that so many writers and directors continually *misused* this beautiful set.

Example: (A familiar scene.) The *Enterprise* is under attack. She's hit by a photon torpedo—*kaboom!*—everything tilts and everybody falls out of their chairs! They climb back into them and another torpedo comes zooming in—*kaboom!*—again, they're knocked to the floor! A third time—*kaboom!* —the camera tilts and they all fall down again!

And Scotty reports, "All defenses out, Captain. The next one will get us for sure."

Several years ago, Bob Justman, associate producer of the show, was asked by a fan about this: "Why don't you put seat belts on the chairs?"

"Because," he replied, "if we did, then the actors couldn't fall out of them."

—But the above scene—and Bob Justman's easy answer—are *wrong*. Both scientifically and dramatically. There has been little thought put into either.

From a scientific standpoint, the scene is fallacious. Each of those torpedoes would have had to have been a direct hit in order to shake the *Enterprise*. If they had been misses—even *near misses*—the ship wouldn't have been shaken at all. Shockwaves don't travel through the vacuum of space. Hence, in order to shake the ship, they must have been direct hits. If they were direct hits, the ship should have been destroyed three times over.

Or try it another way. Let's assume that a near miss *does* have the power to jolt the *Enterprise*. But the *Enterprise* has an artificial gravity—no, not just an artificial gravity, a whole force field to neutralize the effects of momentum, acceleration, and inertia. Assuming the speed and maneuverability already postulated for the vessel, a protective force field is a necessity to keep the ship's crew from being smeared into jelly every time she makes a rapid change of direction or speed. If this is so, a near miss with a photon torpedo would no more be able to rattle the crew of the *Enterprise* than it would be able to dislodge a fly trapped in amber.

(And assuming that such an artificial gravity/force field did exist, isn't it amazing that it was never knocked to hell and gone by one of those missiles?)

Actually, I could just as easily argue the other side of the question:

Well, you see, the *Enterprise* had her shields up. The torpedoes exploded against the ship's force screens and the shock of the explosion was transmitted to the ship via the shields. Or: the shields didn't stop all of the explosion, part of it leaked through. Just enough to shake everyone, but not kill anybody.

Sure.

It doesn't really matter. Whichever side of the question you argue, it's only doubletalk. But when doubletalk is designed to justify a piece of *bad* writing, that's a reprehensible cheating of the viewer. "Let's make it look exciting. We'll have all the actors fall out of their chairs. Three times."

The same scene could have been a lot more tense—and a lot more believable as science fiction—if it had been written with even the simplest awareness of the postulated capabilities of the *Enterprise*.

The purpose of the scene is to dramatize the menace of the attacking ship. Fine. Very simple. Instead of three missiles, just one. The *Enterprise* tracks it all the way in—and can't stop it. The officer at the weapon control console (let's put him at the upper left side of the bridge) reports all of his attempts to intercept the torpedo—phasers, anti-missile missiles, force screens, tractor beams, and various other doubletalk devices—and also reports the failure of each device to stop the approaching torpedo. The torpedo strikes the *Enterprise*'s *last* set of screens and detonates, and in the process knocks out that line of defense. This is all reported on the bridge—at the moment of detonation, nobody falls out of their chairs and no sparks fly from any panels (somebody has invented fuses). The lights simply dim momentarily, then come back up again as (implied) the emergency power supply cuts in.

Kirk calls for a status report and Scotty replies: "All defenses out, Captain. The next one will get us for sure."

And that brings us to the exact same place that the first scene did.

The major difference is one of credibility. The scene with the people falling out of their chairs is visually exciting, but is not dramatically valid. We are abruptly and arbitrarily *told* that the *Enterprise*'s defenses have been knocked out.

The latter scene—admittedly a harder one to write—*shows* how those defenses are taken out, and in the process, it builds to a tense climax. The scene involves the viewer in the destruction of each line of defense and makes him more a participant in the action. The real point of the scene is to leave Kirk with no defenses at all—that's when he has to open his hailing frequencies and start talking. Fast. But it feels a lot better if the writer has brought us to this point *honestly*.

Science fiction is not a western with ray guns and spaceships. It is a genre so demanding that few of its practitioners are more than moderately competent at it. The responsibility to be logical and scientifically accurate, while at the same time telling a good dramatic story, will continually defeat any writer who approaches the field with less than total respect for its requirements.

Because so few screenwriters are well versed in science fiction, STAR TREK should have had a full-time science fiction writer on its staff, someone with a good background in science as well as science fiction. Such a staff advisor could have worked closely with the writers, the directors, the producers and the actors, as well as the designers and the decorators, to make everything as logical, believable, and accurate as possible.

There were too many instances of clumsiness in STAR TREK's production that a science fiction advisor could have corrected. Doubletalk cannot disguise bad writing—and it will only hurt good writing. It's a little harder, yes, to be accurate, but the results are worth it.

Consider:

The *Enterprise*'s corridors seemed awfully roomy, they were about twice as wide as they should have been. In fact, the whole ship was too roomy. Space is at a premium in any kind of enclosed environment. Anyone who's ever been aboard a submarine—or even an aircraft carrier, for that matter— knows that they are designed for the maximum utilization of their volume. Efficency is a necessity, and a spaceship is going to have to be designed the same way.

In fact, the requirements of a spaceship are much more stringent—for instance, the interior atmosphere must be maintained with the correct combination of gases, at the right temperature, pressure, humidity, and ionization, to maintain not just the lives, but the comfort as well, of the crew. The margins for deviation are narrow; therefore, *every* cubic inch of interior volume means airspace that must be maintained—and maintenance requires the expenditure of energy. When you have to conserve your ship's power, you don't waste airspace.

The reason for such broad corridors? They had to be wide enough for a camera dolly, cables and a film crew.

To attempt to show that the ship was cramped would have required the construction of cramped sets—which are harder to work with and would have meant much more in the way of production time.

(So, instead, we're told that the ship has power to waste—it's implied, not specifically said. But if that's so, then we should never see a story in which maintenance of life-support functions become a critical factor for building suspense. A ship can't be both wasteful *and* limited.)

Another example: the turbo-elevators. These were the machines that took the various crew members from one part of the ship to another. Good idea; especially as we are told that the thickest part of the *Enterprise*'s disc is twelve stories thick.

But—the elevators seemed to be the *only* way to get from one deck to another. If the ship's power supply were cut off, every deck would be separated from every other. Oh, well, not really—somebody could always crawl through the air vents, or through the Jefferies Tube, or down one of the ladders which we saw very infrequently. *All except for the bridge*. Cut off the turbo-elevators and you isolate the bridge. Tsk. That's *bad* designing. Illogical.

Another one: the Captain's cabin. Or anybody's cabin for that matter. They were all redresses of the same set. If any of those cabins had a bathroom, it was never shown. There weren't even any doors to *imply* a bathroom.* We were never shown the cleanup facilities on the whole ship—not even the sick bay. And the *Enterprise* was on a five-year mission—isn't at a long time to hold it? Isn't that carrying it a bit too far?

Also, about those cabins—all of the major officers aboard the ship had their own cabins, and roomy places they were too. No complaint here, but what about the crew's quarters? Those were never even shown or suggested. Did each member of the crew have a cabin too? That would have made the *Enterprise* more of a hotel than a starship. Or did they have bunkrooms?

If they did have bunkrooms, how come they were never mentioned or shown? How come we never got into the crew's lives?

Or was the crew just a collection of some 400-odd androids to walk up and down the halls—scenery behind the main characters, to be moved around as necessary, but not really important to the story except as another part of the background to support the overall illusion?†

These examples are not just casual errors in the STAR TREK format. They are part of a general pattern. The glossy surface and flickering lights of the show's gaudy technicolor production could not make up for what was *not* there. In its execution, STAR TREK tended to lack the kind of *deep* extrapolation that characterizes good science fiction.

Consider the ship's galleys, for instance—they were never clearly defined. In "Charlie X" there are references to the ship's cooks, yet when I worked on "The Trouble with Tribbles" I was told that there was only a Mess Officer,

---

*On this one, I was wrong. Elaan of Troyius (from the episode of same name) in one emotional scene did lock herself behind a door, which was presumed to be a bathroom. Or a walk-in closet. When she comes out we'll ask her.

†About this, Gene Roddenberry says, "Well, yes, we did make mistakes. There were things that worked and things that didn't work, and if we were ever to do STAR TREK again, we would make improvements in those areas. The one elevator to the bridge *was* a mistake, and no emergency exit in sight. Yes, we would correct that. And we should have had a head in Captain Kirk's stateroom, certainly.

"We had hoped to build on the basic format as the show progressed. Each year we would have a little more money to spend on new sets and we had intended to add more and more sets gradually to answer some of these questions. My feeling about the crew was that indeed they did have their own staterooms. The services today have always annoyed me, putting up enlisted men like cattle. I think all men deserve dignity and it was my feeling that by that century, we would have come to understand that."

and everything else was done by machines. But what machines?!! A slot in the wall? Whatever a character ordered appeared almost immediately behind it. While this may have been admittedly convenient, the processing machinery necessary to perform this miracle—just the myriad moving parts necessary to bring the food from storage to the wall slot—seems prohibitively wasteful of *space*.

And those damned wall slots were *everywhere*. In "Tomorrow Is Yesterday" we were even shown that the transporter room had a food slot.* It makes you wonder what's going on behind the walls of the *Enterprise*.

A justification can be made for any of these elements of the show's conception. The wide corridors are necessary to prevent claustrophobia in the crew. Separate cabins for everyone are necessary because the culture of the future places a high premium on privacy. Food slots must be plentiful for the same reason—the crew needs to be reassured as to the security of their basic requirements. (And a dumbwaiter system isn't all *that* complex.) Okay—but if you accept this, then what does that imply about the culture that built it?

What kind of a culture would place such a high premium on privacy and security? It does not seem likely that it would be a totally healthy one, or even likely that it would be a spacegoing culture. Space travel implies hardships—insecurity as well as being thrown together with the same group of people for a very long time. The amount of energy needed to establish security and privacy for 430 people is enough to make a starship prohibitively expensive, especially if it is designed in a wasteful manner. The first commandment of the Universe is very simple: Thou Shalt Not Waste. (There are no other commandments, there are only variations.)

These flaws are all part of a pattern—but not a pattern of commission, rather one of omission. And the omission is a serious one. At no point was the *Enterprise* given a background culture.

Oh, we know that Kirk is an Irishman, Spock is a Vulcan, Scotty is a Scot, Sulu's an Oriental, Uhura is African, and McCoy is from the deep South. But these aren't cultural attributes, they're matters of inheritance and have very little to do with the environment that produced this ship and this crew.

---

*Quoting Dorothy Fontana: "There was a food slot in the Transporter Room in 'Tomorrow Is Yesterday' because production people wouldn't let me take the Air Force Sergeant out of the Transporter Room or send an extra for some chow for him. It was, of course, never used again. Same reason, essentially, for never seeing bunk rooms and other variations of crew quarters. Have to build a set which might be used once—for one scene—costly, etc. You had to fight with Bob Justman (Associate Producer) on this. And mostly, writers lost."

In general, the viewers were given so few clues about the social background of the starship that the result was occasionally grotesque. The walls of the recreation rooms were barren even of the simplest decoration. There were no paintings, no screens, nothing to look at, not even patterns of tile or enamel, just a simple stark gray. The basic bulkheads of the ship seemed as grim as a prison, as utilitarian as a hospital.

If these were real people, vitally alive, as intelligent and able as postulated in *The Star Trek Guide,* they would make the impact of their individuality obvious on their "home away from home." They would make the ship their own. They would decorate their galleys and rec rooms, they would make the sick bay a cheerful place with bright walls and colorful artwork. These people are not automatons—and they would not live in an environment seemingly designed for such.*

A starship is not an independent entity—no more than a jet plane is independent just because it can leave the ground.

Imagine for a moment, a fully loaded 747 jet airliner flying from Los Angeles to New York. That's several hundred thousand pounds of airplane and three hundred people. First of all, there's the technology to build that airplane. (Not just one factory in the city of Seattle—but aerospace contractors all over the United States supplying components for every part of the plane, from blades for its jet engines to light bulbs over the seats.) Then there's the technology to maintain it; the schools to train the mechanics, the teachers to teach the stewards; the simulators and mockups on which they'll learn; the equipment with which the plane will be serviced, the specialized trucks and tools and devices; and the men and the training to support *all* of these levels.

There's more than the airplane alone. There are airports. Lots of them.

---

*Shortly after the first printing of this book, I received an angry letter from a young man who was obviously quite upset about some of these criticisms. He accused me of *hating* STAR TREK and demanded to know why I would say such things. I wrote back, asking if his mother had ever told him to dress warmly, finish his soup, and not put beans up his nose. "Obviously," I wrote, "she tells you these things *because* she loves you and wants you to be at your very best. Right? The same is true with these criticisms." (In fact, many of these same questions were first asked by STAR TREK fans themselves.)

Of course, most of these comments apply only to the TV series. The motion pictures were produced with more time, bigger budgets, and a correspondingly greater attention to detail. The films filled in a lot of background. I was pleasantly surprised—and flattered—to be told by Gene Roddenberry that he found this book useful in the planning of *Star Trek: The Motion Picture.* More recently, Harve Bennett, producer of *Star Trek: The Wrath of Khan* and *Star Trek: The Search for Spock,* also noted that this analysis was a help in the planning of both of those pictures.

Now, if we could just get them to dress warmly, finish their soup, and stop putting beans up their nose. . . .

That means the equipment and technology to lay down a perfectly flat run-way two miles long. There are ground controllers—that means radar and scopes and computers. And reservation desks and communications systems to serv-ice those desks. Luggage-handling systems, porters, allowances for taxis, parking lots, restaurants, rest rooms—and the people to clean, maintain, and work in them.

Then you have to be ready for emergencies—so there will be rescue planes and fire trucks and medical equipment on hand. And detectives to protect the passengers and Federal Marshals to look for hijackers with metal detectors and psychological profile charts.

An airplane burns fuel—a lot of it. A 747 gulps enough petroleum in a single flight to drive an automobile for a year. That requires refineries to crack that oil (men to build and operate those refineries) and trucks to de-liver it, tanks to store it. Passengers need meals, that demands another whole service industry. And entertainment—and specialized insurance—and airsick-ness bags in the back of each seat.

None of these things just *happen* by chance; they are designed into the system as it grows. The 747 could not exist until most of the support technol-ogy has already developed. What did not exist had to be built. All of it was oriented to fit the needs of the passenger as our culture has determined them. The very existence of the 747 as the kind of plane it is, is a direct result of what our culture considers important to the traveler. Imagine an airplane with fourteen bathrooms!

That airplane is a piece of living America. (In fact, I'm told it's the state bird of Hawaii.) It is an active vital symbol of our national technology, but it is no more independent of that technology than is a bird independent of the air in which it flies. The air holds up the bird. Our technology holds up that airplane.

Now. Apply that to a starship.

Extrapolate the needs of the *Enterprise*. Her fuel requirements, her crew requirements, her maintenance and training needs, her supply needs, her com-munication and control structures, her relation to the culture that produced her—and *why* that culture produced her.

Think about it.

Do you think the *Enterprise* is really an independent entity?

It isn't. It never could be. Her independence is an illusion, just as the independence of the 747 is an illusion. Sooner or later that ship is going to have to return home to have her exhausted energies recharged. Or, if not home, then to a base with an equivalent technology.

And if all of this is true technologically, then it must follow sociologically

too. The men and women who crew the starship are no more independent of
their cultures than is the starship independent of her technology. They're
going to take their culture with them to the stars—and even if they were
stripped of every physical aspect of their home cities, they would still reflect their social conditioning in their attitudes.

Yet, the *Enterprise* that we saw on NBC television was a strangely stripped
Enterprise. Too often, she seemed to be independent of the rest of the galaxy,
only occasionally taking orders from Starfleet. She seemed also to be sociologically independent. Indeed, there seemed to be nothing at all which could
really be pinpointed as distinctive to the Starfleet culture.

Not in the people. Not in the ship.

Part of the answer is in *The Star Trek Guide:*

> *What is the Earth like in* STAR TREK's *century?*
> For one thing, we'll never take a story back there and therefore don't
> expect to get into subjects which would create great problems, technical
> and otherwise. The "U.S.S." on our ship designation stands for "United
> Space Ship"—indicating (without troublesome specifics) that Mankind
> has found some unity on Earth, perhaps at long last even peace. Refer-
> ences by our characters to Earth will be simply a logical projection of
> current scientific and social advances in food production, transportation,
> communications, and so on. If you want to assume that Earth cities of
> that future are so splendidly planned with fifty-mile parkland strips around
> them, fine. But for obvious reasons, let's not get into any detail of Earth's
> politics of STAR TREK's century; for example, which socio-economic sys-
> tems ultimately worked out best.

Right there, in one paragraph, we are told that we cannot *really* postulate
where these people or this starship came from. We may find out what drives
various individuals aboard the ship, but we do not know, nor do we have
any way of finding out, what drives them culturally—what motivates their
government in sending them out on this mission and equipping them for what
eventualities? We can only surmise from what is implied. Nothing has been
told to us to let us guess what is culturally important, what is approved and
what is taboo.

We can only imply the basic cultural overview by the cumulative actions
of the crew of the *Enterprise* and the people they meet. On our first meeting
with them, because we want to identify with them, we might surmise them
to be like ourselves—but after observing them for several weeks or months,
we begin to see that they have a much nobler outlook than most of us seem

to have. At least, they appear to be more able to live up to those goals that too many of us only pay lip service to in our own lives.

Of course, it's easy to be noble in any situation, when it's only for an hour and you'll be leaving it for a new situation next week. But that's neither here nor there. We also saw that our crew of the *Enterprise* could sometimes be less than noble—quite often we discovered charming human weaknesses. Scotty's drinking, McCoy's sarcasm, Kirk's impetuousness.

To really understand *who* these people are, we have to look to another section of *The Star Trek Guide:*

> *But projecting the advanced capabilities of your starship, wouldn't Man by that time have drastically altered such needs as food, physical love, sleep, etc.?*

> Probably. But if we did it, it would be at the cost of so dehumanizing the STAR TREK characters and surroundings that only a small fraction of the television audience would be interested, and the great percentage of viewers might even be repulsed. Remember, the only Westerns which failed miserably were those which *authentically* portrayed the men, values, and morals of 1870. The audience applauds John Wayne playing what is essentially a 1966 man. It laughed when Gregory Peck, not a bad actor in his own right, came in wearing an authentic moustache of the period.

The giveaway words here are: "1966 man."

Or, what they really mean: "contemporary man."

The crew of the *Enterprise* is in no way meant to be representative of future humanity—not at all. They are representative of the American Sphere of Influence *today.* Their attitudes, their manner of speaking, their ways of reacting, even their ways of making love, are all *contemporary.*

We have met the *Enterprise*—and they are *us.*

The crew of the *Enterprise* is twentieth-century America in space.

And—although it takes a bit of justification—that's the way it *has* to be.

Remember, this is drama we are talking about, as well as *American television.* It *has* to make money.

That means it has to have appeal and that its characters must be attractive and interesting—an audience has to be able to relate to them. Even if the show is alien to the audience's experience, the characters have to be recognizable.

Neither "Gunsmoke" nor "Bonanza" are really about 1880. They are about contemporary men in an 1880 world. "The Untouchables," when it was still on, was about 1966 men in a 1929 world. And STAR TREK also is about 1966–69 men in a 2??? world.

This is the essential appeal of drama. As mentioned earlier, we watch a story because we are really testing ourselves. We are curious as to how we would react in an equivalent situation. In science fiction, we are also testing our culture. Thus, both the characters and the culture have to be recognizable parts of ourselves. They have to reflect contemporary values—not totally, but enough so that the viewer can follow.

STAR TREK is *not* pure science fiction. It is not predictive science fiction, and it is not accurate science fiction.

It was never meant to be.

Anyone who tries to shoehorn the series into that kind of arbitrary definition will be making the same mistake that every hardcore aficionado who grumbles in his beer about SF and the dramatic arts (grumble, grumble) has been making since the very first episode of STAR TREK began.

What STAR TREK is, is a set of fables—morality plays, entertainments, and diversions about contemporary man, but set against a science fiction background. *The background is subordinate to the fable.*

I'm going to quote my earlier definition of SF:

> Science fiction is the contemporary fairy tale, it's the twentieth-century morality play. At its worst, it's merely romantic escapism; but at its best, it is the postulation of an alternate reality with which to contemplate this one.

That definition could almost be applied to STAR TREK, but the difference between STAR TREK and science fiction is that *true* science fiction requires that the background be logical, consistent, and the overall shaper of the story. The world in which the character moves determines the kind of actions he can make, and hence the plot of the tale. In true science fiction, the background is never subordinate to the plot.

As we have already seen, the *Enterprise* and her crew were able to function almost independently of their backgrounds. The only thing about them that remained consistent was their contemporary attitudes.

STAR TREK's backgrounds were always subordinate to the story—and because of that, it never quite achieved the convincing reality of true science fiction. Its use of a science fiction background gave it the appearance of science fiction; but in reality, STAR TREK was a science fiction-*based* format for the telling of entertainments for and about the attitudes of contemporary America.

The format is a flexible one—in other hands, it could be about other people. It doesn't have to be Americans. The Star Trek idea could easily be translated into Russian or Chinese or Swahili or Polish. The basic format is that of reflections of the viewer confronting a wide variety of alternate realities.

These realities are so varied as to provide opportunities for high comedy ("The Trouble with Tribbles"), satire ("Bread and Circuses"), farce ("I, Mudd"), tragedy ("The City on the Edge of Forever"), psycho-case studies ("Space Seed"), morality fables ("Errand of Mercy"), soap opera ("Is There in Truth No Beauty"), theology ("Who Mourns for Adonais?"), melodrama ("The Lights of Zetar"), and even high camp ("Spock's Brain").

As such, Star Trek is the most flexible format for a television series ever to have been postulated for commercial network broadcasting. And as such, Star Trek had the opportunity to be one of the finest dramatic series in TV history.

The reflection of American man—no, make that just Man—freed from the context of the American culture (or any specific culture) and placed in a series of alternate realities, would be a powerful dramatic vehicle for educating, enlightening—and especially for entertaining the American public. If the dramatists scripting the series were allowed to do so with no holds barred.

Just as Archie Bunker was forced to confront his own attitudes week after week, so would such a Star Trek allow its heroes to examine their attitudes in a multitude of situations—and the viewer with them. Captain Kirk would become a symbol not for American ingenuity—but more important, for the American dilemma: how best can we use our strength? Each week, he would be making crucial decisions about problems that we would see relating to our own lives and environments.

There's no question that Star Trek was a show of incredible potential.

But, potential must be realized. An unfulfilled potential is a very special kind of failure.

We'll consider that aspect of Star Trek later.

PART TWO

The STAR TREK Family—
The People Who Made
the Enterprise Fly

THE reality that was STAR TREK was only an illusion—a very skilled and carefully contrived illusion. Even when American television has little or nothing to say, it still can say it beautifully. And when American television *does* have something to say—as with STAR TREK—the illusion is convincing enough to alter the shape of reality. (As witness the fans' response.)

The people who made that illusion work were the STAR TREK family. The cast and crew of the show. The creative talents that worked together to make a totality that was more than the sum of its individual parts.

In writing this book, I spoke with and interviewed all of the cast members of the show, as well as producer Gene Roddenberry, line producer Gene L. Coon, and story editor Dorothy Fontana. I also spoke with other actors and crew members whenever possible.

One theme kept repeating itself over and over. "STAR TREK was a family. It was a special show and we had a special feeling about it. Gene Roddenberry knew what he was doing in the casting and in the production of the show. He was what made it great." Without exception, every person interviewed recalled STAR TREK as one of the high points of their careers.

A couple of notes about the following interviews: The reminiscenes of the cast members are reported all as transcribed off the tapes I made of each session. Their comments on what they liked—and disliked—are included with only the minimum of editing. Editing was for grammatical purposes only.

The comments of Gene L. Coon and Dorothy Fontana are scattered throughout the book in the text or as footnotes. In addition, much of the background material that they presented became the foundation for whole sections of analysis of the show.

William Campbell's remarks are included as representative of the guest star's attitudes toward STAR TREK—also, because his interview was too good to omit. I believe it presents valuable insight into some of the workings of television relationships as well as the difference between series acting and guest-star spots.

Time and space considerations prevented as detailed a report on the sound stage crew as I would have liked. However, the individuals involved were so thoroughly presented in Stephen Whitfield and Gene Roddenberry's *The Making of* STAR TREK that the reader is referred to that work for further information.

Undeniably, the most popular character on STAR TREK was Mr. Spock, the alien First Officer. His mother had been an Earthwoman, his father, a Vulcan. Spock was a half-breed, torn between two worlds.

And because of that, he was the show's most *interesting* character.

But when STAR TREK was conceived—and even in the first two pilot episodes—very little thought had been given to Mr. Spock as a character. The details hadn't been worked out yet, just the basic conception, a half-breed alien without emotions. He was simply *there*.

Gene Roddenberry had thought it would be nice to have an alien on board the *Enterprise,* but the real development of Spock as a character did not come until later—and much of the credit belongs to Dorothy C. Fontana, a thoughtful and sensitive woman who started out as Gene Roddenberry's secretary and ended up as the show's story editor. She wrote several of STAR TREK's best scripts, including the excellent "Journey to Babel." That was the story that introduced Spock's parents and also presented quite a bit of his background.

The impact of Mr. Spock on the show is almost too vast to be clearly defined. More than any other character, he is the one closest indentified with the show—unfairly and unfortunately perhaps, because it is at the expense of so much else that is worthy of attention. When you mention STAR TREK to a non-STAR TREK fan, the reaction is generally, "Oh, yeah—that's the show about the guy with the pointed ears."

The fans took to Mr. Spock—and everything related to him. To many of them he was the sole *raison d'être* for STAR TREK. No less an authority than the *Saturday Review* voiced the opinion that Captain Kirk should be booted off the ship and Mr. Spock put in command. (To which a number of people disagreed vehemently, not the least of whom was William Shatner. Too many of the Spock-fans who expressed this kind of thinking simply hadn't realized that Spock was generally at his best when he had Captain Kirk to play off of. And vice versa.)

Neither could the writers resist Mr. Spock. He was too interesting a character to leave alone. There was too much to do with him. And they did—they used him at every opportunity. Because he was the most interesting crew member for Kirk to take with him on a mission, he was written into more scripts than anyone else. Pretty soon he was on screen as much as the Captain. Within one season, Mr. Spock grew incredibly in his importance to the show—almost, it seemed, until he had taken over the series, if not the ship. When I met William Shatner for the first time in 1967, on the set of STAR TREK, he even touched on this himself. "When you write your script," he said, "remember that Kirk is the Captain of the ship. The story has to center around him and his decisions."

I don't know if he told that to every writer he met—but if he had, there were obviously quite a few who hadn't listened.

A good part of Mr. Spock's appeal, of course, was Leonard Nimoy himself. Before STAR TREK, he'd appeared in shows like *Thriller, The Lieutenant,* and *Outer Limits.* (And even an incredibly bad B-picture called *The Brain Eaters.* Fortunately, it was a very small part and he was heavily made up. If you didn't know it was Leonard, you'd never recognize him.) As an actor, he was not known to the general public—not by his name, perhaps only occasionally by his face. But the casting directors and the producers knew of him, and he was working regularly. He was also training to be a director.*

And then STAR TREK happened.

"For me," says Leonard Nimoy, "it started in 1964 or '65. I did an episode of *The Lieutenant,* a TV series that starred Gary Lockwood.† Gene Roddenberry was the Executive Producer, and he was away when we shot it, so I never did meet him. A month or so later, my agent said he had talked to Gene—he said he had liked me in that show and that he had a part in mind for me in a science fiction pilot he was writing.

"I didn't take it very seriously or think much of it, because the man was only *writing* the pilot—that's an awfully long trip before he gets it done. It has to be examined and reviewed by the studio and the network—and then

---

*There was some concern voiced when Leonard Nimoy was first signed to direct the third STAR TREK movie; but then, when you think about it, he was a *logical* choice. Who else are you going to find who was present at the filming of every episode of the original TV series and both the previous movies? Who else knows STAR TREK as well? (Yes, of course—but he didn't want to direct.) Leonard Nimoy would definitely *not* have to have STAR TREK explained to him.

†Gary Lockwood played Lt. Commander Gary Mitchell in STAR TREK's second pilot episode, "Where No Man Has Gone Before." In that episode, the *Enterprise* tried to go out beyond the edge of the galaxy and Lockwood got zapped into a funny-eyed superman. Lockwood may be better known though for his role as Astronaut Frank Poole in *2001: A Space Odyssey.* He was the spaceman murdered by the computer, Hal 9000.

getting it into production and all that that involves is another whole story. Who knows where I'll be at that time, or whether he might find somebody else? I had learned not to get very excited about that kind of conversation, although it was always nice to hear that somebody was interested.

"But about six months later, he called and said he wanted to meet me. So I went to see him and he was well into it by then. He took me around and showed me the various designs for the sets and the props that were being built, the phasers, the communicators, and wardrobe sketches that were being done. And we talked about this character—the original idea was, from the onset, that this character would be half human, half alien. The pointed ears were specifically established, but the rest of it was somewhat vague. It was in the process of being developed, what color the character's skin would be, the nature of the rest of his makeup—the eyebrows, the haircut, the color of his skin, all came later.

"And so we started serious negotiations. Serious negotiations—in that case, I had no leverage, they made me an offer, we quibbled over a couple of dollars, you know, and made a deal. I liked the idea of the character. At first, when Gene started talking about it, I was a little concerned—it sounded like Mickey Mouse time with the pointed ears. Of course, that was everybody's reaction at first, including the press; but as we discussed it, and as he began to tell me what the character was going to be about and what he hoped for the character in terms of dimension, I thought, 'This is a valid thing—within the genre, this is a valid character. We might be able to make it work.'

"The biggest problem we had developing the character was the ears. It was very difficult—we were with the wrong makeup people. The studio had made a deal with a special effects house that makes monster heads and things like that, and they were going to do the work—they had made a flat deal for X number of dollars to do something like three monster heads and a pair of pointed ears.

"Now, I don't know if you know how those things are made. You have to have a plaster cast made of the area of the face or body where the appliance is going to fit, and then they make a positive piece from the plaster negative—a head, or in this case, the ears. Then, in putty, they work up the shape of the appliance, and then they cast that and make the piece. I went there and they cast my ears, and a few weeks later they came up with the first pair of ears.

"They were gruesome. They were very rough and crude. They were very very porous, almost like alligator skin. The shape wasn't right. Aesthetically, they just didn't work at all. They were awful.

"But this time, they had a makeup man assigned to the show, Fred Phillips, and he started working with me, putting them on, and working with skin colors and eyebrows and so forth. And we both agreed that the ears were pretty bad. He went to the production department and said, 'These ears are being made by the wrong people.' Fred had done an awful lot of appliance work and he *knew* good appliances. He'd started at Universal—he went all the way back to Lon Chaney and Boris Karloff. He told them that there are people who are specialists in the appliance field. These people we were with were very good for shock heads, but for a delicate appliance that we have to really believe is part of the body—like puffy eyes, or a broken nose or scar tissue—it's very delicate work and it has to blend in very evenly with the rest of the face.

"But the studio said no, keep working with these people, because we paid them, we want them to do the job. And about four or five days before shooting, they came up with another pair—which weren't much better. So Fred decided to do it on his own—we were working one afternoon at the studio makeup department—he made a phone call to MGM and said, 'Come with me.' There was a man he knew at MGM who was a specialist in pieces like this. We went over there and told him what we had in mind. He drew us a sketch—which I could see immediately had the right feeling and we did a cast, I was out of there in about twenty-five minutes. And about forty-eight hours later, he delivered the ears that I finally wore. And they came just in time—they came just a day or two before we started shooting the show.

"A pair of ears might last anywhere from three days to five or six shooting days—each appliance had its own little idiosyncrasies, they were all different, some lasted longer than others. Only once in a great while did we get a pair that hadn't baked properly, or something that meant that we couldn't use them.

"You know the ears were painful. They irritated, particularly inside the ear where they had to be glued down. And of course, what we don't realize is that when we talk or move, we do have facial skin movement—and there is a little bit of movement of the ears—so there's a little rub from the appliance. Every once in a while, I'd get a sensitive raw area. But, you know, you can get used to hanging by your thumbs, as they say.

"Meanwhile, Gene Roddenberry and I were having lengthy conversations to develop the character, ideas about how the character would walk, talk, and function. And so we went to work, and I was in that first pilot with Jeff Hunter. I didn't have a heck of a lot to do in it, it was a nice job, I was on it for three weeks—which I think was the longest job I'd ever had in this business in fifteen years. Prior to that, I'd always been in and out in a couple days. I'd had maybe half a dozen jobs that ran two weeks, most of them were one week television jobs.

"So this one was a giant project—very esoteric show, very cerebral. It scared everybody half to death because it cost a fortune and most of the network people didn't understand it.

"And then I forgot about it. I thought, well, that settles that. It's done.

"My contract ran out—but about seven months later, they called me and said, 'We're going to do another STAR TREK pilot and we want you back.' So, we did that, and you know the rest. The rest has all been documented.

"Actually, I felt very comfortable playing the character. I felt, particularly in the first season of scripts, even before we went on the air, that the character was good—that I could stand behind the role. I didn't have to be ashamed or self-conscious in any way. I felt I was finding things in the character, that there was room for exploration. Gene Roddenberry was open to exploration. I felt very good about it—I hoped that the show would work. But I had no idea that the character would become as popular as he did.

"When the fans began to respond, it was exciting—very exciting. There were times when it was even scary. It happened so fast and with such intensity, it changed our whole way of life in a matter of a few weeks.

"The very first thing that gave us a real physical indication of what was happening was a trip I made to Medford, Oregon, for NBC. The show had been on the air a few weeks and my mail was coming in pretty strong . . .— Uh, let me give you an idea of how limited my expectations were. When the first mail started coming in, I answered it myself, responding to each piece personally, writing handwritten notes and handsigning each photograph. And I would do that during lunch hour. Once a week they would give me my mail, so the first week there was about thirty-five pieces, and I thought, 'Well, if that's the mail for the week, I can handle that.' Then the second week there was, I don't know, fifty or sixty pieces. The third week there was a couple of hundred—and after that, it was all over. From that point on it just kept multiplying geometrically until there were thousands of pieces of mail coming in every week.

"Then I went on my first promotion trip—this public appearance I mentioned. NBC called me and said there's this nice little town called Medford, Oregon, that has a Pear Blossom Festival every year and they have a little parade through the town and they'd like you to come and be the Grand Marshal of the parade. John F. Kennedy had done it one year. So, I said, yeah, okay, I'll be the Grand Marshal.

"I went up there and rode in the parade, and what happened was that several thousand people turned out, a very large turnout for this parade. The problem was that they had announced that I would sign autographs in a park at the end of the parade. And as we rode down the street, all of the kids started coming off the sidewalks—the police couldn't control them; there were too few police and too many people—and they surrounded the car, and stayed with the car all the way to the end of the parade. So we were gathering this entire crowd through the city and down to the park. And at the park—there was one man there, he was the park supervisor, who was trying to control the situation—it was physically impossible to get in or out.

"Finally, the police had to come in and get me by force. When I got back to Hollywood, I talked to the NBC promotion department about it, and they said, 'That's the way it's going to be from now on.' They'd been through it all before with people like David McCallum—it had happened to him too, with 'The Man from U.N.C.L.E.' And they said, 'Any time that we send you out in the future, we'll see to it that there's proper security measures for getting into places, getting out of places, privacy, secrecy about where you're going to be and so on. Because it becomes impossible for you otherwise.' And they were right.

"In some cases people *refused* to let me appear because they were concerned about what the results might be. In fact, Macy's department store in New York said, 'We don't want the crowds that you'll bring.' I was offered to them in connection with a promotional tour I was doing for a new record album. And Macy's said, 'We can't handle it.'

"We did a show early in the first season, called 'The Naked Time.'* which was the show in which, at least for me, and I think the audience too, there was the first very definitive—miniscule, but very definitive—study of the kind of schizophrenia that moved Spock, the nature of the dynamic of the split being, the human versus the alien. This was an episode that took place on board the ship. There was a virus that was passed hand to hand, and it very quickly brought about a change in the character of the people it infected. The person's subconscious levels became expressed. And in Spock's case, he started to have feelings. The feelings in him started to overwhelm the control, and there was this fight for control of the being. Would he be an emotional being or a Vulcan? He had to fight it out with himself. And that, I think, very clearly and specifically defined, for a long time to come, the nature of the character.

"There were other shows that were important to Spock for various other reasons. When Gene Roddenberry first came up with the Vulcan mind-meld—

---

*Written by John D.F. Black.

you know, he had a great talent for that kind of thing—what happened was, we had a scene where a disturbed man had been brought aboard the ship and was in sick bay and Spock had to question him to get certain information out of him. Well, as the scene was originally written, it was simply an expository scene where Spock asked a lot of questions and through his garbled conversation the man came up with a lot of information. But Roddenberry rewrote the scene so that we went into the man's mind and *past* his problem— we got past the fact that he was in a psychotic state. That was the first time that we used the mind-meld and it was very successful.*

"When we went to Vulcan the first time and did the show about Spock's impending marriage, it was a very rich and lush show.† We were seeing something about the Vulcan society for the first time—and I came up with the Vulcan greeting, the salute.** I felt that there should be *something*. There was a moment that seemed to call for some signal between Spock and the Matriarch of the planet. Fortunately, Celia Lovsky, who played T'Pau, could do it too. You know, not everybody can do that. If she hadn't been able to do it, we probably would have lost that bit.

"You know, that reminds me of a funny incident. I was in Cleveland one day—it was later in the year—and I was being driven in a car and we stopped at a traffic light. I was sitting in the back seat and a girl pulled up next to us at the traffic light. She looked over and recognized me and she gave the salute. So I rolled down the window and I said, (saluting so) 'Can you do it with your left hand?' She tried—she got about that far (a clawlike gesture) —and said, 'I speak it with an accent.'

"I remember very vividly the day we came up with the Vulcan nerve-pinch. We had a script†† in which Captain Kirk had been fragmented into two characters. It was a Jekyll-and-Hyde type of story where there was the good Kirk and the evil Kirk. And in the scene where they confronted each other and the good Kirk is about to shoot the evil Kirk, it was written that Spock slips up behind the evil Kirk and knocks him out with the butt of his

---

*"Dagger of the Mind," by Shimon Wincelberg (pen name for S. Bar David.)

†"Amok Time," by Theodore Sturgeon.

**The salute is given with the right hand, palm facing the person you are greeting with the fingers spread in the middle. The gesture is very much like the V-for-Victory Peace Sign. When done with both hands close together, it is an old and esoteric Rabbinical gesture, used in certain types of Jewish blessings. The congregation is supposed to cover their eyes, but Leonard used to peek. (Theological humility prevents me from speculating here that Vulcan was colonized by the ten lost tribes of Israel.)

††"The Enemy Within," by Richard Matheson.

phaser. And I rebelled against that—I said that's a hangover from westerns. In the 22nd century, you don't have to slip up behind people—*Vulcans* don't have to slip up behind people and hit them over the head with butts of guns. We should find some other way of doing this. And the director, Leo Penn, said, 'What would you suggest?' And I said, 'Well, I happen to know that Vulcans have this power to render people unconscious through their knowledge of the human anatomy plus a particular Vulcan vibration. And this is the way it's done.' I told Bill (Shatner) what I planned to do, and Bill understood immediately, and I reached up behind him and did that—and Bill just kind of froze up and went unconscious. And that's the way that was born. Roddenberry saw it the next day in the dailies, and loved it. He started including it in future scripts.

"So that's the way that things were developing. Each day was a very creative day for that reason. Bill was finding his things, De Kelley was finding his things, I was finding mine, and it was a very fertile time. There were a lot of good things happening."

Because of Mr. Spock's popularity, and because of Leonard's many other responsibilities, he decided to hire his own secretary—oops, excuse me. Not secretary. Girl Friday. There's a difference. The responsibilities are a great deal heavier.

He hired Teresa Victor in 1967 (she's been with him ever since), and her job is to make his easier. Sometimes she has to be a buffer between Leonard and some of his more overenthusiastic fans.

It's not that the actor doesn't appreciate the fans' attentions—he *does*, they're the ones who have put him where he is—but if he spent as much time with the fans as they wanted, he'd never have any time for acting or directing. And it's the acting that's the *raison d'être* for the whole thing.

Teresa began working for Leonard shortly after STAR TREK went on the air. She had never had any previous experience with the fan phenomenon, so when the head of the mail department phoned her one day and asked, "What should we do with Leonard's mail?" she said, "Well, bring it up here to his office, of course."

And they did. Two huge sacks of it.

And that was just one week's worth of mail. Fortunately, she had the presence of mind to have it delivered somewhere else after that. Within a couple of weeks, it would have filled the office. Shortly thereafter the show's mail was turned over to a service anyway.

When Teresa started working for Leonard, she wasn't too sure if the job would work out, so she and Leonard both agreed to give it a few weeks to

Mr. Spock

An early version of Spock's makeup and ears

First pilot: Captain Christopher Pike and Mr. Spock

Spock confronts his emotions: "The Naked Time"

The vulcan mind-meld

"I should like to file a complaint..."

Starship commander

"The Deadly Years"

"There was a question of how to play a commander
of a ship every week..."

Dr. McCoy and Mr. Spock: friendship...

...and constant quarrels

McCoy with Yeoman Rand in his lab...

...and confronting a medical emergency ashore.

A prematurely aged McCoy: "The Deadly Years"

Scotty

"The logical guy to take charge of the ship."

The engine room

see if they could work well together. If she liked the job and they were getting along, then she would stay on.

After three weeks it was pretty obvious that they meshed well, but Teresa wanted to do something to *show* Leonard how she felt, something that would say to him, "Yes, I am happy working for you."

So she decided to get herself a pair of Vulcan ears and on the day when the trial period was up, she planned to wear them—it would be a pretty obvious gesture.

The first problem lay in getting the ears. She didn't know who to talk to or where to go. The demand for these, the most precious of all STAR TREK souvenirs, was already phenomenal. After all, if Leonard Nimoy's own employee couldn't get a pair . . . Finally, one of the casting directors located a pair and presented them to her just the night before she needed them.

Then she had to figure out how to put them on—and remember, these ears had *not* been cast to fit her, but Leonard Nimoy—she had to use a very strong adhesive. She spent almost an hour the next morning getting them on just right and then combing her hair over them so they wouldn't show until she wanted them to. Unfortunately the tips kept poking through.

All day long she wore those ears, up and down the lot, delivering messages, running errands, taking care of all the big and little things that were her responsibilities. And nobody noticed. No one said a word. Not one person realized that she was wearing a pair of pointed ears.

She was crushed. The few who did notice just looked at her a little strangely and apparently thought that those two odd-shaped projections were part of her *own* ears. Teresa felt so hurt because no one realized—not even Leonard— that she began to wonder if she really was going to stay on.

If the ears were uncomfortable for Leonard Nimoy, who they had been molded for, they were even more uncomfortable for Teresa Victor. By the end of the day she was in real pain and close to tears. Finally, she said, "Leonard, I have something to show you." And she pulled her hair back to reveal her pointed ears. "I am dying from the pain!" He cracked up laughing— but he realized by that gesture how important it was to her that she show him how she felt.

That evening, however, Teresa and a girl friend were supposed to attend one of those parties where they sell cookware or clothes or things like that. Teresa didn't know any of the people there, it was the girl friend's invitation, but she realized she was going to be in a very embarrasing situation—*she couldn't get the ears off.*

All of the people there were strangers to Teresa, and as it was still fairly early in STAR TREK's first season, not one of them had seen the show yet, or knew about Vulcans and pointed ears. For half the evening they thought she had some kind of unusual birth defect, and for the other half they thought she was wearing hearing aids. She could not convince them that she was Mr. Spock's "girl Friday." "Mr. Spock! Who's that?"

For a while, Teresa was having trouble getting pencils and other supplies. So she got into the habit of "borrowing" what she needed from other offices. Finally, Bob Justman wrote a memo—he was famous for that sort of thing—to the studio heads:

> I should like to report to you that pens and pencils have been disappearing from my office at a phenomenal rate. I don't have proof, so I don't think I can logically accuse anyone of these thefts. However, I staked out my office the other night in an attempt to identify the guilty party.
>
> Unhappily, some unknown assailant sneaked up behind me and clamped a fiercely viselike grip upon me somewhere between my neck and shoulder. I lost consciousness within a split second and did not awaken until several minutes later. To my dismay, I noticed that there were more supplies missing from my office.
>
> Whoever attacked me and my supplies must have been endowed with quite superior sense of hearing as I am certain that I made no noise and in fact, was quite careful to breathe as lightly as possible.
>
> There is one very strange fact which has emerged from this incident. I had rather cleverly concealed a naked razor blade within my pencil box so that whoever would be stealing my pencils would have an opportunity to slice open his or her finger. Upon investigating my now empty pencil box, I discovered a slight amount of the oddest green liquid present on the razor blade and around the bottom of the pencil box. I can't imagine what it can be. It certainly isn't blood as we all know that human blood is red.
>
> Incidentally, on the subject of fan letters, I have received three fan letters this season. I answered them post-haste. Please send me fifteen cents to cover postage.
>
> Sincerely,
> Bob Justman

Of course, that wasn't the end of it. Leonard wrote a memo too, also to the studio heads:

> I should like to file a complaint about the first-aid facilities here at the studio. It seems that late one night last week, while doing some very important work in my office, I had a minor accident and cut a finger. I went to the first-aid office only to discover that they are closed after shooting hours. I think it highly illogical to assume that accidents only take place during shooting hours. What can be done?
>
> Spock

Finally, the studio heads replied to all these little notes:

> Come on, you guys! Is that the only thing you have to do all day—write memos?

But Teresa did get her pencils.

Much of STAR TREK's business was conducted by memo. This was by necessity. A memo is an effective way for each member of a team to make the best use of his time. It lets each person record his opinions while they are still important in his mind, and it preserves them until the intended recipient has the opportunity to read them. The advantage is that neither has to have congruent office hours. When Executive Producers, Line Producers and Associate Producers all have dovetailed responsibilities and a limited amount of available time, the memo makes it possible for each of them to handle all their responsibilities more efficiently.

For instance:

> Dear Encino Fats:
>
> Reference your comment the other day I should give you a memo on Bob Bloch's script "Wolf in the Fold," I gave you a memo on it! In fact, a splendid memo, one which I would not have thought would be so easily forgotten by one who professes to admire incisive writing and clear thought.
>
> Yours very truly,
> *THE BIRD*

There. You see how that works? Now isn't that a lot more efficient than a phone call where you might waste ten or fifteen minutes just going over things already discussed?

Memos were also written for more mundane matters. Like getting the show produced.

One of the problems which persisted for all three years of the show's production was that of William Shatner's weight. Shatner is a very athletic actor, and takes great pride in his ability to do strenuous scenes such as fights; he exercised regularly, but as the strain of each season's production began to tell on him, he would begin slacking off on the exercises, and well . . .

As Gene Roddenberry put it, "We found ourselves having to stay away from longer shots wherever possible, as the simple plain lines of our basic costume render most unflattering any extra poundage around the waist. I did get concerned about this since we were playing to an audience that was most weight-conscious—and also very *youth*-conscious, and poundage adds years photographically."

At one point, near the end of the second season, a couple of very concerned memos were written about "William Shatner's Equator."

The memos discussed the possibility of selecting some particularly unflattering film clips, a face view, a full belly body view and sending them to Shatner without comment.

But the pictures were never sent. It wasn't necessary. William Shatner is too much of a professional, he took too much pride in his own appearance to allow the show to be damaged. The *Enterprise* was not going to be commanded by "Captain Fatty."

William Shatner has appeared on such television shows as "Twilight Zone," "Thriller," "Outer Limits," and in such TV-movies as *Vanished* and *The Andersonville Trial*. He was also in the motion picture, *The Brothers Karamazov*. He has worked in television, movies, and stage for far too many years to be unaware of the importance of keeping himself fit. There are too many good parts that require an athletic hero, and those are the parts that William Shatner likes to play.

When the part of Captain Kirk was offered to him, Shatner grabbed it because he believed in the dramatic possibilities of the show. And in the course of the production, he not only made himself synonymous with the role of the starship commander, he brought his wide-ranging expertise in all areas of the art to the STAR TREK set.

Because STAR TREK had many different directors, this meant an increased burden of responsibility on the cast and the rest of the crew to keep the STAR

T<small>REK</small> "look" consistent. Specifically, there were times when, for one reason or another, a director could *not* handle the show—those were the times when William Shatner (as well as the rest of the cast and crew) had to cope with the situation on their own. Shatner's long experience with stage and television proved itself time and time again on the set. Even with experienced directors, like Marc Daniels and Joc Pevney, he did not hesitate to offer his own suggestions.

On the matter of his weight, William Shatner is quite candid and willing to talk. And it is a good example of just how much discipline is required of an actor in a weekly television series.

To quote Shatner, "On the time off between seasons, or prior to starting, for that matter, I'd be involved in my usual regimen of whatever, running hysterically around from place to place, and also doing a lot of exercise. So when I'd start the season I'd be at my optimum weight and everything would be fine, but then as the season progressed and as I got more and more tired, I couldn't get up early enough to work out, and gradually the fatigue began to defeat my ambition to keep in shape. And so I'd gradually—well, deteriorate, to the point where the first shows came on, the first thirteen, and I would see how much weight I had gained. Then I'd go on a crash diet—and I'd lose weight by the end of the season.

"I'd start off slim, and get to my fat period, and then taper off again. And the knowledgeable people who watched the show have written me or told me in person that they've made bets as to what time of the season a particular show was shot, based on the fact of how much weight I had gained.

"They used to leave these lead weights lying around—they were used for counterweighting the camera crane—and the crew would leave them all over the set. So I used to pick them up and heft them a few times between takes, trying to keep in shape that way.—Oh, they played a joke on me with them. That was another practical joke. The weights came in twenty-five and thirty-six pound sizes. And the special effects department went to great time and expense to make a wooden one up and leave it lying where I usually left the ones I worked out with. So I lifted this thing up, I expected it to weigh thirty-six pounds—and it went flying into the air. Luckily it didn't hit anybody, but there was a lot of clowning around with that false weight for a while."

Perhaps the only episode where William Shatner's weight was unimportant was one called "The Deadly Years," written by David P. Harmon. In that script Captain Kirk, Dr. McCoy and Mr. Scott were all victims of a virus that aged them rapidly. They were *supposed* to look old.

In the course of the production each was made up in varying degrees of old-age makeup to indicate the rapid progression of the disease. To some extent, William Shatner objected to this—he didn't want to look old. And if you'll look at stills from the show, you can see that he is wearing considerable less makeup than the other two actors. (I refer you also to the photo section in *The Making of Star Trek*, by Stephen Whitfield and Gene Roddenberry.)

Putting on this makeup was a very lengthy process as it involved facial appliances to give the appearance of baggy eyes, heavy jowls, wrinkles, crow's feet and sagging skin. Appliance work—like Mr. Spock's ears—is always complicated. Each appliance has to be specially molded and then blended into the actor's skin so that no dividing line shows. Old-age makeup requires an appliance for almost every part of the face. Says William Shatner, "I spent three hours in the makeup chair one afternoon, just getting made up, and finally, I was ready about five-thirty or six o'clock. I came out on the set after having spent three hours with this painful—and boring—process of application, and they said, 'Okay, you're ready? Well, we have to quit. We have to cut at six-twelve.' And I said. 'You can't. I just spent three hours getting made up.' And they brought the producer down, Gene Coon, and he tried to go longer, but it was the policy of the studio to quit at six-twelve. So with great reluctance, they quit for the day—and I ripped off three hours worth of work without ever once having stepped before the cameras."

Because he was the star of the show, William Shatner was the focus of its attention. Everything *had* to revolve around him. Neither STAR TREK nor the *Enterprise* could function without Captain Kirk. And if some of the incidents that happened to him were funny or annoying, there were others that were just as moving.

"My father died during one of the shows and I had to leave to pick up the body and fly to Montreal for the funeral. And I did that all on a weekend. I left on a Friday and I came back on a Monday, and we picked up the scene where we had left off.

"I'd heard about his death on my lunch hour, my mother had called me, and the company was willing to shut down immediately. But for some reason I insisted on going on for the rest of the afternoon to complete this particular scene. And I remember vividly, Leonard standing very close to me—almost like a herd instinct, it was a very touching moment—just being there, and trying to comfort me.

"And Jerry Finnerman, the Director of Photography, was standing behind the camera and crying for the whole afternoon. Not only for me, but because *his* father had died on a set some years before. His father had been a cinematographer too, and Jerry had been his father's crane operator. He had collapsed on the set and Jerry had held him in his arms while he died. So now, he was identifying with the death of my father and he was very broken up by it.

"Bob Justman kept running in and out—but he was unable to take it, unable to stand being on the same set, so he'd run out again. Then he'd come back a half hour later to see if he could help. He was torn as a man and as a production manager.

"That was the show with the Horta, you know, the rock monster.* And I know exactly where the scene was that I stopped, and the scene where we picked up again on Monday. But the shots were all usable and nobody ever spotted any noticeable difference."

In a lighter vein:

"I used to keep my dog on the set the last year because I had no place else to leave him—my marriage was breaking up at the time—so everybody got accustomed to seeing this giant black doberman hovering around me, going to my dressing room with me and back and forth to the set. And nobody could get into my dressing room—which reminds me of another story, although it's not about STAR TREK.

"The same dog, his name was Morgan, used to come with me everywhere I went. After STAR TREK ended, I went on summer stock tour. It was the first of four that I did, and the dog came with me and stayed in my dressing room—but he wouldn't allow anybody else in, which was fine with me, because usually in the plays that I did I was on stage the whole time. In this particular play, there was a bit of business where I dropped my pants and the underwear that I was wearing would get a laugh. It was a special kind of underwear because it was commented on in the play. So I had to wear a particular type of boxer underwear.

"Well, one evening I was onstage and we were getting close to the moment where I would drop my pants and I suddenly realized I'd forgotten to put the shorts on. And I couldn't drop my pants—it was essential to the plot that I get this underwear shown. So while I was talking onstage to the character, whoever was on, I edged over to the side of the stage and I said to the stage manager, 'Get my underwear!' Of course, he realized the problem immediately. So I kept on talking and acting in this scene, and I could hear backstage, I could hear him running to my dressing room, I heard the door open, I heard

---

* "The Devil in the Dark," written by Gene L. Coon. The script was written in four days. Monster-maker, Janos Prohaska had crawled into Gene Coon's office wearing a rubber costume. Coon had said, "That's great! What is it?" Prohaska said, "I don't know. It can be whatever you want." Coon replied, "I'll write a script around it." And he did. It proved to be one of the most popular episodes of the first season.

this ferocious barking—and now I realized, I'm still talking and carrying on, but I'm totally aware of what must be going on backstage. This giant doberman would not allow the guy who could save my life into the dressing room. I had about ten seconds in which I came offstage for something or other and I was planning—my mind was leaping ahead to possible solutions—I was planning to change into my underwear at that moment, if I could indeed get the underwear. Well, I didn't know what was happening backstage, but when I came offstage for that ten second bit, there was my underwear waiting for me. And I slipped it on and got back onstage and everything worked out well. It was only when the curtain went down that I had a chance to ask what happened. Another actor in the company also had dobermans, he was very accustomed to dealing with them, and when he realized what the problem was, the stage manager had apparently told him, he went running into my dressing room and told my dog in no uncertain terms, *'Lie down!'* The dog laid down. The guy ran in, grabbed the underwear and ran out. So, I was lucky there that there was another dog fancier in the cast.''

''Getting back to STAR TREK, I remember that the fan reaction was tremendous. I would go out on personal appearances and the fans would just come running. Sometimes there was a danger of them being crushed. It happened at Macy's in New York once, it was very scary; and another time in South Carolina. I had just flown in from New York—it was late at night, about midnight—and I got off this commuter airplane, this smallish airplane and I couldn't see because there were so many lights on it. I didn't know what they were, and suddenly I realized there was a crowd of hundreds and hundreds of people and that all those searchlights were for me. It was absolutely astonishing. They had signs saying 'Up STAR TREK!' And 'Go, Captain Kirk, Go!' It was a tremendous turnout for a small town at this airport, giving it the aura of a grand opening. Well, I had come to appear in a parade—those people followed me all the next day.

''I know that the show is more popular now in its syndicated run than it ever was on network. I know it from the personal appearances I've made across the country that it's the result of it being at an earlier time slot in the independent stations. The network had it on at 8:30 and finally 10:00, but now that it's in the 6:30–7:30 time slots, somewhere around that area, it has outpulled any show at that time, network or independent station. In other words, when an independent station buys STAR TREK, at least up to the point that I was following it, they could be sure that they would have the highest market on any station in their area. I was crisscrossing the country for a while. I was in Seattle, then I flew to Miami, then I went up to New York and then Los Angeles, and in every one of those cities, plus the cities in between, without exception, every station manager told me STAR TREK was more popular than any other show at the same time . . . it's a phenomenon in television history in terms of syndication.

"I think that taken as a whole STAR TREK is one of the best television series ever on the air. I was approached after the first pilot was made. They showed me the first pilot and asked if I were interested in playing the part that Jeffrey Hunter was playing. I was intrigued by it and Gene Roddenberry and I had many talks about what the character would be like, what kind of a person he was, and that sort of thing.

"For instance, there was a question of how to play a commander of a ship every week with the responsibilities he has to bear without getting too heavy and pompous. That was a problem. I didn't solve it until about halfway through the first season. I had to learn not to take myself so seriously. I was being told to do certain things, but there was no precedent to follow. We were establishing our own precedent, and I found out as soon as I began to see it on the air. I realized what I had done wrong and began to change. In a play, you get immediate reaction from an audience and can start to change immediately, but until you're on the air on TV, you just don't know. There were things I had to create, like Captain Kirk's sense of humor, that was one of the things I began to develop.

"I've been an actor for many years and a director too. I feel I know a great deal about the way to make a film. I know what I would do in given instances. I don't like to impinge my feelings about a scene or a moment on a director who knows what he is doing because he may have a point of view himself. Certainly Marc Daniels is a first rate director, but there are times when I can say to somebody who I respect—why don't you try it this way . . . and because they respect me, they'll accept an idea from me where they might throw it away out of hand from some other actor. Besides which, as the star of a series, you have more influence than you would under normal circumstances.

"I felt very strongly about every area of the show. If I could see a point in the story line that could be improved, I would not hesitate, but leap eagerly into the fray and say, 'Here's what I think.' There were many times when the point was taken and used, and there were other times when they said, 'We can't do that.' And I accepted that. There were times when I suggested dialogue or script changes or ways to play a scene. There were times when directors finked out for one reason or another, either personal problems or lack of talent. Jerry Finnerman and I would complete the show.

"There was one show, I've forgotten the name of it, which somebody said to the director, if you bring the show in in five days, you'll get $500 extra. And it was a show I was mostly alone in. I did fourteen pages of dialogue in one day. The average was nine or ten pages a day, but I did fourteen. The show came in on time, the director got the 500 bucks and I didn't even get a thank-you."

There were occasionally problems on the STAR TREK set. Not all of them were *easily* solved. But all of them were eventually solved. For instance, Gene Rodenberry recalls: "One little incident that happened was one of the assistant directors asked me to go to the stage and talk to Bill Shatner about not being available when the camera was ready to roll, he was either on the phone or in the bathroom, or whatever. I went up to talk to him and Bill Shatner said, 'All right, Gene. It's reasonable for you to say this, but may I suggest something to you? I am in practically every scene in this show. Now there's a certain amount of personal business I have to conduct, there are times when I have to use the john, there are times when a friend will drop in on the set to say hello, and so on. The reason that it looks that I am late more often than other people is that I am in more scenes. Another person who has a smaller part can do these necessary things and it will never be noticed.'

"I said, 'My God, Bill, you're quite right. There is a certain amount of personal life and professional life an actor has to keep up and you're absolutely right. You're bound to appear more often late than others because you are in every scene. Forgive me for not seeing that first.' And we shook hands and that's how most of our problems were really solved.

"We had an exceptional relationship. Not just Bill and I, everybody on the show. We hardly ever had a problem that in the end we couldn't sit down and resolve."

One of the problems, however, was "The Great Shatner and Nimoy Feud."

There wasn't one. Not really.

—There were rumors, but they were unfounded. They were born out of the show's popularity. But, as rumors, they caused trouble.

When so much attention is focused on anything or any*one*, even the smallest incident will be magnified out of all proportion. A discussion becomes a disagreement. A disagreement becomes an argument. An argument becomes a fight. A fight becomes a feud.

Look, a movie set is a lot of things. It's a tourist attraction, it's a sweatshop, it's an altar for idol-worshippers, it's a political convention, it's an encounter group, it's a hostility session—but to the people who have to work on it, day in and day out, it's a *family*.

And STAR TREK was one of the happiest families. Probably it was one of the most congenial sets in Hollywood—most of the cast and crew members seemed to think so. Even the casual visitor was likely to notice that this particular set was a fun place to be. In fact, there were times when the studio had to restrict the number of people allowed to visit—they were starting to interfere with the shooting.

Like all families, however—even the happiest—the STAR TREK family was not without its little bumps and crises. And it was these that gave rise to the persistent and annoying rumors of a feud.

In the STAR TREK family, Gene Roddenberry was the father-image—affectionately known as "The Great Bird of the Galaxy" or sometimes just "The Bird." As a producer, he is one of the most skilled. The hardest problem for any producer is keeping his regular people happy and functioning at their best—and this is one of the things that Gene Roddenberry is very very good at. Nothing but *nothing* is every allowed to get in the way of production. The producer's goal is to get a good show on film and into the can. And that means that the cast and crew *have* to be kept happy. Gene Roddenberry should have been called "The Man with the Silver Tongue." He could charm the venom out of a cobra—and make the cobra enjoy every moment of it.

He gave frequent parties for the cast and crew, he was called "the Pearl Mesta of Paramount." He encouraged a good practical joke, and he set up some of the best himself. ("Steve Carabatsos was our story editor for a while. Matt Jefferies got hold of a weather balloon and we got some helium. We poured about a pint of cheap perfume in it and then we put the balloon in his office and blew it up so it completely filled his office and pushed the door closed against it and waited for Steve to come to work. He opened the door and walked right into this thing and we knew the only way he could get into his office was to break it, and breaking all the helium and air mixed with perfume would make his office smell like a Turkish whorehouse for a month, and indeed, that's what happened.") And he saw that there was a STAR TREK "blooper reel" for every season, an expense that most producers won't go to.

Gene Roddenberry always did what he believed to be best. His basic goal was to see that STAR TREK was the best TV show that he could make it.

Along about the middle of the second season, the little grumbles and gripes began to get annoying, almost out of hand. In this case, the hassle was not limited to Shatner and Nimoy—there were complaints from all of the actors.

You see, by this time, the show was beginning to settle into shape. Most of the development of the *Enterprise*'s capabilities and her characters' personalities had already been done. We had seen the Vulcan nerve pinch and the salute and the mind-meld. We had seen two or three super-computers driven crazy with illogic, we'd met the Klingons and the Romulans, and we'd determined the relationships of the various principal characters. Nearly every other episode had some girl tumbling into Captain Kirk's arms. Some of these things, once determined, began to turn into *shticks* and formulas and overworked devices.

The cast began to chafe. For a variety of reasons, each of them was unhappy with many of the scripts that were being sent down. For one thing, the show was a hit; it was established by now that STAR TREK had the most devoted fans of any TV show on the tube. Every member of the cast was concerned with making his character interesting and important. *And* keeping true to the original concept that these are warm, intelligent *human beings*, who have dedicated their lives to the stars.

For instance, Nichelle Nichols was very unhappy with the fact that so few of the writers were giving Lieutenant Uhura anything of importance to do— she felt that she was being used as a token Negro, opening and closing the hailing frequencies and staying safely in the background in most of the episodes. James Doohan felt that Scotty had not been treated as importantly as the Chief Engineer of a vast starship should be. After all, he was third in command after Kirk and Spock. And he really hadn't been allowed to be much of a human being either. James Doohan is an accomplished actor of considerable experience—he wanted to use his abilities to the fullest.

DeForest Kelley was generally unhappy that Dr. McCoy was not being used as a real doctor; too often, he felt, McCoy was being slighted. In the original conception, the Medical Officer was as important as the First Officer; but lately, it seemed that a lot of scenes were being written for Spock and Kirk, when the nature of the information being presented demanded that it be the Medical Officer who deduces and explains what is going on. De felt that he wasn't being given enough to do.

Shatner and Nimoy were unhappy too.

Now, this was not a major crisis—but there was a deterioration of morale. And Gene Roddenberry felt that much of the grumbling was unwarranted. He was aware of the problems and was working to solve some of them.

So he wrote THE letter.

It was a very confidential piece, sent only to the cast, only the regulars. No one, not even Gene Coon, saw copies of it. There was five pages directed to William Shatner, four or five pages to Leonard Nimoy, half a page to DeForest Kelley, half a page to James Doohan, and so on.

In this letter, Gene Roddenberry—the silver-tongued bird of the galaxy himself—took his actors to task and gave them all a proper bawling out. What was said to each is unimportant—what is important is that it *worked*.

Afterwards, things settled down. Somewhat. With only an occasional bruised ego, the cast went back to work.

But shortly after that, Gene Coon and Gene Roddenberry walked onto the set and De Kelley came up to them with murder in his eye and a copy of the letter in his hand. "Now, *this* is exactly what I'm talking about. Shatner gets five pages. Nimoy gets five pages. And I get only half a page!"

About this incident, Gene Roddenberry said: "A time did come during one of the years when I felt some criticism of the major performances were in order, which is the producer's job, of course. But I decided to keep it soft. I think it's safe to say that it is impossible to make any show with a group of actors who are proud of themselves and their performances—and have reason to be—and have them work together ten hours a day, under the pressures of television production, day after day after day without their feuds coming and going. They have it on every show, it happened on STAR TREK. I think it's to the credit of all the performers on STAR TREK that the fights rarely interfered with performances and most of them were over just as soon as they started."

Both Leonard Nimoy and William Shatner can confirm the truth of this. For instance, Leonard Nimoy says, "Bill and I are both very committed to and concerned with the work that we do, and we both tend to have strong personalities—we're both Aries—and we both have strong feelings about what's right and what's wrong. So, yes, there were times when we had differences of opinion about how a thing should be done or whether it should be done at all. But, we are very good friends, we're very close. We have a very very close relationship, even though we don't see each other a lot. But that's not by choice—Bill has done a lot of traveling in the last couple of years and so have I. It's just the nature of the business. But when we do meet, it's babble time. The stuff just pours out of us and we turn each other in a way that's really unique. I don't really know of anybody else in my life that does that—that I have that kind of thing with. I went to Chicago just to surprise him on a television show. They called me and asked me if I would do it and I said I would be glad to. And not only was he genuinely surprised, but he was obviously terribly moved. It was really a terrific thing. And we sat on that TV show for about an hour and we just *babbled* about old times.

"The whole feud thing, I think was amplified out of proportion by the fan magazines* who needed something exciting to write about. And it's much more exciting to write about arguments on a set than to simply report that all is peace and quiet and that the show is being done professionally.

"The one problem that I did run into in the time that Bill and I spent together was that we'd be together in the makeup department in the morning and we'd start talking about something that happened the previous day. And we'd get so animated and so involved—we'd get so hilarious and hysterical just laughing that we literally couldn't even sit in the chairs. We'd have to get up out of the chairs to laugh it out. And by the time 8:00 came around— you know, I'd be there at 6:30 in the morning, Bill would arrive at 7:00 and it would start—and by 8:00, many days, I was just wiped out, exhausted emotionally, from having talked and laughed so much. Sometimes it was pure craziness in there. And then I had to go out and start a twelve-hour day of shooting, and I would walk out *limp*."

William Shatner's reply to the same question was almost identical:

"There was never any feud. There were, on occasions, mostly between Leonard and I, a difference of opinion and sometimes, in a moment of pique, one or the other of us would get angry. You've got to realize that for three years, all of us—but particularly, Leonard and I—were thrown into each other's company for twelve hours or more a day. And here were two people who had never met before, we never asked to be married to each other—but we were, in effect, *married*. We were more constant companions than each other's wives. And, if you use that as a basis for judging the relationship, we had a far happier marriage than most marriages are. We got along famously.

"And, I think, any analysis of our relationship with each other has to be based also on the feelings we have for each other now, which is very interesting. I hadn't seen Leonard for three years, not since the cancellation of the show. The first time I saw him was only for a brief second in the commissary at Universal Studios. We just kind of clutched each other, pounded each other on the back and said 'Hi, how are you?' But then, a couple of months after that, I was playing in the Chicago area and I was doing a live television show, a talk show, and while we were on the air, the host asked, 'What do you think of Leonard Nimoy?' And I began to praise Leonard. And the host said, 'Well, I'm glad you said that, because—' And in walked Leonard. They had flown him from Los Angeles to Chicago, to appear on this hour show. Well, we just laughed and giggled our way through the whole program—and I think that demonstrates more than anything the basic good fellowship between us."

---

* Not to be confused with *fanziness*.

End of paragraph, chapter and feud.

DeForest Kelley, who played sarcastic Dr. McCoy, used to love clowning around on the set. Like all the actors, he couldn't resist a good joke.
  For instance:
  "We'd had these tribbles everywhere. They had them in the prop room
and they kept showing up here and there for weeks after we filmed the
episode. A tribble might show up as an extra breast on Nichelle or something like that. I guess everybody was still kind of tribble happy and every
time we got a chance to work a tribble in somewhere, we were working
them in. Instead of pulling out a communicator, somebody would pull out a
tribble. They'd continually pop up somewhere. Pull out a drawer and somebody would reach for something and there'd be a tribble there. So I delivered one. I don't remember what show it was, but I was performing surgery
on someone—probably Mark Lenard in 'Journey to Babel'—and after a supposed incision, I took a tribble out of him. I remember doing it and having
the whole crew crack up completely. It took weeks to get all the tribbles off
the set.
  "Another time, we did a show with Shatner where he was playing a man
and a woman both. I think it might have been 'Turnabout Intruder.' Anyway,
he had this very dramatic scene and I was checking him over and he had his
moments of becoming quite feminine every so often. And he had a line something like, 'What do you think it is?' And I looked at him very sincerely and
said, 'Captain, you're pregnant!' He almost fell off the table. Shatner loved
that stuff.
  "Of course, Shatner loved to do it to people too. He was an artist in it,
certainly with me. You know, we all had our differences here and there, but
we had this thing going, and no matter what we thought of the other one, he
could look at me in a certain way or do something and crack me up completely.
But he's a very in-control actor under very adverse circumstances.
  "There were some things that weren't so funny at the time, but they're
funny to think back upon. The first year of the show, I was driving an old
'57 Ford that I had, and Leonard was driving an old Studebaker or something like that. By the time we were into the second year, we found ourselves in the position of being able to afford new cars. So I bought a new
Thunderbird, and Leonard bought a new Buick Riviera. We were both very
proud of them. You know, they had stereo radios and were just lush. We'd
back in every morning in our same spots, side by side, all three of us, parked
on the lot there. The third space, was Shatner's of course. He went from a

Corvette—that's what he had when we started—to something like a Pontiac sports car. A GTO, something like that. He was always the hot-rodder of the group, the motorcycle king, the athletic one.

"But anyhow, I got off early one day and I went out and got in the car, and I had left the wheels turned when I had parked in the morning. Leonard was just coming around the corner of the soundstage, I didn't really see him until a moment later; I started the car and the wheels were turned and I went right into his new Buick.

"So here comes Leonard on his bicycle, and I'm out looking at the cars. And I said, 'Leonard, I wrecked our cars!' And he said, 'You're kidding.' And then he looked over and saw it and he almost fell off his bicycle. It would have been a great shot—there we were standing there and exchanging insurance information, me in street clothes and him in his costume and ears. It was very funny—and at the same time, it wasn't.

"You know, I remember how I came on to STAR TREK. Paul Fix was the doctor in the first couple episodes, and then I came on. It's a strange thing with casting. Roddenberry is a very talented man and he has a great knack for casting—I've done other things with him. I've seen how he works and it's not easy to get principals together where a certain chemistry works. If you don't have that chemistry that's flowing between three people or four, it doesn't work and you can't force it. It's one of the things that was a major factor with the three of us, me and Leonard and Bill. A lot of people thought there was a great deal of luck involved in it, but I think a great deal of it was shrewd casting.

"When Gene first called me in for this show, and to meet with the director, he said he wanted me for the doctor. At the time I thought it was Roddenberry's decision to say yes or no. So I thought I had the part, but apparently somebody didn't want me, I don't know who, because I didn't get it. Genc was doing another show, called *Police Story* with Rafer Johnson and myself and the late Steve Ihnat. It was a threesome thing going again, and it was a hell of a show, a very good show. It should have sold, but it didn't. In the meantime, NBC had made the first pilot of STAR TREK, but they couldn't get together with the late Jeffrey Hunter. That's when Shatner came into the picture, so they went ahead and made the second pilot with him.

"Now, *Police Story* was shown on one of these audience reaction things and evidently I got lucky and I received a good response. So I called Gene Roddenberry after I found out *Police Story* didn't sell. He had already made the second pilot on STAR TREK and I called him to thank him, to tell him I was sorry that the show hadn't gone, and he said, 'Well, don't hang up.

De. Something has just happened.' And he said that the network was impressed by the response on that other show and that he wanted me for the doctor on STAR TREK. So that's how the whole thing started.

"Now, to be perfectly honest, I had never been much of a science fiction fan. I read very little of it. But I saw the pilot that Jeffrey Hunter made, and I was absolutely fascinated by it. I had never seen anything like it. I walked out of the projection room—I felt *stoned*! You know, really! It was the first time that I had ever seen any science fiction that had impressed me so much. And I thought, well, it's either going to be the biggest hit on television, or the biggest flop. I didn't think there would be any middle road at all. So when I was finally called upon to be in STAR TREK, that's when I began reading science fiction.

"It was a fascinating time—particularly the first year. The first year was very hard work. It almost killed us all. We were working terribly long hours. We were pushing to get these things done and done right. We all felt we needed so much more time than we were getting. I was pleased with it, but I felt that McCoy wasn't being used to his fullest extent. I began to see and feel the possibilities for him, and I think they did too. In the second year they began to expand him somewhat, and in the third year, they really began to get to him.

"Our first year was the kind of a year, even though it was experimental because we were really trying to find our way, we were trying to set the characters and give each character definition, Bill and Leonard and myself, we were all looking for ourselves that first year—but we did some material that I think people enjoyed most, which was more science fictional than some of the stuff we did later.

"We did a lot of crazy things on the set. In the beginning, when everything was rosy, everyone was having a lot of fun working with the show. And after working long hard hours, you do certain things to break some of the tension that builds up. You need a good laugh, and then you go back and work some more.

"I remember when we were doing the Halloween show—'Catspaw'—and Nichelle and Bill and Leonard and Walter and myself were behind huge double doors in this big castle, and we were supposed to burst through these doors and come running into this place. We were all standing around in the back and we were laughing about whether we were going to go in according to billing, Shatner, Leonard and me, then Nichelle and finally Walter. Well, Bill said, 'The hell with it, let's just bust through the door all at once like we're supposed to.' And Nichelle was standing there, and I said, 'Okay, the last one out's a nigger-baby.' And Nichelle, she got the biggest kick out of it, she cracked up completely. And then we all came out of this door, just roaring with laughter, falling down. Of course, it ruined the take. The director yelled 'Cut' and we had to start over, but it's an example of the good rapport we had.

"I always wanted the show to do a script that featured Nichelle and myself. Something where the two of us were thrown onto a planet where there was a great racial problem, only reversed. The fact that I am a Southerner and she is black, and that we're trapped on this planet together could have been a very good story.*

" 'The Deadly Years'—we did that second season, that was an interesting show. I was in makeup from five to six hours. I had to look very very old. I only worked half a day on that show because I was in makeup the other half. I'd sit in the chair for a while, then I'd take a break, go to the john, come back, and they'd work some more. It was a tremendous makeup effort. There were three makeup men working on me all this time, on my hands and on my face. Leonard was lucky on that show. He was blessed by the fact that Vulcans don't age as fast as humans. But I enjoyed it.

"You know, the fans remember these things. The shows that are mentioned to me when I go back east are 'The Trouble with Tribbles,' 'The City on the Edge of Forever,' and there was another one, 'Shore Leave.' These are the ones that are mentioned most to me. I've never seen it where fans remember individual episodes of a show before, they remember them by the titles, who was in them, everything.

"I used to have my scripts from the first two years stacked out in the garage. I had all of them, and then I received a letter from a Catholic organization, some nuns back east in Pennsylvania someplace, asking me if I had a script that I could send them that they might auction off for some charity and so I packed the whole bunch of them up and sent them off to them, but at that time I never realized that everybody was so hungry for the scripts. But even if I had, it would still have been the thing to do. I don't think I have a STAR TREK script left.

"The greatest fan letter I ever received, I still have it somewhere, I opened it up and there was a cardboard inside and pasted on it was a marijuana cigarette. And it said, 'Dear DeForest, you have turned me on so many times, I would like to repay the favor. (signed) One of your female fans.'

---

* As a matter of fact, the idea was one that very definitely *had* been considered. A script version had even been written. And rewritten. And rewritten. The story involved a planet where blacks were the masters and whites were the slaves, but either the premise was too touchy for television or nobody could quite make it work. The script never reached a form where Roddenberry or Coon wanted to put it into production.

"But, I remember, the fan reaction came as a complete shock to me because I had no idea the popularity that STAR TREK had generated. The first time I really became aware of it was on a trip to New York. It was on a Saturday and we said, well, let's go to a matinee. It was kind of a rainy afternoon, so we went right into the theatre, the lobby, and my wife Carolyne said, 'I'm going to the ladies' room.' I said, 'Okay, I'll wait here for you.' There was this vacant candy stand and I was leaning against it and a couple of women saw me and they came over and handed me their programs to sign and I signed them, and a couple more came over and handed me their programs to sign and I started to sign them and after about ten minutes there was a whole mob. I looked up, looking for Carolyne, and I couldn't see her. I was in the middle of a seething, actually a seething mob. And finally, I saw Carolyne coming up, just her head, coming up the steps from the ladies' room. I literally was surrounded and I couldn't get away and I started to make the move and I couldn't get away and Carolyne waved at me and I waved to her and she pointed like this, 'I'm going to the seats.' They finally had to call the ushers and a security man—the women were getting up out of their seats, mind you, in the theatre and coming into the aisle to get to me.

"This was a complete shock to me. And they were all standing up in the balconies and yelling 'STAR TREK' and 'McCoy.' It was wild. Finally, they got me down to my seat and when I sat down, we were in the middle of a row of nuns, sisters on each side of us. So people are in the aisles and they're passing programs over and the nuns are handing me their programs and I'm signing them. It was such a mess that they were holding the curtain of the show, there was so much noise. This nun that was sitting next to me, she said, 'This must be a terrible annoyance for you wherever you go.' I said, 'It's the first time it's ever happened to me. I wouldn't know.' 'Well,' she said, 'you must remember something. With every little blessing, there comes a penalty.'

"It was equally as bad getting out of there. I wanted to go backstage and say hello to Joel Grey, but I couldn't. The ushers came and got me, surrounded me, got me to the side of the theatre and put me in a cab like a mechanical doll or something. That was the first time I was ever mobbed and it was completely shocking."

Mr. Scott, the Chief Engineer of the *Enterprise*, was played by James Doohan, an actor of no small ability and considerable background in radio and television, as well as motion pictures. At one time, he was known as the busiest actor in Canada, working seven days a week, nine–fourteen hours a day. "If I didn't have my book full up for the next six weeks, I figured I was in a slump."

Like all the members of the STAR TREK family, James Doohan has a sly sense of humor. "I remember some of the practical jokes that were played on me when I was working radio. Things like setting the last three pages of your script on fire or putting a blank page in front of you, things like that.

"Of course, some of the things that happened on the STAR TREK set grew out of mistakes. In 'Catspaw,' we were coming into a dungeon and I tripped down the steps a couple of times. They only recorded one, I think. It's in the blooper reel. I was supposed to be very serious and kind of blank in my mind. I certainly was blank about that final step. I tripped and everyone broke up.

"I got onto STAR TREK through a fellow named Jimmy Goldstone. I had read for him about ten days before I read for STAR TREK. I forget the name of the show, but the producer said I looked too much like the star. I did an English accent too, but I didn't get the job.

"Jimmy Goldstone was flipped anyway, so he called me up about ten days later and said would I mind coming down to Desilu studios on a Saturday morning and reading for this new pilot which was just starting. So I got in there and there was Gene and Bob Justman and Joe D. Agosta, who was head of casting at the time, and a couple of other people I didn't know. And they handed me a script and said, go ahead, do some accents. So I did about five or six accents, Russian, Irish, English, German, and Scottish. And then they asked me to do a couple again. According to Gene I entertained them for about two hours, I thought it was only forty minutes. Anyway, they picked the Scottish, and then we did the pilot. In the pilot I had very little to do. I think I had about three lines. I think they didn't consider they'd be using the engineer very much, and so I had a contract for five out of thirteen episodes, and as soon as they began working with it they began to feel that they would be using the character much more and that if Leonard and Bill were going to go down to a planet that the Chief Engineer is the logical guy to take care of the ship. You don't put the doctor of the ship in charge. So they began to find out that Scotty was more useful, so I got thirteen out of thirteen, which was very nice. And it just kept getting better and better.

"Actors can put a lot of things into a show. I remember, for instance, I suggested Scotty's dress uniform be a kilt. They immediately grabbed onto the idea. They sent to Scotland for the Scott tartan, which is one of the really old tartans. There are really only about four, and the Scott family is one of the originals. They sent to San Francisco for some other stuff and had the uniform made and it looked pretty good. It was only too bad they didn't have it earlier. There were other episodes when it might have been used.

"Personally, I didn't like the flare legs on the trousers. I didn't like the way they stuck out, I thought that they came on kind of fey. But after a while, it worked out, I got used to it. I think though, that it might have been just as good if they had just had a band of red down the trousers, you know, red for engineering, blue for scientific, green for command, and so on.

"You know, the engine room was just a piddling little thing when they started. They didn't think they'd ever be going to it. Then they found out they *had* to go to it, it helped to create a lot of suspense. The very fact that you were there and did all sorts of things, helped the show a great deal, so each year they added to it . . . Like they added the upstairs section with the ladder leading up to it, and later the Emergency Manual Monitor. Things like that.

"There was a time when I wrote down, from what I knew of science and atomic energy, all the functions of the ship and the reason why certain things worked. Like the force field and the tractor beams where we pulled something in. To me, it seemed that the ship could cone the energy out to a certain distance—the further out, the less powerful it becomes—and all we would do is focus the cone back in, and that would be our tractor beam. Why not? I've got it all written down somewhere. I had to have all of that figured out not just for myself, but also in case the fans asked, how does this work? So I sat down there for a couple of days and figured the whole thing out so I could talk about it—the transporter room breaking down matter into its component parts, the warp drive engines, and so on. Just as an actor, I had to know what my character was doing and *why*.

"I think STAR TREK was one of the greatest creations that has come out of television in the United States, and it really should be brought back. But, of course, only with Gene Roddenberry in charge, because I don't think anyone else can handle it and has the range that Gene has. I don't know of anyone else that has that possible range of understanding. I think there might be more leeway if it were done as a series of movies, once every few months or so. Then you could have a really good STAR TREK movie, and have it as a series—like the way *Planet of the Apes* has been handled. But you see, the problem with these things is that even if they're willing to spend a couple of million on them, you still have to have an executive producer who will make sure that it doesn't come out like trash. That's why it needs a Gene Roddenberry. Because he won't allow it to be trash, Gene has integrity.

"The fans recognize it. That's why the show won't die. I've been to STAR TREK conventions, and I think they're great. They're very enthusiastically put on, and I was surprised at the people. You might think that STAR TREK fans are a bunch of kooks, but they're not. It's just their interest that makes them out of the ordinary and makes some people say, 'Oh, STAR TREK nuts.'

"I'll tell you, I don't remember what was first season and what was third season—but the fans, they know exactly what was done and when, but I don't. I can't remember them. They start talking to me about certain scripts, and an actor really forgets certain lines, but they say, 'Oh, but you said so and so and so,' and I say, 'What? What?' I can maybe remember the line, but not the context.

"You know, when I changed my hair, the fans noticed it immediately. I just wasn't happy with it, but I didn't like it combed back either. I thought it looked like hell. But when I went to put it back the old way, Gene didn't like it. He decided I'd have to have a new hairdo, so he sent me to Sebring's. After that it was better, I was able to make it match more easily. It hasn't changed much since then, now it's just a little longer.

"Sometimes, some of the fans created problems. Like one girl was invited on the set and she was there from eight in the morning to seven at night, and she would just either stand there and look at you with that dead look in the eyes or she would ask you fifty times a day if you'd like a cup of coffee. And you know, she was there for two or three days. One of the actors got really bugged by it, and he had to go to the executive producer to get that girl off the set. She was driving him crazy, he couldn't work, couldn't plan, couldn't do anything; no matter where he went, she followed him. Fans don't realize that it's very upsetting. When they come in, meet you and talk to you, it's okay, but when they just sit there and they just look at you with that worshipping look—it can really be terrible, like all the actor has to do is look at the fan and she's going to be cured or something. I honestly think that people should not be allowed to stay on a set longer than forty-five minutes unless it's business, because it's just too much. Particularly when it's that kind of adulation.

"We had closed sets for a while, then they opened again, then they closed again, and it got pretty bad. The second assistants are very busy and the actors don't like to go to them all the time and say, 'Please get rid of this person or that person, they're bugging me.' So, there really ought to be some kind of time limit put on all of these things. But then you'd have to hire someone to go around and say, 'Your time is up and your time is up.'

"I don't think the fans realize sometimes what they're doing. I was moving from one apartment to another apartment and I still had a couple of weeks left in the old place, so I left some stuff there and I went back every now and then to get it, just short trips in my car. One day some kids met me out in the old apartment building saying, 'There's a woman in your patio.' And there was this eighteen-year-old girl, an exchange student who lived in Pasadena or Arcadia, and she'd been waiting there for eighteen hours, all night, she'd been waiting on the patio. It really shook me. So I took her down to the drugstore and bought her a soda and then put her on a bus and sent her home. But it really shook me.

"But those are the exceptions. Most of the fans have been great. There were a group of kids here from Detroit—from the STAR TREK Association for Revival. I gave them some film clips and some autographed things on STAR TREK stationary (which I'm fast running out of) and also some scripts. My point in giving them the film and the scripts was that these kids wanted me to come to a convention they were holding, and so they were going to pay my expenses to get there. Well, I wanted to help, so I said, 'What can I do?' And then I came up with this idea. They could sell some of the autographed scripts, and if I gave them a pile, then that's their expenses and everybody benefits.

"I'll tell you, STAR TREK was always a fascinating show for an actor, especially the content. If it was a choice between another good show and STAR TREK, I think I'd take STAR TREK, even though I may have a better part in the other show. I'd still take STAR TREK. It's one of the best things I've ever worked on."

Ensign Chekov was introduced to the *Enterprise* in STAR TREK's second year. At first, Walter Koenig, who played Chekov, was not a contract player; rather, he was hired on a show-by-show basis. But as he began to fit so well into the STAR TREK ensemble, he became more and more important, until by the third season, he was upgraded to a regular supporting player.

"When the show was still in production," says Koenig, "I was being pushed by *Sixteen* magazine, so I received an enormous flood of letters. At one time, I was getting about 650 letters a week . . . which was about the same as the other people on the show were getting at that time.

"Some of them I got into correspondence with, the ones who were most interesting or most touching or most intelligent; the letters that were a little bit more than 'Would you please send me a photograph?' All girls, I think. They wrote me from all over the country. I remember one girl, I think she was in New York, she kept writing to me and it really seemed to me like she had a lot of problems, but she was an interesting girl. But she was always denigrating herself and putting herself down. There was a big lapse between her eighth and ninth letter, and then finally she wrote to me and told me that she hoped I wouldn't stop liking her, but she was black. Well, that was silly.

Ensign Chekov

Chekov in environmental gear: "The Tholian Web"

Mr. Sulu

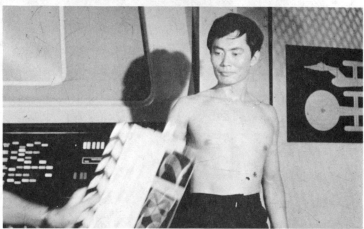

"The Naked Time"

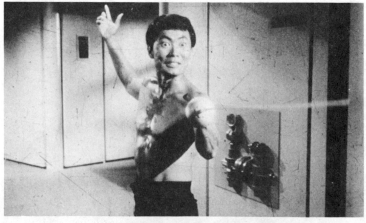

"The fencing caused a little havoc on the set."

Lt. Uhura

Uhura singing: "Charlie X"

Uhura and sulu: "Mirror, Mirror"

Trelane, "The Squire of Gothos"

I wrote to her and said, 'Absurd . . . I'm Jewish, so what the hell does that mean? Why should it make any difference one way or the other? And she responded to that, and we went on writing for a few months after that.

"I had kids writing me from deaf school too. I used to send them scripts and things. And I got letters from college students; we had long drawn-out debates about what we were doing and what I was doing specifically on the show. Now that the show has moved out of the states, I've gotten letters from all over. I've gotten them from Korea, Vietnam, Germany, England—the show was very big in England. There were letters from behind the Iron Curtain even. I got some from Hungary or Czechoslovakia or someplace like that—I couldn't tell, they were in a foreign language.

"I still have most of the letters. I have them out in my garage. Five mail sacks full. I finally had to dispose of some of them though. I just didn't have any more room. All that mail—I never did get used to it.

"We were shooting 'The Gamesters of Triskelion.' There were three of us, Bill, Nichelle and myself, and we had just landed on this planet—but we were dislocated, we didn't know where we were, and we were looking around and all of a sudden we hear a voice saying, 'Hello, foreigners' or something like that. And in my zeal, I turned to Bill and instead of saying, 'What was that?' I slapped him on the arm like we used to do as kids in New York. And he turned to me and looked like 'Who is this fellow?' and whacked me right back. I had just gotten so much into the scene that I hadn't realized what I was doing.

"I had a thing about that particular episode. Firstly, it was one of the shows that I had a pretty good part in to begin with, but the director was a former song-and-dance man who was—I can't recall his name—just sort of tap dancing his way through this thing, literally as well as figuratively. I had this big scene where this homely girl comes into the cell with me and says, 'Let me be your mate.' Something like that. We had a very funny relationship set up, because Chekov didn't want to have anything to do with her. Because I was the junior member of the cast, my scenes were relegated to the end of the day, which is quite understandable, I'm not complaining about it, but on this particular day we were pressed for time. So rather than covering me by shooting over her shoulder and covering her by shooting over my shoulder, the director only did it one way—they shot it over my shoulder at her. Which meant if I were to look at her, all the audience would see would be the back of my head. So he suggested I do this—every time I have to deliver a line I do a profile and not look at her, which really didn't leave a lot of room for spontaneity; so I would say something and I'd turn profile, then I'd say something and look at her, and then I'd turn profile and say the line, and I was very disconcerted and very disappointed in that. They never did get around to shooting it the other way.

"The same kind of thing happened to me in another very big scene, and another director who was pressed for time. He shot my scene without even a rehearsal. It was supposed to be a full view, and as it turned out, the most prominent part of me was my left ear.

"But I was very lucky that I was able to be so much a part of the show. There was a set of circumstances that was very fortuitous for me in the second season. George Takei and I were being featured about equally on the show, and then George was cast as Captain Nim in *The Green Berets*. That was filming in Georgia. So he left for ten weeks, and during that time, rather than dividing up the parts between myself and him, they were able to give me more to do, and I got a lot of better shows than I had gotten at first.

"There was one thing that happened that hit me in a funny way. A sad thing, really. I was getting an awful lot of mail, but I was getting it a month after it was sent because it was coming through the United Fan Mail Service. Some of it would go to Paramount first and then the service. And some of it would go to NBC and then to Paramount and finally the service. And finally, I would get it. Anyway, I got a letter from a couple of parents who had a little girl who was ill, quite ill, and she had heard that I had a dog, and she wanted a snapshot of my dog, and the parents asked if I would send her the snapshot of the dog, which I did as soon as I got the letter—but this was three or four weeks after it had been sent. I sent the picture with a little note on the back and I got back a reply from the parents, thanking me, but telling me that the child had passed away. It was really quite sad. But the interesting part of the episode was that they asked me if I wanted this to be publicized, they would be glad to send it over to their local newspaper. But I said no, I didn't want publicity that capitalized on someone else's grief. But it was interesting the way people come to think about TV shows and actors.

"There were nice things that happened too. There was a little girl from Pennsylvania who had been corresponding with me, very sweet girl about fifteen and quite bright. She mentioned that she and her mother would like to come out and visit the set and I took it all quite literal and said, 'That'd be great. If you come out, we'll have to say hello.' And that must have sounded like an invitation because they came right out. She was a very lovely kid and the mother had made every effort to make the whole trip happen, it must have meant an awful lot to both of them. Well, I had alerted the rest of the cast, and it was really beautiful. Everybody was just terrific to her. They knew she had come in from Pennsylvania and they were all really sweet. Nichelle, Bill, Leonard, everyone—so the kid was in heaven. She and her mother spent the whole day there with us and she really had a ball. She stayed in town for about a week after that, and I took her out to lunch one day. We still correspond. She's in college now, studying literature and drama.

"One of my most depressing moments, one where I felt the most defeated, happened at the beginning of the third season's production. I had talked to Gene Roddenberry. I had gone over to his house, he was extremely generous with his time, and explained that I wanted to know what was going to happen with the character of Chekov, and I was asking in the most subordinate way, I mean, I wasn't being pushy or insistent. Well, he showed me a memo he had received from Mort Werner, the NBC executive, about the character of Chekov, about getting him more involved in the show, getting him in more stories and so on. He wanted to know what Gene was going to do with Chekov as he had gotten a very good reaction from the audience.

"Well, after that, I received a copy of a memo that Gene had sent to his executives that Chekov should be developed more, should get involved with girls, should be proud—but in a good way, and so on. He wanted the character developed. All of this sounded terribly exciting, and I thought, here at last I would get a chance to do something more often than one out of every six or seven shows. But, of course, that was when the show was still scheduled to be shown on Monday at 7:30. That was a marvelous time slot; all the kids would be up and able to see the show—especially the age group that would react best to Chekov. But then the show was moved to 10:00 on Friday nights and I knew that was it for Chekov. And for the show. We all knew it. When Gene left we were all very depressed. It was one of the most depressing moments of the show.

"I always felt that among the people who were in support of me—besides Gene, of course—was Bob Justman. Bob was a gentleman to the core. An extremely nice man. I remember how touching it was when he left the show. This was in the third season. He gave all of us little personal notes, thanking us for cooperation and thanking us for part of his life."

George Takei is one of the smiling-est human beings alive. He radiates energy. As Mr. Sulu, the Helmsman of the *Enterprise*, he was able to discipline and project a great deal of that vitality and maintain the presence of a consistent character, despite the fact that he was one of the least used of the regular cast members. Very few of the scripts gave him chances to show off his acting ability. As George says, "I used to have my lines memorized even before I saw the script. 'Aye, aye, sir,' 'Coming to new course,' and 'Phasers locked on target.'

"You know, it's been eight years since I made my first STAR TREK. I wasn't in the first pilot—the one with Jeffrey Hunter—but I was in the second one. We shot that at MGM. The whole concept of STAR TREK was one that I was very excited about doing. I had never done a series until then, so the idea of working on a continuing character was a real challenge. Of course, Gene Roddenberry was the key to the series; if they tried to do it without him, it would be a mistake. What STAR TREK was, would not be there. But if Gene were to be in charge, I would have no reservation about doing it again.

"I didn't have much to do the first year, so I worked on them to beef up the part. There was one script where I was able to have a little fun. That was 'The Naked Time' where I got to do a little fencing. That was a lot of fun. I really enjoyed that. I knew nothing about fencing at the time. John D.F. Black who wrote the show came on the set one afternoon and he engaged me in conversation and said 'I'm planning something in a script for you and it's going to involve a little fencing. Can you fence?' And I said, 'No, but I can learn.' I was being very honest when I confessed that—but that's what any actor would have said, 'I can learn.'

"So I dashed out and started taking lessons immediately. It turned out I really enjoyed the exercise and the beauty of the whole sport. It was a fun thing, so now it actually has become a hobby of mine. I still work out when I have the time—which isn't as often as I'd like because I'm so busy with other activities.

"The fencing caused a little havoc on the set—there was some concern while we were shooting because I'm a pretty rambunctious person and I was constantly working out on stage. I have a tendency to get involved in what I'm doing and sometimes I forget that other people might not share that same involvement—so who didn't I slice? You know, you'd expect Shatner to grab a sword and fight back, but he didn't; he feigned mock terror and ran away.

"During the second year of the show, I had a chance to play Captain Nim in *The Green Berets* with John Wayne. This meant I would have to be away from STAR TREK for several weeks—in fact, that developed into a real hassle. There was one particular script that was really a nice one, a good one for Sulu. It was 'The Gamesters of Triskelion' and I wanted to do it very much. Roddenberry had showed it to me before I took off for Columbus, Georgia. Well, we had some rain and that delayed the shooting of the picture and they had to change the schedule, so there were more than a couple of weeks of just sitting around. I spent a lot of time hiking—it's beautiful country there— but it was frustrating because I wanted to come back and do that show. So I talked to John Wayne, who was also directing as well as starring, and he thought well, maybe he could let me go so I could dash back to L.A. and do that segment and then dash back to Georgia and resume filming. But this was a great frustration. We were doing some night shots, and they needed one particular shot before I could take off. I had to take the early Sunday morning plane in order to be in Los Angeles for the early Monday morning call. So we were shooting all night Saturday and then we had some mishap with one of the explosions and that took up most of the night. And this one particular scene that we had to have before they could wrap up on the night shots could not be gotten, so John Wayne said, sorry about that, but we need you for Monday night's shooting, we can't let you go. So because of that one shot we couldn't grab on Saturday night, I had to stay over and had to miss out on that episode. It was very frustrating, I had really wanted to do it. As it turned out, they rewrote it for Walter. Ensign Chekov got all of Mr. Sulu's lines. I've got to admit though, that despite my disappointment, I was pleased that Walter was able to do it. All of us shared the common problem of not really having enough to do to satisfy us, so if I couldn't do it, at least another good actor and a good friend was able to benefit from it.

"You know, in the back of your mind, you always have these glimmers of hope that a show will be a smasheroonie, so you do whatever you can to help it. I have relatives in Milwaukee and Denver, and whenever I would go back there, I would always do a little promoting. The year before the show premiered even, I wrote them to let them know and they talked to the local newspaper people and said their relative was coming and would they like to meet him and so forth.

"The thing about a television series is that when you're exposed on a regular basis, it does give you that much more visibility. The fan following is therefore multiplied. I'd been doing things before, but never getting the kind of fan letter response that STAR TREK afforded me. We all had to learn how to cope with it. I answered my mail as best as I could, without encouraging the fans too much. The ones that were really intelligent, very sincerely intended ones, I found to be personally stimulating and I answered them in kind. There are a few people who still maintain that correspondence with me—they write letters of substance, so STAR TREK did afford me some interesting pen pal relationships.

"I had people come and visit me at the studios from quite a long distance. There was a girl who watched STAR TREK in Japan, and was a great STAR TREK follower there. I don't think she came all the way just because of STAR TREK— she wanted to visit America, but she wrote and asked if she could visit the set, and so I showed her around. She didn't speak English, so I had to translate for her. I felt like a Universal Studios tour guide. Miss Japan, who competed in one of those international beauty pageants, also made a special request to visit the STAR TREK set. She didn't speak English either, so I served as a translator for her as well. That was a lot of fun.

"You know, I think the whole actor's thing of 'I want to be alone' is ridiculous. Public appearances are part of our job, and I think most actors enjoy the fan adulation. It's rather a singular kind of privilege to be placed on a pedestal like this. I know that I've been doing some political work, and I know some of the things I am able to do specifically because I'm an actor and can attract a certain following. So there are certain advantages that other people don't have that actors do. Whenever I hear other actors complaining that they don't like the whole thing of being mobbed and so on, I think it's ridiculous. It's part of the career, like it or not, and one has to learn to deal with it. And with it come very special privileges. I enjoy it. And yes, I use it too. But most of all, I enjoy it."

Of all the STAR TREK cast members, Nichelle Nichols, the lovely Lieutenant Uhura, is one of the most lucid on the subject of the show, and science fiction in general; she displays an amazing savvy not just of STAR TREK'S appeal, but of its importance as a part of American culture—and from that, she makes the leap to the ultimate considerations of science fiction: "Where are we going and why?"

Nichelle loves to talk about the show, and she can hold an audience spellbound with her descriptions and analyses. For instance, in November 1972, the International Fantasy Film Convention devoted one of its sessions to STAR TREK. Guests included Nichelle Nichols, Dorothy Fontana, Walter Koenig, George Takei, Majel Barrett, and Gene Roddenberry. While waiting in the VIP room, a reporter asked if he could interview a few of the group. Chairs were pulled up in a circle and a casual rap began.

—Forty-five minutes later, the convention chairman reluctantly had to break up the session because the STAR TREK cast was needed to speak to the rest of the convention. But for those forty-five minutes, a true *happening* had occurred. Nichelle Nichols had all but dominated the talk, holding a delighted group of listeners spellbound with her vision of why science fiction—not just STAR TREK—could be one of the great vehicles for spreading human understanding. Above all, she showed that Lieutenant Uhura was capable of a lot more depth than she had ever been allowed to show on the tube.

Nichelle is reluctant to talk about the real Nichelle but at another time she spoke on a more personal level about her own experiences. "I think we had the most fun in the first year of the show. It was the best year as far as I'm concerned. It was the best produced, and there were the best directors that we had. We were alive and we enjoyed the scripts and that was when we had the best scripts. We had very few good ones after the first year and a half.

"In the third season, as far as I was concerned, we were just marking time. There were occasionally moments of value, but the things we had set as the tone and the mood of the show, the brotherhood of man and the family of the ship, were completely lost. We started doing silly old cliches like beasties from outer space, where before it had been not beasties, but alien beings, alien only that they were alien to us, different—alien *meaning* different. And I thought that was the beauty of the show at the beginning, and I think that's what Gene Roddenberry most intended and regretted most that the show lost. I do.

"My first job in television was on *The Lieutenant*, with Gary Lockwood. It was a very good role, but it was a feature role, and after I did it, that's when they found out it was my first role on television. I'd done a lot of theatre before that, though. I'd had experience, but I didn't know camera moves, I didn't even know what my key light was—that's how they found out that I had never done television before. The director came over to me and said, 'You're doing a brilliant job. I like the sensitivity that you're getting, but stay in your key lights.' And I said, 'Huh? What?' And finally, he said, 'Don't you know where—haven't you ever done a TV show before?!' And I said no, and they said, 'What?!!' He said 'Cut. Everybody take five.' And he came and put his arm around me and walked down the set and he said, 'Are you putting me on?' And I said, 'No, I'm not.' So after he explained about key lights, they took me around, laughing like hell, and everybody was congratulating me because here this was the third day of shooting and they didn't know it, except occasionally I got out of my key light. The key light is the light that's focused on you, and if you move out of it, you throw a shadow in the wrong place, either across yourself or another actor. They explained a lot of things to me after that and I learned a lot.

"Anyway, after I finished that show, I got a formal legal document from Gene Roddenberry and MGM. It was very long and I couldn't figure it out, and I got scared to death. I thought, what the hell is going on? So I called my agent who already knew about it and it turned out that they were elevating my billing from just a feature role to an introductory co-starring—and that was marvelous. That was my first introduction to Gene Roddenberry. He's very devoted to his friends, to people he likes—and his sense of humor— well, Gene does the whole thing. One day, during the shooting of that show, he went to makeup and had himself made up as a hunchback. He had this big horrible hump put on, and a big nose. He had his eye pulled down, he was hideous. He had this old coat on, and it was the third day of shooting and I didn't know him. I had only met him once, and so he did this right after he found out that I had never done a TV show before. Apparently the director had told him I was doing a good job, and he couldn't believe that I had never done any TV before. So, we were out doing this night shooting, and I turned around and saw this hideous-looking man, smoking a cigarette and wearing this old tweedy English kind of coat. And he kept watching me. And then he kept coming near me. And I began to get a little bugged. And finally I went to the Assistant Director, not to bother the director, and I said, 'Who is that creep that keeps bugging me? He keeps walking over and saying hello, and I don't want to be nasty because I seem to know him from somewhere.' He says, 'I think he's a friend of the producer's.' And I said, 'Really?' And I went back to do my shot.

"Well, I was waiting while another shot was being set up, and this man is stalking me again, and finally, I'm just about ready to turn around and ream him out when I noticed something that had fascinated me about Gene Roddenberry, and that is that he always smokes his cigarettes between his middle two fingers. And I looked up, and he said something about my being lovely and I turned to snap at him and I saw that cigarette, and I said, 'Look you—' And then I realized, and screamed, *'Mr. Roddenberry!!'* right in the middle of a take! Somebody else's take. Well, the whole damn set just completely broke up. There was pandemonium for the next half hour, with Assistant Directors trying to pull things together and everybody else just cracking up. Lights had been knocked over and they had to redo the whole damn thing. Gene said he enjoyed that incident more than anything, that it was precious to him. And he remembers it to this day in a very kind way.

"Anyway, then I got that letter from him and I began to realize that this man Gene Roddenberry is quite a person. He has a great depth to him. I met him subsequently over the next two or three years. I would see him occasionally on a set or at the studio, and on these occasional visits, I would stop in to see him or say hello if I was down for an interview and each time he would tell me, 'I have something in mind for you. If it comes about, it will be very very interesting.' Okay, the first time, the first few times, the first year, you think that's groovy. The second year, you begin to think that's very nice of him still to even remember, and you remember fondly the things that happened on *The Lieutenant*. And now *The Lieutenant*'s over. And by now it's 'Hello, Gene,' 'Hello, Nichelle.' And sure enough, I take off for New York for a job, and I get a call from my agent, 'Get back here, quick!' 'What are you talking about? I'm not coming back to California!' So they sent me a ticket and I came flying back for an interview. What is the interview?

I don't know, but as long as they sent me a ticket—well, he says, 'It's a series that's going on called STAR TREK.' Well, my agent assumed that I knew it was Roddenberry, but I didn't. So I went into the interview—I was competing with four or five other top actresses—and there was Gene Roddenberry. I said, 'Gene, I didn't know you had anything to do with this,' and I gave him a peck on the cheek and sat down. There were other people sitting there, Joe Sargent, the director, Bob Justman, the associate producer, and so on. And they asked me to read—Lieutenant Uhura had not been written yet—so they asked me to read Spock's part to see how I sounded. So I asked them to tell me something about Spock. And they started to tell me about Lieutenant Uhura. I said, 'No, don't tell me about————.' She wasn't even named yet. Well, they thought that the character of Spock was closest to what they had in mind for Uhura, so to get an idea, they would have me read Spock's lines, so I said, 'If you're asking me to read his words, tell me what his character is and let me do that character. Then you can see if I can act or not! Don't ask me to do a character you haven't written, because you don't know if it's going to be exactly this or exactly that. I don't know what she's going to be either. When you find out, then I'll act her.' And they all turned around and looked at each other like I'd just hit them in the head and said, 'You know, that makes sense.' So I read Spock's part and I took on the stoicness of Mr. Spock and did that number. So Gene said, 'Do you think she'd look good in pointed ears? We could call her a Vulcanita.' All this was in fun, of course, but I still didn't know I had the part. They asked me to wait, so I sat down in the outer office and waited. And I waited, and I waited, and I waited, and everybody left. The other actresses had gone in and come out, nobody was left to wait, but me. And I was still waiting and waiting. My agent came by then, he saw me and said, 'Hey, what's happening? Are you still here?' I said, 'Well, they told me to wait.' And he said, 'Okay,' and he left too.

''Well, what had happened was that they'd all gone to lunch. I hadn't seen them leave—that's how the offices were set up—and I waited an hour and a half. Finally Joe Sargent popped in and he said, 'Hi, are you still here?' And I said, 'Yeah, you told me to wait.' And he said, 'Didn't anybody tell you—you got it!' And I said, 'You're kidding!' And he said, 'No.' He put his arm around me and said, 'I understand you haven't done too much television before. But I've heard good things about you. It's going to be a pleasure doing this show with you, big talent.' And I beamed. It made up for sitting so long.

''We started shooting within a matter of weeks. Mine had been the last part cast. Everything else was set. I was the last, because in the second pilot, 'Where No Man Has Gone Before,' the communications officer had been a man. As a matter of fact, it was Lloyd Haynes, who later became the lead on *Room 222*. I guess things happened for the best; if he'd been tied up on STAR TREK, perhaps he wouldn't have done *Room 222*.

"I remember some of the things that happened on the set. One script, I got pretty tired of doing the same thing over and over. We were doing this scene repeatedly and I don't remember what it was, but there was some technical difficulty, and then there was a problem with lines and then it was a problem with blocking and I think Kirk had to come in and I'm supposed to swing out to him, and say something like, 'Captain, the Klingons are—' and he says, 'Can't you handle it, Lieutenant Uhura?' And I snap back at him, 'Captain, I'm doing the best I can.'

"You see, everyone was supposed to be losing their tempers in this scene. We kept doing it over and over and it kept going on. Everyone kept blowing his lines and it got kind of silly, couldn't get it right. So, on the next take and I'm stifling a yawn, almost nodding, Bill says to me, 'Am I keeping you up, Lieutenant Uhura?' and everybody cracks up. Up to this time I'm the only one who hasn't blown it yet. So he comes back in on the next take and goes, 'Ahem! Any word, Lieutenant Uhura?' I said, 'Captain, the Klingons, etc., etc.' He says, 'Lieutenant Uhura, can't you handle it?' I said, 'Why shoah, Shugah, Ah can do anything y'all want. Why didn't y'all just tell me all along, honey? Whatevah your little heart desires.' That broke the ice. I thought Bill would just about have a hemorrhage. He really broke up, laughing. And they caught him on camera. I truly didn't know I was going to do that until I actually did it right in a take and the director, whoever it was at the time, yelled, 'Cut! What the hell was that?' But we all got it right on the next take.

"Two of my favorite shows were 'The Trouble with Tribbles' and 'The Tholian Web.' In the latter one, we think Kirk is dead and I see him floating through the walls of my quarters. That was fun to do—of course, I enjoyed anything that I was able to get out of uniform. Like 'Plato's Stepchildren.' That was the one with the controversial kiss—television's first interracial kiss—but it was a big copout. Bill had to kiss me because these aliens were forcing him to, but they were so concerned about how controversial it was that we played too hard against it. Bill fought it as if he didn't want to kiss me. And the letters came in by the pounds saying, 'I don't care what ship he's the Captain of, if he's got a woman like that in his arms, he's not going to be afraid of kissing her.' I thought it lost all its impact the way we played it.

"I loved it when I got a chance to sing. I have this crazy tremendous range, and when they found out, they used it to as high as I could go. You know, there were people who thought it was an instrument. One of the songs, either Gene Roddenberry or Gene Coon wrote. I did three different episodes where I sang, and in the first one, NBC objected—that was 'Charlie X'—and they said, 'What are you doing? Making this a musical?' And then they saw it and they said, 'Hey! It gives the show a human quality, do it again sometime.' They didn't even wait for an audience reaction.

"On one of the songs we had a very ethereal thing. We had a rendition of it that was out of sight, but it was too now, too hip. It had just the tinge of sultriness and it could have gone wrong. It was called 'Beyond Antares,' I should have recorded it. Anyway, when I took it just a little lower, it had a throaty quality—that was the one that Gene wrote, and what was marvelous about it was that we had Laurindo Almeida and full accompaniment. We had a harp and we had Lucille Ball's music director, Marl Young, he played the harpsichord, and Laurindo Almeida laid in a beautiful beautiful guitar background. I really enjoyed that. I love being in a recording studio.

"You know, I've seen very few of the shows. I don't like to watch myself. Except to criticize. If you start watching yourself too much, you begin overcompensating. You become stagey. Besides, you can start falling in love with yourself. You get into a heavy narcissistic kind of playing and you don't want anything imperfect.

"There was a script where Lieutenant Uhura was supposed to take over the helm because all of the top officers were down on a planet—and then they rewrote it so that she *didn't* take over the helm. They wrote me out. Well, I got furious. I pitched a bitch! This was another copout. To his credit, Gene Roddenberry admitted it: but this was the third season and he wasn't producing. The attitude was that you can't have females taking over a man's ship. But I think Bill would have gotten a personal kick out of it, because it would be the right thing to do. How can you have a mixed crew and suddenly stop in terms of responsibility? In the same light, I resented and balked at having to play the delicate little thing. I refused to do the clinging helpless female. If we were really a starship crew, the whole crew would be well trained and physically fit. They'd know karate and all kinds of defense procedures, and they wouldn't crumble the minute someone gets hit. When you're out in space, in a dangerous situation where the ship might be blown up at any time, you're not going to have some female that goes, 'Ooooh, Captain, save me, save me!' And all those other stupid things that used to bug me like, 'What is it? What do you think it is, Captain? What are we going to do, Captain? Will we make it, Captain?' All those female things, delicate how-are-we-going-to-do-it-without-you-Captain things. Completely unbelievable, and *especially* so from Lieutenant Uhura who is efficient, no-nonsense, stoic, balanced, brilliant. She knows that whole panel and all of a sudden she's supposed to become little lady milquetoast? Ridiculous! Just not so.

"So you battle, because you care, you've got to care about that damn show, you really do. Even in the third year, when I thought I didn't care, I found myself going and telling directors, I'm sorry, but you can't do that— even things that didn't have a damn thing to do with my role, or my sphere. You know, we all did. We'd say, 'Didn't anybody tell you that this is so on the *Enterprise*?'

"I got into difficulty only once with a director, and then it might have been a matter of male ego and my feminine vanity or pride that got in the way. Everyone was working under tremendous pressure, and he yelled at me, and I asked who the hell he was yelling at? I said Uhura wouldn't do it, and he said she would do it, and we couldn't straighten it out. It was one of those kind of things. To his great credit, he came to me when he found out he was wrong, and it was very funny. As he was coming to me to apologize, I was going to him to apologize. And we were constantly saying, 'No, no *you're* absolutely right.' And we stood there trying to apologize so hard, we started fighting all over again! That was Jud Taylor. We stood there and looked at each other and we were still mad and I not letting him apologize and he not letting me. He said, 'Just shut up and let me tell you I was wrong.' And I said, 'Would you just shut up and listen?' And we finally looked at each other and started laughing. All of this happened during lunch, so no one really saw it. It was an empty stage when all this took place. So, after lunch, everybody's waiting and waiting and so we staged a big thing. '*Miss Nichols!* . . .' '*Yes, Mr. Taylor!* . . .' That sort of thing. 'Would you please accept . . .' 'Oh, yes, Jud . . . of course,' And I made cooing noises, 'I will . . .' And we were just oh-so polite to one another, and finally he came up to me and we did a waltz. The cast and crew caught on then and broke up. I guess the zany things that went on were why we were so closely knit.

"One of my favorite people was Jerry Finnerman, the Director of Photography. On my very first day there, my very very first day there, I had just done makeup, I was still in my street clothes, and I see this man, and he's got a riding crop and a little beret on and he's kind of walking around the set, but when he saw me, he says, 'Hey you . . .' with the crop yet, and he walked over and he said, 'You're Nichelle Nichols, aren't you?' And I said, 'Yeah,' I didn't know who he was and he thought I did. Or he assumed that I should—but I didn't know who ANYBODY was! Right? So he says, 'Just a minute.' And he walks over to me and takes my face in his hand and he looks at me this way, and he turns it that way and he says, 'Yes, I'm going to do great things with you.' And I said, 'Like hell you are!' And I flew.

He's gonna do great things with me, huh? And then somebody said, 'That's your cinematographer,' and I said, 'Oh, my God!'

"But Jerry was beautiful, he realized what it sounded like. He had a great sense of humor, but I guess he was embarrassed about it, so he came very seriously to the makeup room when I returned and he said, 'Would you introduce Miss Nichols and me?' And I said, 'Someone told me who you are and I didn't realize.' And he said he was sorry, he hadn't realized that I didn't know who he was. And he explained about the 'great things.' He said, 'I meant you have great planes to your face, and I want them to highlight your cheeks.' And he really did mastermind my makeup for it. I think he did marvelous marvelous angles. He was always very conscious of me because he said I was his pride and joy. I don't know if he had ever really, really worked with any black people before to this great a degree. He said the coloring, and if you've seen it in color, you know, is very very beautiful.

"We were doing a scene and we had one of *those* directors or Assistant Directors, one of those chop-chop, let's get it going sort, and we were behind time and we were just about ready to shoot and they said Action, and Jerry said, 'Wait a minute.' The director said, 'What's the matter?' And Jerry says, 'I have to fix a light on Uhura.' And the director says, 'Can't we let it go?' And Jerry says, 'No, it'll only take a minute to fix.' So he starts yelling up to one of the gaffers. 'Bring a junior'—that's a type of light—'bring a junior down. Put it across here and—no, lower, lower.' And then he says. 'Naw, that's not right, you've got it on the black—she's *black*. She's black!' Well that's lighting talk, he meant that he wasn't getting enough light on me. And he kept yelling up, 'No, that's not it, she's black, she's *black*.' So there's silence like you've never heard. There was such a hush when he realized what he was saying. And he looked at me and he said, 'Uh—ulp . . . uh, Nichelle—' And I said 'But *comely*.' And of course, it broke up the whole set, everybody laughed, it broke the tension and everything. And of course we went on about that for months. For the rest of the show. Any time anybody would get upset about something they would pull that on me. Somebody would walk over to me and they would say—especially Leonard or Bill—they'd walk past me and just over their shoulder they would say to me, 'But *comely*.' Which would never fail to break me up, bring me out of whatever I was in a snit about.

"We pulled a joke on Leonard once. In the script, a panel had blown and we were in a desperate situation, a two-seconds-to-destruction kind of thing, and I had to crawl underneath and fix this panel, Uhura being the expert on it, you know. So I put on these overalls and I climbed down there, and they had explained how dangerous it was, not just to me, but to everybody on the ship, everything depends on my accomplishing this. Kirk wasn't on the ship and Spock was in command and he comes the closest he does of ever showing any real emotion by showing real concern.

"So I was doing this and the camera was set up underneath this panel, they had pulled this board back and the camera was right in my face and here I'm working on this panel and Spock is supposed to come in and say 'How's it going, Lieutenant Uhura?' And I'm sweating a bit and I say, 'Mr. Spock, I don't know if I can do this.' And he says, 'If anyone can do it, Lieutenant, you can.' And that gives me the courage to go on. Well, it was a very difficult shot, we were just about nose to nose, so I had to okay this gag with the director. He thought it was a great idea. So he says to Leonard 'I'm going to change a little something here. When you say "If anyone can, you can" stay there, because I want to catch just a tinge of concern that she doesn't see. Wonder if you examine it, you might have to fix it up after her.' And Leonard went to bat for me. He said, 'Well, I see no reason for that. She's efficient in what she does.' But finally, they got it through to him that he should stay there for a moment because he was supposed to leave. So he comes in and I'm doing this panel and the cameras are rolling and I say, 'Mr. Spock, I'm not sure I can do this,' And he says to me, 'Lieutenant, all our lives depend on it, and if anyone can, you can.' And I said, 'He loves me . . .' And then I sang, 'He loves me . . .' And I went into this opera thing. 'Once you have found him, never let him go . . .' And *he* said, 'Carry on, Lieutenant.' He absolutely was frozen. So that was all he could say, 'Carry on, Lieutenant.' That bloody Vulcan, you could never break him up.

"I'll tell you one thing about STAR TREK—and I've worked with a lot of companies—all in all, from Matt Jefferies who did the sets to Irving Feinberg, the prop man, to everyone you worked with, the sound men and the light men, they had a very personal attitude about that show, a very personal pride, a personal sense of ownership. There were times when even a sound man wouldn't let something go by—it may not have had anything to do with sound—but he knew it didn't belong on the *Enterprise*, it wasn't part of the format—and he would speak up. And this fascinated me. Even through the third year, when we had new people (a lot of people by that time had gone on to other jobs) the pride in STAR TREK never stopped. It never stopped, and that's what made the *Enterprise* work."

William Campbell appeared in two of STAR TREK's episodes: "The Squire of Gothos," in which he played Trelane, the penultimate spoiled brat, and "The Trouble with Tribbles," where he was seen as the oily Klingon, Captain Koloth.

As a result of that latter appearance, he almost became a STAR TREK regular. Gene Roddenberry had felt that Captain Kirk needed a regular adversary, a Klingon counterpart with whom he continually bumped heads. When Campbell was called for the part of Captain Koloth, this possibility was mentioned—that he might be hired for as many as thirteen shows per season. Campbell was very excited about it. "After 'The Trouble with Tribbles' was aired, I felt Wow, because I got such a response from playing the Klingon. Even the neighborhood kids teased my wife about being 'Mrs. Klingon.' People were writing to me about the eyebrows and the costume, and the way I played the part. And I thought to myself that whatever the makeup man had done to me must have been distinctive enough that this will go; this Captain of the Klingons will be a good adversary, a good part. Kirk needs him like Flash Gordon needs Ming of Mongo. They respect each other's abilities, even though they're still adversaries.

"I was really disappointed when the show wound down. The one great thing about STAR TREK was there was a marvelous lot of social content there. I could see why they felt they needed a continuing set of villains. I think it must have been very difficult for the writers of the individual episodes; the show had already gone for fifty-two episodes and each time they had to come up with a completely different set of characters. A continuing villain could have solved a lot of problems—and it could have given them some new story potentials. All the different conflicts with the Klingons could have been shown. All these elements could have been utilized.

"I didn't get into any of the other Klingon episodes, though, because the next time I was approached to do one, I was already involved in something else, so I couldn't do it. They had thought of the part as signing another contractee—and of course, I would have done it for Roddenberry and Coon. Even though the part was a heavy, he was a good heavy, distinctive, you know. The other Klingon, his aide, was the nasty one, and I thought that was a good idea; it gave them depth.

"I got a lot of fan mail after that episode—and the fan response wasn't just in terms of being a Klingon, but it was more or less in regard to the tribbles. The actors weren't really the stars of the show, those little animals were. They really intrigued whoever watched it. One little girl even made a tribble and sent it to me. I received a lot of mail about both STAR TREK episodes I did. And it seems to me that the fans of STAR TREK are unique in that they know every show. And they know who's been on every show and they have their favorites. I've known other actors who've done other episodes, I won't name them, but I've asked, have you ever heard from any of the STAR TREK fans, and they've said no. And I think that proves that the fans had their favorite shows. They're very sophisticated about scripts in the genre. I mean, they can *talk* about them. Which is one of the reasons why I consider those two STAR TREK episodes as high points in my career. I've done a hundred TV shows and somewhere around sixteen pictures; either starred in some big ones or co-starred in some big ones, or starred in some moderate ones, like *Caryl Chessman*. In television, though, I played guest star on many shows. But both the STAR TREKS I did, were high points. It's a piece of film that I can be proud of.

"For 'Gothos,' I was contracted by Gene Coon. Now, I had never worked for Gene, but we were friends, and Gene said to me, 'I have a part here for an English fop, and I know you can play it because I've seen your work in other pictures.' But the casting director, Joe D'Agosta, said, 'Gene, Gene, Campbell could never play an English fop. I've never seen him do anything like that.' Gene tried to explain to him that I had played sinister roles and could do this because it was kind of comedic sinister. And Joe just didn't think so, so Gene asked me to read for it. He said, 'Bill, I would never ask you to read, but Joe doesn't think you can do it. I could press it through without Joe, but if I do and it doesn't work, I'll never be able to live with him again because the next time I try to suggest someone, he'll say, "Will you leave the casting to me?" ' As it turned out, I did the reading under the worst possible conditions, because I had the assistant to Joe D'Agosta, who was not an actor, feeding me the lines. But within one paragraph, Joe said, 'Let's go to wardrobe.' And we went.

"You know, I went into that show with the full realization that 'Squire of Gothos' was my show. Not Leonard Nimoy's, not William Shatner's. I mean, I was the focus of attention. There was an incident, for instance, where I played a judge. The judge was supposed to be an English judge that said, 'And you were called here because you have committed the crime of treason against the government, etc., etc.' And it was specifically an English courtroom. The judge described in the script and the dialogue was all English. My mental image of the judge was with the robe and the little wig that sits on top of the head—as opposed to the French wigs, which are always very long and curly and very ornate. Well, they sent me to Max Factor and they put the wig on me and I found it was a French wig. I told them that at Max Factor, and the hairdresser there said, 'Well, we'll comb it out and redo it. We know what you want.' So on the day of the scene, the wig box was opened up and it was the French wig, all done up curly. I refused to work the scene in that. Shatner's position in that instance was that I should wear it because who cares? I explained to him that two people should care: one, and for important reasons, is myself, because I'm playing the character, and in order to feel the character I must have the proper paraphernalia. Number two, *he* should care because if I were the star of a show, I would want everything in it to be absolutely perfect. Of course, I'm not blaming Bill for his attitude, he wanted to get the show into the can. I know from the response I received from that show that I was right, because I received three or four very good roles because of that part. It broke me out of the image of being simply a tough guy who could play Caryl Chessman or whatever. Oh, but finally, Gene Coon came down on the set and the question was presented to him. Now, if Gene had said to me, 'Bill, it doesn't matter, go ahead and do it.' I would have reluctantly gone ahead and done it. And as a matter of fact, it *wouldn't* have made any difference. It wasn't the thing that would make or break the episode, and the chances are that few people would have cared. But Gene said, 'Immediately go down and get another wig.' So somebody went and got a wig, it only took twenty or thirty minutes, so they picked up another shot in the meantime. After it was over, I don't think that Shatner felt that I was wrong, he just never felt that it was important. But it was important to me.

"I'll tell you how important that script was to me—I hurt myself doing it and really badly. I mean, I didn't realize it at that time. But we had this sword fight sequence, if you remember, and we did that on the stage. So they had merely poured sand over the linoleum. And I had on these high French-type boots, they were leather-heeled, and in one of the sequences where Shatner and I are running after each other, I did a header and came down on my shoulder. And my shoulder came out of the socket. The pain was excruciating and I jumped up and threw it up in the air and it popped back in. Luckily. But by the time I returned home that night, I was black and blue on the entire left side of my body. Of course, they called the nurse down to the set when it happened, but there was nothing she could do for me. I managed to finish that day despite it.

"The unique thing about STAR TREK was that Shatner and Nimoy were really interested in that show. They were aware that I had been given a hell of a role and they wanted to see it emerge, so they stayed on the set, and as a matter of fact, Bill Shatner gave me some marvelous suggestions. The crying sequence at the end was an example. It was very sensitive, but it could have gone both ways. It could have been ranting and raving, or it could be that almost plaintive thing. As it turned out, we shot it both ways, but Shatner said he liked it more subdued, and so did I. That was the shot that was used, and it was better.

"There was a funny thing that happened. We were rehearsing the sequence with Nichelle Nichols and Bill Shatner introduces her, and I say—the line was supposed to be, 'Ah, a Nubian maid. Captured in the sun.' Something like that. So I came up and said—I didn't realize I was saying it, 'Ah, a Nubian slave—' And Nichelle says, 'I'll kick you in the ankle!' It had been a Freudian slip on my part, but she took it very lightly. It was a very funny moment.

"I got a tremendous amount of fan mail out of 'The Squire of Gothos.' A lot of people asked me why I didn't get roles like that more often. You know, nobody hated me at the end. They didn't even hate the character while he was doing it to the Captain and crew of the *Enterprise*, because the way he played it, it was all a game. 'You've got to play my game.' Well, that was his childish petulance, and people picked up on it. So they didn't get mad at him; and then at the end, everyone felt great sympathy for him, that his toy was being taken away. It was a very well conceived character.

"But then, STAR TREK was a very well conceived show. I enjoyed doing it. As I said, it's one of the high points in my career."

PART THREE

The STAR TREK Phenomenon

SAVING Star Trek

ONCE upon a time, there was a lady named Bjo Trimble, and she loved Star Trek so much—she still does—that she could not bear to see it die after just two seasons.

So she wrote a letter to NBC in late 1967 telling them that Star Trek was a good TV show and they should keep it on the air. Then she asked a few of her friends to do the same.

About a million of them did.

Bjo (pronounced Bee-jo) was one of Star Trek's first fans. She wrote to Gene Roddenberry, the show's producer and creator, almost immediately after the first few episodes had been telecast, and asked if she could meet him. Of course, he was delighted to. At that time, neither the cast nor crew had any idea of the eventual public response to the show—and they were all a bit scared about whether or not the series would be a success. Star Trek was, quite frankly, one of the biggest gambles in TV history.

Gene Roddenberry was impressed with this perky little redheaded lady, and gradually she became the fan liaison for Star Trek. She felt that there was much that the fans could do to show their involvement with the show. Perhaps a letter campaign . . .

The idea was *not* pulled casually from a hat. Bjo already had a pretty good idea of the intensity of reaction to Star Trek, she was handling some of the show's fan mail for Roddenberry—but in addition to that, she herself had been a science fiction fan for a number of years. And that was her real advantage.

Let me explain this.

First, forget all previous definitions of the word *fan*. To use the word in

91

any of its more common connotations would be a misnomer and a disservice. If you approach science fiction *fandom* with the traditional definitions, you'll never understand it.

There's something about science fiction—it stretches the mind. After you've spent a few afternoons with Heinlein, Asimov, Sturgeon, and Clarke, everything else is mundane. Dull. After you've spent an evening saving the Earth, exploring the galaxy, discovering immortality, probing the depths of the mind, touring the far future and achieving *The Answer to it All,* who cares about the dishes or the six o'clock news? Once your mind has been thoroughly boggled, you want to keep that sense of wonder—you don't want to lose the wider horizons that science fiction has given you.

It's not enough for the *trufan* to escape for just an hour or two into an alternate universe. He doesn't want to be a tourist. He wants to be a resident. So he sets out to build his alternate worlds for real, and makes them so totally convincing that he alters a portion of the actual realtime continuum. He makes it come true.

Creating alternate realities and making them real enough to live in is the business of science fiction writers; they do it for a living. The science fiction fans do it for fun.

A fan—short for fanatic—collects books, collects magazines, collects cover paintings and still pictures from films, collects comic books and original artwork, collects film clips and old props and anything else even remotely related to his central interest.

And he writes. Incessantly. A fan writes his own amateur fiction, most of it pretty bad, and inflicts it on his friends. But an SF writer has to start somewhere, and many of them start out as fans. It's when a fan becomes so good at making his realities believable that others are willing to pay for the privilege of sharing them that he becomes a pro.

Other fans become critics. A fan critic is the hardest kind of all—he does it because he likes it. He'll write reviews of new movies and analyses of old ones, he'll write complex criticisms of the latest novels, and even more involved critiques of other reviewers. He'll do in-depth studies of individual writers in the field and he'll write long articles about ideas and machines and the overall shape of the universe. He'll write about *anything* that suggests itself to him.

And then he'll publish it.

A *fanzine*—look it up, it's in the dictionary—is an amateur magazine, generally mimeographed, sometimes dittoed, occasionally offset-printed with full-color covers, and looking better than the prozines. The fan publisher pays for it himself and generally edits it himself too; all the articles and artwork are voluntary, and generally the fan sells just enough copies to other fans to break even on the whole thing. If he generates any ego-response, then the effort was worth it and he starts planning another issue.

Fanzines are probably the most important avenue of communication between fans. Besides being ego-builders, a good fanzine also garners status for its publisher. Most fanzine editors trade copies of their zine for copies of other zines, a semi-incestuous practice which results in interminable comments and reviews on each other's zines. However, the reviews also create what might best be called "The Dandelion Effect." (Blow on a dandelion. You'll see what I mean.)

An editor sends copies of his fanzine to other editors, who review it and publish the address of the first editor. Anyone who reads the reviews and is interested in obtaining a copy of the first fanzine can then send for it by mail. Depending on the nature of the zine and what it publishes, it is possible to build a circulation of several thousand. But at that point the fanzine becomes a very expensive hobby. Fanzines generally are not profit-making operations.

The real interest is in writing and publishing and in being responded to by others.

And that kind of interest results in Amateur Press Associations—and there are many of them. Each member of an APA prints up to fifty or sixty copies of his zine (as many as is required) and contributes them to the distribution, which is collated and then mailed, or delivered by hand. In return for his one zine, each APA-member gets forty or fifty in return, many of them with public comments to him about his latest APA-zine.*

Organized (you should pardon the expression) fandom touches about five thousand people in the United States.

Disorganized fandom reaches a lot more. I make no guesses at the number— but every really *intense* fan is merely a nucleus at the core of ten or twenty other human beings, whose interest in science fiction is not quite so rabid, but who enjoy the contact with someone whose interest is.

Fandom is like a small town spread out across the United States—and throughout the rest of the world too. There are science fiction clubs in almost every major city; if there isn't a club, there is at least a nucleus of fans.

The lifelines of fandom are the U.S. mail and the telephone system. Fandom

---

*Since this was first written computer bulletin boards have also become a popular channel of fan communication. Perhaps someday *most* fanzines will be electronic. . . .

depends upon communication—communication is the name of the game. What is being communicated is often less important than the fact that the communication exists.

Fans have large address books—no, make that files. Fans have large postage bills—fifty dollars a month just to keep in touch is not uncommon. Fans are—well, fans.

In *The Crying of Lot 49* by Thomas Pynchon, a woman named Oedipa Maas discovers a vast underground network of secret communications, a sort of second postal system, which spans the country and touches all sorts of sub-worlds and tangential cultures. It reaches into computer companies and gay bars and stamp collectors' homes and used-book stores and organizations of Iowa Masons and drug addicts and anywhere else that other levels— *separated* levels—of cultural activity have developed. Fandom is something like that. Without the secret recognition signs though. (Mention the name Heinlein, that's enough.)

Science fiction fandom can touch a large number of human beings in a very short time. It's a seemingly amorphous grapevine with no discernible structure at all—until you get into it. Then you find that the apparent lack of structure is really the chaotic overlaying of hundreds of lesser structures, interrelated and interdependent. Big structures appear in fandom only when massive amounts of energy are directed into the system—then the fans organize and channel that energy, they focus it and distribute it.

If the input is STAR TREK, then what is the output?

A letter campaign to save the show.

And more than that.

Science fiction fandom has existed in the United States for more than fifty years. Properly, it began with Hugo Gernsback's magazines and the Science Fiction League. It's a healthy and viable subculture and will probably go on for decades. But a few years ago, it gave birth to a giant—or maybe a monster—called STAR TREK fandom.

The midwife was Bjo Trimble.

Bjo Trimble is a pert, redheaded little ogre of a woman with incredible talent, vitality, enthusiasm, ability and aggressiveness. She writes, she paints, she cartoons, she designs clothes, she does professional makeup for movies, she does offset layouts and pasteups, she compiles indexes, and if someone were to invent a new art form tomorrow, Bjo would be a master of it by next Friday.

All human beings are unique—but Bjo is uniquer than most. She has a husband, two beautiful daughters, a houseful of cats and books and breathtaking artwork, and a dragon in the basement. (Honest.) Once when a door-to-door canvasser asked her what the most important appliance in her home was, she replied without hesitation, "The typewriter." (She does not have an automatic dishwasher—she *does* have four typewriters.)

Bjo Trimble is an organizer—and one of the best. If Bjo can't do it, it can't be done.

She and STAR TREK fandom were designed for each other. There probably isn't anyone else who could have done what she did—at least not half so well. It was largely because of her efforts that the STAR TREK Phenomenon developed as it did.

Bjo is a science fiction fan. That doesn't mean that she participates in *all* the activities that were listed above, but she is familiar with them. Because of her fannish activities, she doesn't have just an address book. Not even address files. No, Bjo Trimble has *mailing lists*.

When she got the idea of a "Save STAR TREK" letter campaign, she had about eight hundred people she could contact. Most of them were science fiction fans themselves and many of them had mailing lists of their own.

Chain letter—? Uh-uh. More like chain reaction.

But at this point, Bjo can tell the story herself:

"We decided to try—on a fairly small scale, really—a sort of letter-writing campaign to convince NBC to pick up the show again.

"I had seen a good deal of the mail coming in, not only to STAR TREK, but other shows as well, and most of it struck me that the people were writing the wrong thing to get their point across. Like for instance, letters that started off, 'You big dumb shit, put the show back on!' And obviously, nobody is going to finish reading a letter like that.

"So, I wrote up a list of dos and don'ts, which are now being copied by similar campaigns for other shows, on how to write a reasonable and intelligent-sounding letter to get your point across. One of them was that you should put your letter in a legal-sized envelope, because it looked more businesslike; don't put 'Gene Roddenberry' or 'STAR TREK' on the outside because then it would go straight to the fan mail department and not be opened by the NBC studios. Address the NBC people directly—and, of course, we listed their names and addresses—and then, on the *inside*, that's where you start in about wanting the show saved. NBC couldn't afford *not* to open these letters—without outside identification, they had no way of knowing if they were important or not.

"We mailed out these flyers listing all this information to about eight hundred people—the mailing list of the last big science fiction convention, so we were reaching right away much of science fiction fandom. My main point in the covering letter was, 'See how many other people you can reach.' And people would then write back and say, 'Send me more flyers, I can run them through my local company paper.'

"One man xeroxed his letter and sent it through all the departments of the largest Polaroid division. And Polaroid turns out to be one of the holding companies that owns the NBC corporation. Employees above a certain level own stock in the company, so that provided a little irony because they were writing in to NBC as *stockholders*.

"MENSA, which is a kind of social club for geniuses, copied our letter entirely in their official newspaper, and that went out to about six thousand members of the organization.

"Several college newspapers either duplicated the letter or told people where to write.

"The *Kansas City Star Tribune* phoned us and we gave them an hour and a half interview about what we were doing, and got hundreds of letters in response because they reprinted our address in the article.

"High school kids would write in for more letters and pass them out to friends and so on. Several high school newspapers repeated the information.

"One employee of NASA wrote us from Texas. And a SAC officer, out of the main SAC base, wherever that is, wrote and asked for fifty copies. This kind of thing went on for weeks.

"Thousands of letters later, and somewhere around four or five hundred dollars worth of postage, we found we had created a monster. We were sending out as many flyers as we could afford, about eight or ten letters a day, or whatever we could afford postage for.

"Gene Roddenberry gave us a great many film clips and so on, odds and ends of things around the set, to sell to fans and friends, so that we could defray some of the expenses of the campaign. Well, the stuff went like wildfire and I knew then that fans—all STAR TREK fans, not just our friends—would dig the chance to buy this kind of stuff.

"I told Roddenberry this, but at first he didn't believe me. And then after we took several cartons of STAR TREK trivia, a Spock shirt, some Spock ears, a tribble, some scripts, some film clips and so on, to a convention, he was convinced. We had to fight the people off of the stuff. The auction of this material brought in over four hundred and seventy dollars. (By the way, the auction was to benefit the Trans. Ocean Fan Fund, TOFF, to help bring a Japanese fan over to the United States for the next World Science Fiction Convention.)

"Roddenberry was impressed by this evidence of the show's impact, and we had done some research on other costs and kinds of merchandising, and that's how STAR TREK Enterprises was born. We set it up for him. We made up a mailing list from the fan mail and from the letter-writing campaign and that was the list we used when we sent out the first catalogs. STAR TREK Enterprises sold scripts, decals, film clips, insignia stickers, color postcards, writer's guides, memo pads, letterheads, cast biographies, bumper stickers, flight deck certificates, and monthly newsletters.

"But all that came later. First, we had to get STAR TREK renewed. That was our central concern.

"Our campaign kept building and building as word of it got around. This was early 1968 already, and there had been protest marches against NBC in Los Angeles, New York, and San Francisco. All in all, I'd say we sent out about four thousand flyers to people all over the country.

"Were we having any effect? Well, we began hearing rumors. NBC had called Gene Roddenberry's office to ask, 'What are you people doing down there? And, of course, Gene said, 'Who? Me?' NBC was sure that Roddenberry was behind it all. We had his blessing, of course, and his help, but he wasn't *actively* behind the effort. It was entirely a fan enterprise. We were trying to reach as many people as possible and get them to write NBC if they cared at all about STAR TREK.

"One of the things we stressed in our flyers was individuality. A lot of people had said, 'Oh, write me a letter and I'll sign it.' Or, 'Can't I just mimeograph something off?' I came down very hard on this, I felt it wouldn't help us at all—and my theory was born out by the fact that a letter-writing campaign was recently tried for the country-music program, 'Hee-Haw.' And it failed. And when asked why it failed, one of the studio executives replied that it looked as if it had come from an extremely small group of people who were trying to force an issue, because *all* of the letters were the same. That was why I very carefully didn't even write a sample letter. We were following along blindly thinking that if enough people wrote in to NBC, they would have to notice us. As a result, all of our letters were individualistic, and I think that was an important point in our favor.

"At last, Gene Roddenberry's secretary, Penny Unger, heard that the mail to NBC had topped one million pieces, and we were all pretty jubilant about that. Other shows had been renewed because of letter-writing campaigns in the past, and in those cases, it had taken a good deal fewer letters, so when we heard that more than one million people had written in, we felt pretty good. One NBC official was reported to have said that a hundred and fifty thousand letters would have done it.

"At any rate, NBC came on the air with a precedent-making announcement one night, right after STAR TREK—I wish I had a tape of it—that the show *had been* renewed and would everybody *please* stop writing in. This was pretty indicative that we had flooded them way too much with mail.

"Of course, STAR TREK fans, being what they were, promptly turned around and flooded NBC with thank you letters, still written on legal-size paper and envelopes and nothing to identify them on the outside. NBC had to open these letters too! An anguished vice-president called Gene Roddenberry and pleaded, 'Gene, how do you turn them off! Please!'

"You see, all those letters *had* to be opened. NBC had to hire extra girls just to handle that sheer bulk of mail, to open it and sort it and tabulate it, and the costs started adding up. Anyone who's ever run a business can tell you, office hours can be very expensive. Just the sheer job of opening thousands of pieces of mail a week—just *opening* it—requires more man hours and more office hours than the average business can afford.

"A few weeks later, NBC told *TV Guide* that they had gotten two hundred thousand pieces of mail. And in subsequent years, that number has steadily dropped. Recently, NBC was admitting only to a hundred and fifty thousand, and more recently, only fifty thousand letters. But I know we generated more than that.

"I was at a party, business people mostly, and a man who was fairly high in the computer business was there with a friend, also in the computer business—this friend had been working with NBC at the time of our campaign. He heard someone mention my name, Bjo, and he walked over and asked, 'Bjo Trimble?' I said, 'Yes . . . ?' I'd never met this fellow before in my whole life, but he started laughing. 'You have no idea,' he said, 'how many people would like to meet you—especially at NBC. Your name is very well known.'

"I said, 'Why?'

"And he said, 'Well, you broke down the machines at NBC in New York.'

"I said, 'No, I didn't—I never even touched them.' Anyway, he explained that—and I don't understand computer work—in some way, in trying to tabulate the load of mail—apparently they were trying to break it down to find out what kind of people were writing in—the overload of mail was so much that the machines couldn't handle it. He was one of the people called in to repair them, and the talk was all over the place that more than one million letters had come in. So this is how that one million letter figure was verified by an entirely separate source. So, I know—and NBC knows—that there were over one million letters. Whether or not they want to admit it, that's how many there were. NBC claims that the whole thing was engineered by a hard core of fanatics—but there just aren't that many science fiction fanatics in this country. Most of that mail had to come from STAR TREK fans—and even if people were writing in two or three letters apiece, that's still more than the hundred and fifty thousand minimum.

"Actually, we probably touched a lot more than a million people—we'll never know for sure. You see, in that one million letters, petitions were counted only as one letter. I myself have seen petitions with from three hundred to eighteen hundred names on them. And one boy, with a remarkable amount of enterprise, in a small Texas town of three thousand people, managed to get over two thousand names on his petition. He must have gotten everything short of the family pets to sign. And there were a lot of petitions.

"Eventually, we had an NBC man from Burbank come out and talk to us on the STAR TREK set one night, and he asked us if we would tell them how we had done it. How had we reached so many people so fast? And how had we gotten the information to them about who to write and how to address the envelope and how to phrase the letter politely? Of course, we didn't tell him. We might have to do it again someday.

"The mail campaign was a lot of fun—and we made a lot of friends through it. Quite frankly, it expanded our knowledge and dealings with people by a great deal, so in spite of the fact that it was expensive getting all those flyers run off and mailed out, it was well worth it. It was worth it to have proven the amount of power that people have if they work together to accomplish something."

STAR TREK'S FANS

Not all the letters went to NBC.

STAR TREK received a considerable amount of fan mail itself.

For instance, there was one little boy who had evidently learned business form. His letter had his address and the date at the top, Desilu-Paramount's address, and the identification, "To STAR TREK." Then, it started out: "Dear Mr. Trek . . ." And went on from there, a very personal letter.

Then there was the woman who wrote a seven-page letter, in which she very carefully explained that she was a happily married woman and this was not prurient interest, *but* she pointed out that red-blooded people have all of their extremities pink, and since Spock was supposed to be green-blooded, she wanted to know—with reference to particular extremities—if they were green.*

Bjo Trimble handled STAR TREK's fan mail for a while. "We opened all the mail," she said. "Whether it was marked personal or not. After a while, you got the feeling of being a voyeur—especially after reading seventeen-page letters to William Shatner describing in *great* detail what certain women had in the way of daydreams about him. And you know, you really wonder, if they're making it up out of their own mind, and if they are then they've got a great future in dirty books—and if they *aren't*, then what kind of literature are they reading and where are they getting it? I haven't read very many more red-hot things than we opened in the STAR TREK fan mail. It was amazing.

---

*Yes, *they*. Idle speculation around the set had it that the particular extremity this woman was inquiring about was forked. . . .

Really.

"We got one marvelous letter from a woman who pointed out that she was not at all prejudiced, and she really believed in equality and all of this, and since we had a Russian, which she sort of agreed with, and a Scotsman and an Oriental, there was really no need to have Nichelle Nichols . . . and so we sent her an autographed picture of Nichelle and our thanks. . . .

"One little boy had a birthday coming up soon and sent a full-page letter listing all the things he wanted. He wanted a bicycle and a catcher's mitt—and he named the brands, by the way, on all of these things—he wanted a suit of clothes, he wanted a scout uniform, he wanted one each of everything there was on the entire *Enterprise,* props, uniforms, one of the panels from the bridge, and he ended the thing with '—and twenty-five dollars for incidentals which I haven't thought of yet.' We sent him an autographed picture of Mr. Spock. You wonder at the crass nerve of some of these people, but he pointed out that we—meaning the entire *Enterprise* crew—had a good deal more money than he did and could afford this for him for his birthday.

"There was one boy who wanted a *working* phaser sent to him—but *not,* in case his little brother asked for one too, to his little brother. We kind of wondered how that family was getting along. . . .

"One kid wanted one of Dr. McCoy's hypodermics that *worked*—and he wanted it *full.* And he named the stuff he wanted it full of. And it was the cordrazine or whatever that sent McCoy off into the twentieth century in 'The City on the Edge of Forever.' I don't know—I think he was going to become the biggest pusher in his neighborhood or something. . . .

"We got letters with—what I hoped were inadvertent—innuendos. One girl wanted William Shatner to come to her graduation and stay overnight at her house and go with her to the prom. She pointed out that this would give her a good deal of status among her girl friends—especially his staying overnight at the house. And then ended her letter with, 'In case you'd like to know what you're getting into, here's my picture . . .' We're still not awfully sure if she understood what she was saying or not. . . .

"And we got one little group of kids from Colorado who had decided that—after seeing 'Mirror, Mirror,'—that Kirk needed a 'Captain's Woman.' They wanted Stefanie Powers ('The Girl from U.N.C.L.E.') to play the part. And after about the fifteenth letter from the fifteenth different child on this point, I finally wrote back to the two ringleaders and I said, 'I'm not awfully sure you understand what a "Captain's Woman" is, but she's not a very nice lady and I suggest you talk to your mother . . .' We never heard from them again. It really tickled us though, we kept getting these letters: 'Kirk needs a "Captain's Woman," ' and I kept thinking he'd probably agree . . ."

There were other letters too.

After "The Trouble with Tribbles" was telecast in 1967, for a while, almost every letter received included a request for one of the tribbles. (These were little fuzzy creatures that bred like crazy till Captain Kirk was up to his neck in them.) "Surely you have so many of them . . ." was the general theme, "you can certainly spare one or two. I know you must have millions. I saw them on the show." Nope. Only five hundred. But how do you explain that to twenty million fans?

Some of the letter-writers thought that the tribbles were actually alive. They wanted to know what animals were used and where they could get one. And one gentleman was highly outraged that STAR TREK had been mistreating living creatures by cooping them up in a hot storage compartment, then dropping them onto a soundstage floor and photographing them under hot lights. Had the animals been properly fed, watered, and cared for? He didn't think so.

In point of fact, any time any kind of living animal is used in film work, there are very strict production codes to prevent their mistreatment. The days when a film producer could stampede a herd of horses off a cliff just for an exciting shot are long past.

One of the main focuses of the fan mail, of course, was Mr. Spock.

Leonard Nimoy's characterization of the half-alien, half-human First Officer touched a particularly responsive chord in a lot of little girls—and a lot of big girls too. The pointed ears and arched eyebrows suggested great strength and masculinity with a healthy hint of controlled *evil*. But Spock's conscious suppression of emotion, as well as his unavailability as a sexual object, made him (in the words of one of these young ladies) "A safe rape. You could love him without risking your virginity."

Actually, it may have been more than that. Deep down inside, each of these little girls—and the big girls too—believed that she was the one who could warm up Mr. Spock. If she could be given half a chance, she could get through to him.

—And if she couldn't, well then that was just proof that no one could.

Mr. Spock, as a character, touched the *right* emotional chords. He suggested the Devil. He echoed of satyrs and Pan and elves and other unholy things—but he suppressed it. He suppressed the half of him that was human and prey to earthy desires. His self-control was an almost visible thing. His knowledge was never carnal, his being was totally rational, and a fan could approach his character on the mental level without ever having to worry about reacting physically.

And that was just right for the fans.

That many of STAR TREK's most rabid fans were teenagers was no coincidence. It was Mr. Spock that they were focused on. They identified with him and the central conflict in his life—the continuing need to control himself in an emotional environment. Most of them felt the same way themselves. Adolescence is one of the most difficult times in a human being's life. The child is having to decide what kind of an adult he is going to be. His body is changing rapidly and forcing the decision on him by giving him adult capabilities. There is no escape from this messy business of emotions and love and mating and—scariest of all, *sex.*

Mr. Spock had the answer though. Suppression. Control. Logic is the god, and emotions don't exist; relegate them to the dark underside of the mind and never never let them show. This is one of the reasons that science fiction has such an appeal to teenagers; when the adolescent has trouble accepting his transition to adulthood, he casts around for alternate worlds to live in, worlds where these difficult things don't exist or are suppressed. In Mr. Spock, they found not just an answer, but a role model.

If rabid STAR TREK fans are "Trekkies," then within that group is a subcult of "Spockies." Girls—and some boys—who focus not on science fiction, not on STAR TREK, but only on Mr. Spock. The fan mail proved this over and over. It was not all Leonard Nimoy's appeal that attracted the fans to him, but the concept of the character he played. The alienness.

For many viewers, this was their first glimpse of another kind of reality— one where things from space are not automatically monsters. This was their first real meeting with something from another planet—and it was *friendly.* They wanted to know more.

For instance, after the episode "Journey to Babel," the fan mail poured in at an incredible rate. But it was not for Spock. The show had dealt with Spock's parents, played by Jane Wyatt and Mark Lenard—and for two weeks, the letters to Mark Lenard topped even those coming in to Leonard Nimoy.

Later on, in the third season, the phenomenon was repeated again, when an ancient Vulcan philosopher showed up in "The Savage Curtain." Again the fans were intrigued—and again they wrote in. They demanded to see more of Surak, who was played by Barry Atwater.

Clearly, it was not just Spock alone—although he played a large part in it—it was the whole Vulcan concept: cool, rational beings, in complete command of themselves, non-violent, curious, and super-intelligent. Whatever emotions they had were under control—or else channeled and heavily ritualized, as for instance, the seven-year sexual cycle, which, when it did occur, was irresistibly strong. Nimoy's performance added a dimension of enormous, *unused* strength, and of dry humor occasionally. But probably, the keynote appeal of Vulcans was their controlled strength.

The majority of STAR TREK's fans, however, were not so limited in their involvement as the "Spockies." Most of them were primarily intrigued with the show's format: the idea of a giant starship exploring the galaxy, each week touching upon strange and exotic new worlds, experiencing fantastic adventures and meeting incredible beings, was clearly one of the most dazzling formats in television. Also one of the most difficult. Former producer, Gene L. Coon believed it to be "the hardest show in television history to write for."

Unlike other television series, STAR TREK demanded more involvement from its viewers. A certain familiarity with advanced technology was implied, but the show had so *many* devices and wonders that it simply could not present all of them in every episode. Phasers and spaceships can be taken for granted by an uninitiated audience, but try and remember—how many episodes did you have to watch before you began to *understand* the transporter? Or the ship's computer? Or the sick bay? Or Vulcans?

The background of the show was too broad. A whole new culture had to be presented. The only way to do it was cumulatively, from show to show. It took at least four or five weeks of steady viewing to gain a degree of familiarity with Gene Roddenberry's universe, but there were always new discoveries to be made and you had to watch regularly to keep up with them. At the end of the first year, only the broad outlines had been sketched, the details still had to be filled in.

Both as television, and as science fiction, STAR TREK had its weaknesses, but despite whatever drawbacks it had, it still succeeded in fulfilling the functions of both of those mediums. As television, it entertained, and as science fiction, it stretched the mind. STAR TREK widened a lot of horizons—right out to the edge of the galaxy. And maybe even a little bit beyond.

And the fans responded.

If STAR TREK demanded an involvement, the fans were more than willing to meet it. STAR TREK fandom grew in direct response to the show. It grew slowly at first—the phenomenon wasn't really recognized as a social force in its own right until STAR TREK had already been on the air for two years. And few people realized the extent of the phenomenon until the show was

"You can certainly spare one or two..."

"Mr. Spock touched the *right* emotional chords."

Spock in his demonic aspect: "Mirror, Mirror"

Surak, Vulcan's greatest philosopher...

...and one of his alien captors

Star Trek's secret message? Kirk and Spock
in "Patterns of Force"...

...and in "Operation—Annihilate!"

already off the air. (If they had, it might not have gone off the air, but that's another story.)

Trekkies have often been compared with groupies. In one respect, the comparison is apt. Groupies follow rock stars around, hoping to share in the fame and magic of the superstar experience. Trekkies respond to STAR TREK the same way—but much more intensely. And in that respect, the comparison with groupies is unfair. For one thing, being a Trekkie involves a hell of a lot more work.

All that a groupie has to do is devote herself slavishly to her particular rock idols, collect their albums and newspaper clippings, and attend their concerts and try to get in backstage. The responsibilities of a Trekkie are much more demanding.

A Trekkie not only keeps careful tabs on everyone involved with STAR TREK, she—(generally, Trekkies are adolescent or post-adolescent girls, but not always)—she collects film clips, publishes fanzines, writes her own STAR TREK stories—usually with herself as heroine, she keeps scrapbooks, she sews up costumes and uniforms for herself to match the ones on the show, she learns how to make herself up as a Vulcan, she corresponds endlessly with other Trekkies, and so on. . . .

And there are the conventions.

There are at least a dozen science fiction conventions every year. The World Science Fiction Convention, at which the International Hugo Award for excellence in science fiction is presented, usually commands an attendance of several thousand fans and writers from all over the world. Major regional conventions usually have attendances of at least a thousand, and even a small local convention can depend on two or three hundred people from the surrounding area, minimum. And there are somewhere in the neighborhood of two hundred of these local conventions a year. Although the main focus of all these conventions is science fiction, comics or movies, STAR TREK is always well represented.

There are always a few Trekkies who show up to trade their film clips and wear their costumes and sell their STAR TREK fanzines. They flash each other the Vulcan Peace Sign and exchange such logical salutations as, "May you live long and prosper."

If a convention holds a masquerade ball, there will always be several STAR TREK costumes. If there is a huckster room, there will be plenty of STAR TREK memorabilia. If there are any panel discussions on science fiction and the dramatic arts, STAR TREK will always be mentioned.

This is not to imply that all science fiction fans are Trekkies, or vice versa.

On the contrary, the two groups are quite distinct. Science fiction fandom existed long before Star Trek, and science fiction fans regard Star Trek as only a part of science fiction, a TV show moderately enjoyable and better than most. On the other hand, the most devout of Trekkies tend to regard Star Trek as the *raison d'être* of science fiction, as if all the rest were merely preparation and Star Trek the proper pinnacle of accomplishment.

This dichotomy is mainly a matter of attitude. There is no civil war between the two groups. Fans are generally a pretty tolerant lot: "I won't pee on your tree if you won't pee on mine."

Science fiction fandom has seen a lot of changes in the past thirty years. The development of the Star Trek phenomenon is just one more in a succession of violent wrenches to the fannish consciousness. The subculture has gone through at least eight or nine generations of fans, and science fiction aficionados have seen a lot of their dreams come true and many of their predictions realized. Fandom itself has almost risen to respectability along with science fiction.

Many of the older fans still remember that science fiction began as a "junk" literature, and it has a long heritage of pulp fiction in its history, stretching back beyond Buck Rogers and *Thrilling Wonder Stories,* back to before World War I when Hugo Gernsback was publishing "scientific fiction" stories in his *Modern Electrics Magazine.*

To the more seasoned SF fans (anyone who has been around for five years or more) Star Trek is just the contemporary form of "junk." That is, at the moment, it's the lowest common denominator in science fiction. Its appeal is on the gut level and its stories tend more toward action than idea. It is science fiction for the masses. Hence, many of the older fans are a bit skeptical of the hardcore Trekkies.

Nevertheless, Star Trek's science fiction still attempted to stress a maturity of approach against a generally credible background. Despite the restrictions of television production, every effort was made to keep the special effects and other production values as accurate as possible. If Star Trek is now "the lowest common denominator," then that just demonstrates science fiction's amazing capacity for growth. In the B-pictures that were being made in the fifties, and even the early sixties, like as not, the spaceships were stock shots of old V-2s—and later on, Saturn Vs and other missiles. Alien planets were usually Griffith Park.

Until very recently—i.e., post-Star Trek and post-*2001: A Space Odyssey*— TV and motion picture handling of science fiction (with rare exceptions such as George Pal's efforts) was thirty to forty years behind science fiction in the written form.* It was still rooting around in old-fashioned space opera, bems (bug-eyed monsters) and the like. STAR TREK represented an extraordinary leap, and most of the science fiction world recognized it.

STAR TREK may very well be the spiritual descendant of Buck Rogers, but the difference is a couple of orders of magnitude—especially in sophistication and credibility.

Science fiction fans have a slogan-derived acronym to express their attitude toward fannish activities: FIAWOL—it means, "Fandom is a way of life." Conversely, other fans, who don't take the thing too seriously, insist on FIJAGH: "Fandom is just a goddamn hobby."

On the other hand, STAR TREK fandom may be something else altogether.

In Los Angeles, a fellow named Roger Heisman managed to glom onto the actual *Enterprise* shuttlecraft, the full-size mockup that was used in several episodes, particularly "Galileo Seven." He kept it on his front lawn with the intention of restoring it, inside and out. (The interior of the shuttlecraft never had an actual set inside it; Heisman is building one.) He also made himself a STAR TREK uniform and props such as phasers and communicators. His props were so accurate as to be indistinguishable from the originals.

In Poughkeepsie, New York, Michael McMaster and Art Brumaghim built their own bridge set and a transporter room to make their own STAR TREK movie. The set covered a half-circle, from Mr. Spock's science station to Mr. Scott's station to the right of the elevator. There was a captain's chair and a pilot console. They also made costumes and props identical to those used on the show. The effect was so accurate that they even fooled Gene Roddenberry with it. At a STAR TREK convention in Detroit in October 1972, McMaster handed Roddenberry a photograph and asked him if he could identify what was wrong with the picture. Roddenberry stared at it for a while and finally said, "Well, the Captain is wearing glasses—" And then he realized what he was saying and took a closer look. "This isn't my bridge set—!" McMaster and Brumaghim's effort was truly a labor of love; their plans were based entirely on the floorplan of the bridge in *The Making of* STAR TREK, and microscopic study of film clips ordered from STAR TREK Enterprises.

Many female STAR TREK fans have made costumes that they can wear, costumes based on various episodes or characters. Others have formed STAR TREK clubs and act out various episodes. This author's personal favorite is the sweet little old lady in Southern California who has tape-recorded every

*To discuss the science fiction movies and TV shows since STAR TREK would require a whole other book. At least. (I'll let someone else write it, thanks.)

single STAR TREK episode—for the express purpose of later dubbing in her own voice over the leading lady's.

These people are "STAR TREK nuts" but most of them are *good* "nuts" because they can still relate to the rest of the world—and they've channeled their interest into constructive outlets: building, writing, and creating. Those occasional few who go off the deep end, do great damage not only to themselves, but to others as well. And in the truly *extreme* cases, this kind of fanaticism can actually be dangerous. For instance, one girl ran away from home to go to Hollywood and try to move in with Leonard Nimoy. She chased after him for months, in general making his life miserable. In the process she managed to interfere with shooting schedules, personal lives, and the nerves of everybody she came in contact with.

There's an explanation for this kind of rabid devotion. It involves, first of all, the medium of television and the star system. Week after week, television brings the actors into the individual's home, forces a kind of pseudo-intimacy, creates the illusion of friendship where no relationship exists at all. The people on the tube are giving off signals of "I like you, you're a part of my tribe and my family," but unfortunately, most of that is only a *performance*—and when a fan meets the actors and tries to respond to those perceived signals of intimacy, he or she slams up against the brick wall of "Who are you? You're not in my tribe or family. I don't even know you." It's very frustrating. Television creates the illusion that one has shared a meaningful experience with the actors, but in real life, the fan finds that the actors have not experienced it the same way.

All stars run into this—there's only one William Shatner; there are millions of William Shatner fans. All of them know who he is, but to him, they're all a sea of blurred faces. He can't even begin to make the effort. He has to concentrate on being William Shatner the actor first, because in the long run that's the best way that he can serve *all* of his fans. The same applies to any man or woman who becomes a star.

This is why it's so hard to meet your favorite movie star—or even to get a letter to him or her. (It's actually easier to meet a United States senator.) A star's privacy can become a very precious thing.

The good news is that a great many actors and actresses are very much aware of the debt they owe to the fans. George Takei perhaps summed it up best. He was explaining his frequent attendance at STAR TREK conventions: "It's a responsibility. It's part of the job."

STAR TREK was saved for its third season by a massive letter campaign that brought in more than one million letters. But in addition to that, Gene Roddenberry *had made a personal effort to save the show.*

"I went to NBC," recalls Roddenberry, "and I said, 'I love this show. I think it could run for as long as "Gunsmoke" if you'll give it another season, and so, NBC, I am prepared to make this offer: if you'll put STAR TREK on for a third year, I will come back, I will come out of the Executive Producer spot. I will go back and personally line-produce the third year the same way I did the first year. I guarantee it to you that if I have to work 14 hours a day, we'll have the same kind of scripts we had, the same kind of attention, and all I ask in return is that if I do that, you'll give me a good time slot. Don't kill the show with a bad time slot, because you've moved us twice now into increasingly worse spots.'

"NBC said to me, 'Yes, okay, we accept your offer. You can have either 7:30, Monday, or 8:00, Tuesday.' And I said fine, 7:30, Monday was fine and I was prepared to do it. A few weeks before the schedules came out, I received a call from NBC, from one of the executives, and I was having breakfast at home and remember clearly and the first words of the executive was, 'Gene, baby . . .' and I almost knew I was in trouble right then. He says, 'We've really done something for you. The Research Department has been working very hard about the ideal spot for your show and we're going to do even better for you. We're going to put you at 10:00 Friday night.'

"I said, 'You're mad. What are you talking about, you're doing something for me?' He said, 'Please, our research people have really a lot of reasons for this.'

"Well, I learned later in the day that their real reason for it was that *Laugh-In* had insisted on the spot they were going to give us* and it was obvious to me that 10:00 Friday was death so I said to the network in subsequent meetings, 'I will not go back and put that kind of effort, risk of life and health and everything, to a show that cannot make it no matter what I do.' Oh, and at the same time NBC had also, instead of giving us a full year's commitment, only picked us up for 13 shows, a half a year. The only clout I had to fight the network with was would I or would I not produce. Obviously, I had no other weapon. I could not get them to change the time.

"I retreated so far, finally, in an effort to save STAR TREK as to say, 'All right, if you'll give me a firm commitment for a full season, 22 episodes, I'll even produce it then. I'll take a chance that even in this bad time slot

---

*"Laugh-In" was scheduled for 8:00 Monday and refused to be moved to 8:30. As they had a bigger rating than STAR TREK—they were the smash hit of 1968 and '69—they had more clout. STAR TREK was outvoted.

that if I can have a commitment for the full year that somehow we'll pull it off.' The network refused to budge even there.* I said, 'If you won't, I will not produce it.' They refused to budge and I was left in a situation of having used the only threat I had. I was stuck with either backing off entirely and producing it anyway, which meant that in future dealings with NBC, they would never believe my word again. Or I could keep my word. So I was really forced to break off from the show, and I could see it was going to die and I spent that year trying to develop new projects for the following season.

"Later, I also found out that there would be no fourth season, no matter what. I was told that they didn't understand the show and they didn't like it and that was generally it. I suppose if we'd gotten smash ratings they couldn't have done anything about it, but there's no chance of getting smash ratings in that time slot. That was a great sorrow to me, but I have my own career to think about. If the show was going to be dead anyway, I was better off keeping my executive producer position which left me time to develop things for the following year. Since STAR TREK was gone, I had to have something else, and I spent the time writing a couple of features.''

About the third season, in general, Gene Roddenberry was brief: "I think a show needs its creator with it, or if it doesn't have that it has to have someone who has continuity with the show, who you had developed to take over that position, and unfortunately, always intending to stay close to STAR TREK, I had developed no one to take it over except Gene Coon who, unfortunately had gotten sick and then had a commitment over at Universal. So I brought in people who were well recommended and they saw the show their own way.''

So STAR TREK went off the air. Its last episode was "Turnabout Intruder.'' The *Enterprise*'s five year mission had been aborted two years before completion.

It may have been the biggest mistake NBC ever made. How wrong they were.

Because almost immediately, STAR TREK went into syndication.

What this meant was that the seventy-nine episodes that had already been filmed were to be rerun—*endlessly*—on local stations all across the country.

---

*The network always suspected that Gene Roddenberry had engineered the mail campaign. NBC never quite understood what it had in STAR TREK and probably would have cancelled it in 1968, had it not been for the mail campaign. Thus embarrassed, they had to keep it on the air—but they were not committed to keeping it alive. Hence, the bad time slot. It has always seemed to many of the fans that NBC was definitely trying to kill the show. It was too expensive for them and it wasn't a big enough hit. Demographics have since proven the Nielson ratings wrong on STAR TREK.

Syndication is the sale of a package of episodes to a single market, i.e., a television station. That market can use those shows in a variety of ways, but the most usual is to "strip" them. "Stripping" means running one episode per weeknight, and this was the practice that was generally used with STAR TREK.

In 1966 STAR TREK had been on Thursdays at 8:30. In 1967 it moved to Fridays at 8:30. In 1968, although it had been scheduled to appear on Mondays at 7:30 (we'll talk about that later), the show eventually came on at 10:00 Fridays. What this meant in terms of viewers is obvious. There weren't any—at least not enough to justify a fourth season. It seemed as if NBC were trying to ignore the show, pretend it wasn't there, and had shuffled it into a dark corner where they hoped eventually it would just die away. By their actions, it looked as if they were trying to kill STAR TREK. Ten P.M. was just too late an hour for a whole generation of eager, would-be STAR TREK fans.

Apparently, the local station managers had more sense. When they got their hands on the STAR TREK reruns, they knew what to do. They scheduled them for 5:00 and 6:00 and 7:00. Never any later. They knew which audience they wanted to reach—and reach it they did.

All the teens and pre-teens who had never seen STAR TREK before suddenly discovered a whole new universe of excitement; it was the same thrill of discovery that the first generation of Trekkies had experienced only three years before, and it was happening all over again.

Almost everywhere it was scheduled, it whiped up the ratings race. More than one station manager was delighted to discover that he had captured the lion's share of the local viewing audience with STAR TREK.

Between the hours of 4:00 and 8:00 P.M. are when teens and pre-teens do most of their viewing. That's valuable commercial time—time to schedule a show that they will be sure to watch, time to sell commercials specifically oriented toward their consumer needs. Teenagers are one of the most volatile consumer forces in America, one that advertisers are constantly trying to reach. If they're watching STAR TREK, then that's the vehicle to reach them by.

The result of this is that not only did STAR TREK find a whole new audience, but that same new audience discovered STAR TREK fandom.

Although it might have seemed logical to expect that the movement would have died away with the show, it was an erroneous assumption. Because once a social structure forms, it does not easily disband. Once the links are put into place, they tend to remain in place.

Example: Bjo Trimble. Before her letter campaign, she had a mailing list of about eight hundred people who were interested in science fiction. *After* that campaign, her list had grown to twelve *thousand*. And one simply does not throw away a mailing list. If a fan is interested in STAR TREK, he might also be interested in J.R.R. Tolkein, and science fiction conventions, and *Planet of the Apes,* and fanzines and related memorabilia.

And Bjo Trimble was not alone. There was S. Cornelie Cole in Texas, and Carol Lee in New York, and the Basta sisters in Detroit, and others too numerous to mention.

These are the people who published STAR TREK fanzines, and ran STAR TREK fan clubs and wrote letters by the score. Especially intense were the fans who did *not* live in New York or California. These were the people who didn't have the convenient access to the studios or the stars. To them, the excitement was distant—unless they provided their own excitement by *making* their own. All they had was their intensity—and be damned if they were going to give that up.

Their precious links with others all over the country had been formed mostly through the mail and over the telephones (hundred dollar phone bills were not uncommon). Ostensibly STAR TREK was the reason for all that communication—but just because STAR TREK was gone was no reason to stop communicating. The links had been established, they were going to be *used* whether STAR TREK was still around or not. A whole new world of friendship had been opened for a great many people who hungered to stretch their horizons. Anyone who thought it would be easily dismantled just by the cancellation of a TV show was a poor judge of human nature.

A couple of examples here to prove a point:

Leonard Nimoy was on a promotional tour one time. When he walked into his hotel room in Chicago, the phone rang. He answered it—it was Susan from Colorado. He chatted with her for a bit, then hung up. A few minutes later, the phone rang again, this time it was Diane from Miami. He chatted with her for a while, then begged off because he had to get ready for an appearance that evening. A few moments later, the phone rang again. This time, it was Gail in New York. Intrigued, Leonard asked how they all knew where he was. Oh, replied the girl. Susan from Colorado called Diane in Miami who called her in New York, etc.

On that same tour, he ended a phone conversation in one city, flew to another, only to find the same girl waiting on the phone for him at his new hotel room. She had found out his whole itinerary and was prepared to talk him across the country.

This is the STAR TREK grapevine in action. A more subdued example, but one more far-reaching in its consequences, is the incredible film-clip caper.

To properly appreciate this, you have to understand that there are a limited number of 35 millimeter film clips from STAR TREK floating around. While STAR TREK Enterprises was in business, they sold sets of these film clips to fans. The clips could be mounted in slide holders and projected exactly as any other 35mm slide. The clips are in full color and are literally a piece of the show.

These are actual clips of unused STAR TREK footage. Shots of the *Enterprise,* of Kirk and Spock, of alien beings and strange planets, of weird sets and weirder characters—anything and everything in fact that had ever appeared before the cameras. These are the beginnings and endings of shots, the parts that are edited out, these are duplicate work prints, outtakes, unusable sequences and other assorted sweepings from the cutting room floor. They're of no worth to anybody—except a STAR TREK fan.

(Want to play STAR TREK Trivia? Two Trekkies and a pile of slides. Each one picks a slide and has to identify it—what show is this from, who are the actors involved, what characters do they play, and what's going on in this scene? A real Trekkie can identify the episode by the characters in the scene, the cut of a costume, or even the lighting of a background. Miss three times, and obviously you're just a Klingon imposter.)

These film clips are in great demand by the fans—after all, being able to project Captain Kirk or Mr. Spock onto a wall-sized screen can be almost as exciting as an episode itself. STAR TREK's visuals were almost always dramatic— if you've ever seen them projected, rather than just on a TV screen, you know what I mean. And if all you ever had was just a small black and white TV set, then a color slide is even more overpowering.

The interesting thing is that these film clips came out of Paramount in batches—and were being released in batches by STAR TREK Enterprises. For example, in late '69, they were still only working on the episodes of late '67. That is, when the show went off the air, they were only halfway through the second season.

But one of the people who keeps tabs on STAR TREK fandom noticed a funny thing. There were slides from the third season floating around. And there shouldn't be. Not yet. STAR TREK Enterprises hadn't gotten that far.

For a while, this was a minor mystery among certain circles—where were these film clips coming from? Certainly from no source that anyone knew or would admit to. Not even the big-name fans, the presidents of fan clubs, or wheeler-dealers knew.

Finally, one of the sources was pinned down, a teenage girl who admitted how she had gotten her clips. When STAR TREK went into syndication, each local station began cutting bits and pieces out of each episode, to make more time for commercials.*

This little girl had gotten a phone call from one of her friends in another city, who had heard about it from a friend in still another city. (And so on.) It seems that somewhere, some little Trekkie had approached the local station in her area, gotten friendly with the film cutter, and asked what he was doing with the pieces he was cutting out of the STAR TREK shows. He told her that he was throwing them away. They were no good to anyone. She got friendlier then and said, "Oh, don't throw them away. Save them for me. I collect them." Just how friendly she had to get in order to accomplish this goal is not known. (But I suspect that very few film cutters resented this attention.)

In any case, she then proceeded to phone all of her friends in other cities where STAR TREK was being syndicated. And shortly thereafter, other film cutters at other local stations found themselves being approached by young girls who were only too eager to be friendly in return for one small favor. . . .

And then they called their friends in other cities. . . .

STAR TREK has been syndicated in over 150 markets. You figure it out.

The extent of the STAR TREK Phenomenon can be partially gauged by the number of fanzines and fan clubs devoted exclusively to the show.

For instance, the fanzines.

All it takes to produce a fanzine is one fan and a typewriter. And some enthusiasm. Journalistic ability is no prerequisite at all, but a good mimeo is. A fanzine is judged as much by its reproduction as by its content.

The average fanzine is published at the whim of the fan. That makes it about as regular as a spastic colon, and gives it approximately the same life expectancy as an Italian government. Which is to say, not very and not long.

But despite all this, fanzines have one saving grace. They're fun.

In general, a fanzine is a fairly accurate reflection of what is going on in its writer's mind—whether the writer intended that or not.

Further, as an avenue of communication, a fanzine functions as a scatter-gun. It allows a writer to communicate not to just one person at a time, but many people. And a fanzine is a time machine too—the writer's words are being preserved on paper and thus sent into the future so that other fans, months and years removed, can share the writer's feelings and reactions.

---

*I know. I cringe too at the thought. Some of these cuts were horrendous. Whole episodes were emasculated by the ill-timed dropping of a single scene. Unfortunately, this was necessary to make that all-important commercial time available—otherwise the station couldn't afford STAR TREK in the first place. Fortunately, most of the episodes held up well; they were able to withstand even that amount of abuse.

STAR TREK fanzines are all of this. Generally, they drip with enthusiasm for STAR TREK, its cast and crew. The articles tend to be analyses of the show in general or reviews of specific episodes, articles about individual cast members or the characters they play, fan-written STAR TREK adventures, and occasionally interviews or news reports. STAR TREK fanzines also contain excited reports of STAR TREK activities at recent conventions, and in the days when the show was still in production, often published articles by fans who had been lucky enough to visit the actual sets.

The fanzines began shortly after STAR TREK appeared on the air. As the Trek-fans discovered science fiction fandom, they began to adopt more and more of its conventions. (Pun intended, but more about that later.) Articles about STAR TREK in science fiction fanzines turned into STAR TREK fanzines with occasional science fiction articles.

As the STAR TREK Phenomenon developed and grew, more and more of the Trekkies, many of whom had never heard of science fiction fandom before STAR TREK, began to put out their own zines. They paid little attention to either tradition or structure—but then again, few fans do—substituting enthusiasm instead. In science fiction fandom, however, gross displays of enthusiasm are considered neo-fannish, hence *gauche*. But because of the nature of the two fandoms, they must share the same space-time continuum.

Some of the fanzines that have been published include *Eridani Triad, Pastaklan Vesla* (A Horta Press Publication), *Spock's Showcase, Terran Times, The Nimoyan, Retrospect* (Spotlight on Leonard Nimoy), *Deck 6, Faunch, Grup, Babel, Vorpal Sword, Anti-Matter,* Spock's Scribes' *Storyteller, Impulse, Leonard Nimoy Power, LNSTFCCF* (Leonard Nimoy Star Trek Fan Club of Concerned Fans), *Masiform-D, Nimoyan Digest, Nuts and Bolts Work Sheet, Pentathlon, Spockanalia, Star Date, Star-Fleet Communications, S. T. Phile, T-Negative, Kevas & Trillium, The Voyages, The William Shatner Letter Exchange, Gonomony, Guardian of Forever, Kraith Collected, Log of the U.S.S. Enterprise, NCC 1701, LNAF* (Leonard Nimoy Association of Fans), *Nimoyan Federation, Overload* (A Scotty zine), *Quadrant, Star Base Omega, Star-Borne, Stargram, Star Trek Song Book, Tholiam Web, Triskelion,* and *A Taste of Armageddon.* (No, I do not know where you can order any of these.)

Since the early seventies, STAR TREK fandom has been a phenomenon— and many people in the film industry have been baffled by the intensity of the fans' involvement with the show. It's beyond their experience to see an audience *care* this much about the stories, the actors, the characters, and all the myriad details of production.

It is clear that STAR TREK has become a cultural artifact. There are references to it everywhere. The series has been parodied on "Saturday Night Live" (with Chevy Chase playing Spock), on "Fridays" (with William Shatner playing William Shatner), and even on "Mork and Mindy"—with a surprise beam-in by a very surprised Captain Kirk. There have been references to it in *E.T.* ("Can't he just beam up?" "Hey—this is reality.") and *Close Encounters of the Third Kind.* (An *Enterprise* model can be seen in Roy Neary's hobby room.)

On "Bosom Buddies," Kip Niven once flipped open a stapler as if it were a communicator and said to it, "Scotty, beam me up." References to the series have shown up in various comic strips such as "Peanuts" and "B.C." and "Doonesbury." In "Funky Winkerbean" the computer plays STAR TREK games as a running gag and in "DRABBLE" the mother goes off to STAR TREK conventions on a regular basis, and the characters in "Bloom County" love to play STAR TREK.

A murder mystery titled *Two Plus Two* starred a detective with a cat named "Tribble." (If his date didn't recognize the reference, he didn't ask her out again.) Puzzle magazines routinely include trivia questions on STAR TREK. *The New Limerick,* edited by G. Legman, includes a whole cycle of STAR TREK limericks.* And STAR TREK bumper stickers can be seen everywhere. The most common one says, "Beam me up, Scotty!"

STAR TREK is not only an arcade video game, there seem to be several hundred different versions of it available for home computers. The first STAR TREK game was written sometime in 1966 or '67 by a long forgotten amateur computer hacker; but the classic version was the one written by Mike Mayfield in October 1972. This became the "standard" STAR TREK game when it was put into the Hewlett Packard program library and distributed onto a number of HP Data Center machines. In the summer of 1973, David Ahl (now the publisher of *Creative Computing* magazine), translated the HP version into Basic-Plus for a Digital Equipment computer and added some improvements of his own to the program. Since then, the game has been copied, adapted, upgraded, and published in so many different places that it's impossible to keep count. There are versions of STAR TREK available for just about every

---

*Speaking of limericks:

Since I first wrote that damn script for Gene
And the electrical picture machine,
   Fuzzies have chased their creator
   From here to Decatur;
Nobody knows of the tribbles I've seen!

computer on the market. (Most of them are in public domain and can be obtained from local users groups.)

Most of the games put the player at the controls of the *Enterprise*—his mission to patrol the galaxy and shoot Klingons wherever he finds them. The game is generally played on a two-dimensional grid, and most of the STAR TREK computer games are fairly simplistic.

The most sophisticated and complex STAR TREK computer game of all is STAR TREK Colossus. It took Dr. Phillip E. Bailey more than two years to write, and it is obviously a labor of love; the game fills two floppy disks, and the rules fill a third. The documentation includes a detailed set of blueprints for the *Enterprise,* and a complete crew and equipment list. The player is not only responsible for moving his characters throughout the ship—putting out fires, delivering dilithium crystals to replace broken ones, etc.—at the same time, he must do battle with a Klingon battlecruiser that is stalking the *Enterprise*. The game also produces a variety of rather startling graphics; using only the alphanumeric characters of a standard video terminal, the program displays long, medium, and close-range scanning views of the Klingon battlecruiser—approaching, retreating, flanking, and even exploding, should the player be skilled enough to outfight the Klingon commander. (There are several different battlecruisers and captains. Your computer will give you the appropriate identifications when the ship shows up on the screen.) There are also starbases for refueling, repair and replacements of injured or deceased crew.* (When the real *Enterprise* is finally built, this will be the simulator they'll train Kirk and Spock on.)

And then there are the *academic* concerns:

STAR TREK has been studied as a religious phenomenon, a psychological phenomenon, an example of American cultural monomyth, and even as a sexual phenomenon. The series is a favorite topic for graduate theses, and those who are close to the show are used to getting phone calls and letters from researchers (almost invariably female) who are careful to explain that they are not *really* "Trekkies"—they just want to do the definitive study of the show. (Curiously, many of these researchers have produced documents that use the "evidence" in STAR TREK to support a variety of different positions: religious, sexual, psychological. Several of these studies even reveal Gene Roddenberry's carefully conceived "master plan"—ignoring the evidence that much of STAR TREK was invented during the course of three years of production by a variety of writers and directors. So far, the only paper that hasn't been written is "STAR TREK, A Rorschach Test for PhDs.")

---

*I was so upset when I accidentally killed Dr. McCoy that I haven't played the game since.

One woman (characterized by an observer as a charter member of "size-nineteen STAR TREK fandom"), used to corner people at STAR TREK conventions and read to them from her 150-page (single-spaced) study about Spock and the planet Vulcan. Her authorization was a letter from Gene Roddenberry (sealed in plastic.) The letter was actually one of those very polite acknowledgments, routinely sent out by the secretaries, something to the effect of: "You sure did a lot of typing here. Gosh, we're impressed that you like us so much. Thanks."

In the mid-seventies STAR TREK fans organized themselves to orchestrate a letter campaign to then-President Gerald Ford, asking him to name the first space shuttle, the *Enterprise*. NASA officials were startled—and more than a little stunned—when President Ford actually did name the shuttle after the starship. When the *Enterprise* was first rolled out at Edwards Air Force Base, they played the STAR TREK theme song, and Senator Barry Goldwater joked that none of the astronauts were qualified to fly this ship because none of them had pointy ears.

What is interesting about all of these examples of the pervasiveness of STAR TREK in the American culture is that they are all *spontaneous*. Neither Paramount Pictures, nor anyone else involved in merchandising has created them. Rather, they have all occurred as spontaneous expressions of individual affection for the show, its characters, the actors, the starship *Enterprise*, and the larger context of optimism that all of these elements represent.

Truly, STAR TREK has transcended its origins as a simple TV series to become a larger expression of American culture. Paramount is no longer the owner of a property, as much as they are the custodians of a national treasure.

Indeed, it is the fans who act as if they are the actual owners of the show.

Howard Zimmerman, editor of *Starlog* magazine, has had nearly a decade's worth of experience with STAR TREK fans. He says, "Oh yes—they think they own the show because for a very long time they were the only ones keeping it alive. Paramount didn't seem to care, Paramount wasn't bringing the show back, so Paramount was the enemy. Now . . . the fans resent it that Paramount has taken it away from them. They resent the studio, the producers—anyone who violates what they think STAR TREK should be. I guess the fans think that Paramount should make STAR TREK movies just for the love of STAR TREK alone, and let fans write, direct, and act in the pictures. A lot of the fans don't recognize that STAR TREK is an economic entity too."

But even beyond that, there is a dark side to STAR TREK fandom that troubles many long-time friends of the show. Indeed, some of the more extreme STAR TREK fans have exhibited behavior that can best be described as self-destructive.

Early in the production of *Star Trek III*, one of the more rabid fans of the series arrived at Paramount Studios. He walked into Harve Bennett's office and *demanded* a part in the third movie. If he wasn't given a respectable speaking part, he threatened to have *his* fans (a fan with fans?) organize a massive boycott of *Star Trek III* on the east coast.

Harve Bennett listened politely—and then had the man escorted off the lot and permanently barred from the studio. The man hung around Hollywood for three weeks, found he was getting nowhere, and eventually returned home (where presumably, he set about organizing his threatened boycott.) But incidents like this present a very real danger to a production company. A producer can seriously hurt himself when he falls out of his chair laughing.

Another, more serious case:

In the 1973 edition of this book, I wrote about a young man with a rather startling resemblance to Mr. Spock. He had heightened this resemblance with an appropriate haircut, a careful trimming of his eyebrows, and a deliberately blank manner. He copied Spock's precise way of speaking and even the famous eyebrow lift. Of course, he wore a STAR TREK uniform. He looked like a teenage Spock. Moreover, he *acted* like a teenage Spock, and the effect he had on many of the young women attending the west coast STAR TREK conventions was . . . ah, dramatic. The young man had so totally submerged his own personality that whoever he had once been was no longer available. He had *become* Spock.

Unfortunately, in the real universe—there is no Spock. He's only a fictitious character. There is no planet Vulcan. There is no Vulcan mind control. There is no Vulcan purging of emotions. Not in the real world. Not in the world you and I wake up in. But this young man had so wanted it to be real that he put himself into a fatal psychological trap. He was trying to turn himself into a Vulcan, and that was something he could not *possibly* become—because he still had his own emotions and his own feelings—and there was no way he could rectify having those feelings and still be Spock. After a few years, he tried *not* being Spock—but that didn't work for him either, because he'd so suppressed his own identity that that didn't exist for him any more either. Eventually, he came up against feelings that he couldn't contain as Spock and not knowing how else to handle them, he committed suicide to end the pressure.

An equally disturbing phenomenon has developed among a group of female STAR TREK fans. To them, STAR TREK is not about the *Enterprise* or its five-year mission, or the noble vision of humanity among the stars—it is specifically about the relationship between Kirk and Spock.

More specifically, these women entertain themselves by writing stories in which Kirk and Spock are homosexual lovers.*

Kirk?!! And Spock?!!

The stories are collected and circulated in mimeographed fanzines. More than one unsuspecting STAR TREK fan has stumbled unwarily into these zines at some convention or other. The result is usually a startled expression and the question, "Is this what STAR TREK fandom is really about?" (It is most definitely *not* what STAR TREK fandom is really about, but more than one young would-be fan has been prohibited from attending TREK-cons or reading TREK-zines because his/her parents have seen this material.)

The network of K/S fans—as they call themselves—is small, but very active. Some of their stories are very explicit. And some of the artwork accompanying—well, never mind.† These women use scenes from the episodes and specifically from the STAR TREK movies to justify their belief that this is the *secret message* of STAR TREK. (Imagine what could be made out of Spock taking Kirk's hand to tell him about ". . . this simple feeling." Remember, the one that's beyond V'GER's comprehension?)

While the K/S ladies have never been vocal enough to be a problem, their projection of their own sexual fantasies onto STAR TREK has at times been a nuisance for those who actually have to produce the show. Eventually, Gene Roddenberry, in his novelization of *Star Trek I*, had to acknowledge their unwelcome invasion of the universe he had created by including a footnote (ostensibly written by Kirk himself) explaining that Kirk and Spock were "just good friends." (This did not even slow the K/S ladies down.)

One long time STAR TREK fan summed up her feelings about the K/S phenomenon this way: "I really don't mind the stories. Some of them are even quite well written. What does bother me though is the sado-masochism in them. Too many of the stories involve beatings and rapes—sometimes even between Kirk and Spock. I just find it difficult to believe that this is an accurate portrayal of the behavior of two of Starfleet's finest officers."

Even more candid are the comments of a gay male STAR TREK fan: "The K/S stories I've seen are offensive. It's a woman's idea of what gay men are like, and it's way off base. Besides, I like Kirk and Spock the way they are."

What anyone wants to believe in the privacy of his or her own head, of

---

*I am not making this up. Honest.

†This is a PG-rated book and I'd like to keep it that way.

course, is his or her own business. It's when you start messing around in other people's universes that you have to follow the rules of the local creator. If nothing else, it's good manners.

Perhaps the best place to see STAR TREK fans at their worst is at a STAR TREK convention.

In the beginning, STAR TREK conventions were put on by groups of fans (with previous science fiction convention experience) as an expression of love for STAR TREK. In those days, it was like the gathering of a large enthusiastic family. The first STAR TREK convention in New York attracted over three thousand people, and the first STAR TREK convention in Los Angeles attracted over five thousand people. The first conventions in Detroit and New Orleans also attracted crowds numbering in the thousands.

The committees that put on these first conventions had not done so with the expectation that they would show a large profit—they were as surprised as anyone to discover how many people would show up to express their affection for the defunct TV series.

But it doesn't take much mathematical ability to multiply a twenty dollar admission price by 5000 attendees and come up with a very exciting number. And just about *anybody* could put on a STAR TREK convention.

Very quickly, some very unsavory anybodies *were* putting on STAR TREK conventions:

A 1976 convention in New York, organized by a team of entrepreneurs attracted over thirty thousand people to the Statler Hilton Hotel—a facility not designed to handle crowds that large. Many attendees had to wait two or three or four hours to get in to see a two and a half hour personal appearance of the STAR TREK cast. (At that same convention, William Shatner was hit with a pie. The man who threw the pie was put up to it by a local science fiction writer with a penchant for bad manners. Some STAR TREK fans who've recently learned the identity of the author intend to return the compliment at the first available opportunity.)

The following year, an attempt to repeat the event in Chicago failed disastrously. Due to some very bad planning, and even worse advertising, the Chicago "Space Circus" attracted less than a thousand attendees and was forced to close after one day. None of the guests were paid their speakers' fees.

One convention organizer was fired by his own committee because he was unable to account for all of the income of the convention. Another convention entrepreneur disappeared, leaving behind thousands of dollars of bad debts.

Although most of the STAR TREK conventions have been put on by fannish groups—many of whom have done so specifically to raise money for local charities—the bad press earned by the entrepreneurs and the embezzlers has had a dampening effect. Many of those who were responsible for the first STAR TREK conventions in New York and Los Angeles no longer wanted to be involved. It isn't worth the aggravation, the suspicions, or the accusations. (The Los Angeles STAR TREK convention made large charitable donations to a school for retarded children, the Motion Picture Country Home and Hospital, and the American Cancer Society—the latter in honor of Gene L. Coon—but the committee was still accused of not being idealistic enough in the service of STAR TREK.)

But even at those conventions where the committee is operating in a context of integrity, the fans cannot always be depended to. At one New York STAR TREK convention, a man was caught hawking "official STAR TREK program books." The truth was, he was a local printer; his nine-year-old son had cobbled the "program book" together out of pictures from magazines and books (including several from the earlier edition of this volume.) The captions had been added with a typewriter. The man had put the whole thing together with the express purpose of cashing in. When he was confronted, he just shrugged and said, "Why not? Everybody else is getting rich off STAR TREK. Why shouldn't I?"

In those early days, the dealers' room sometimes had a definite sense of piracy. One fan was once caught selling bootleg copies of STAR TREK scripts. Another was quietly selling bootleg videotapes of episodes. There were other ripoffs too. (A company that had purchased a license to sell tribbles finally gave up in the face of massive fannish ripoffs. Again, it wasn't worth the aggravation.)

Some of these practices were stopped when committees realized they were offending their guests. It makes no sense to honor a star in the banquet hall, while someone is ripping him off in the dealers' room. Several dealers were stopped by Paramount Pictures—lawyers from the studios visited the New York and Los Angeles conventions, but even the worst offenders managed to stay in business for quite a while before the studio managed to catch up with them.

But even moving beyond the commercial aspects of STAR TREK fandom, the behavior of individual fans has sometimes caused guests at conventions to wonder why they bother.

One STAR TREK author once appeared at a STAR TREK convention and found himself booed by the audience. A young woman accosted him in the lobby and proceeded to violently upbraid him for all the mistakes in his book. Another cornered him (literally) at a party for the purpose of "correcting" his thinking about the show. And finally, at a panel discussion, the poor man found that many of the fans weren't there to ask him questions, but wanted instead to call him to account for his crimes against the genre. The man has not been to a STAR TREK convention since. "I thought I'd been invited as a guest, not a defendant."

But—

The best place to see STAR TREK fans at their very best is *also* at a STAR TREK convention.

Because despite whatever else occurs at a STAR TREK convention, the attendees have come because they are *inspired* by the show—and their actions demonstrate where their hearts are.

Examples:

On the last night of one of the New York conventions, one of the guests found a lady crying in the lobby. She'd lost her wallet and all her money and had no way to get home. The guest took her to the convention hospitality suite and told her to wait there, then he found the convention committee chairman and related the problem. The chairman said, "No problem at all. How much does she need?" The woman was given thirty dollars busfare home.

Several hours later, she showed up again with a sheepish expression on her face. Her wallet had slipped down into the lining of her jacket and she hadn't lost it at all. She wanted to return the thirty dollars—and thank the committee again for their thoughtfulness.

A 1977 STAR TREK convention in Seattle, hosted by the Puget Sound Star Trekkers, hosted a blood drive in honor of Robert A. Heinlein, who has a rare blood type; Heinlein's life was once saved through blood donations and he has been a regular supporter of blood donorship ever since. The convention was one of Heinlein's rare public appearances, and the only STAR TREK convention he ever attended.

At the very first STAR TREK convention in Detroit, a seventeen-year-old fan with multiple sclerosis and permanently confined to a wheelchair came to the masquerade as Captain Christopher Pike, as seen in "The Menagerie." Before the convention was over, Gene Roddenberry had made him Starfleet's first honorary admiral (Admiral George LaForge).

The original New York STAR TREK Convention Committee always made a point of making their conventions handicapped-accessible. Spaces up front were always made available for wheelchairs. People with guide-dogs always had facilities available for their dogs, and blind people who used canes were given oral maps of the hotel. In fact, two blind fans met at the first New York STAR TREK convention, and by the time of the fifth one, were not only married, but had already had their first baby. (The baby was sighted.)

Bjo Trimble, in her book *On the Good Ship Enterprise*, tells of a young girl who waited quietly in line for a chance to shake William Shatner's hand. She got to the head of the line just as William Shatner announced, "I'm sorry I must go. Just one more—" There was a little boy standing just in front of the girl, who had also been waiting politely—who now lifted his hand desperately upward. The girl saw the little boy, Shatner didn't—he reached for her hand—and she lifted the little boy up so he could get the last handshake instead of her.

Many of those who worked on STAR TREK share this spirit. One little boy whose family was returning to Japan wrote to his favorite STAR TREK author asking about the animated STAR TREK TV series. It wouldn't be on the air until after he was already back in Tokyo and he was afraid he would never get to see it.* The author arranged for the boy and his family to tour the Filmation studios where the show was being produced.

When George Takei appears at conventions, he almost always invites the whole convention to come jogging with him. Just be in the lobby of the hotel at seven A.M. Not surprisingly, he almost always has a group of young women to jog with. (Hm . . .)

There are *spontaneous* conventions too—and spontaneous demonstrations of goodwill.

In San Jose, while fans were waiting in line for the first showing of *Star Trek II*, an unknown fan showed up with a small videotape recorder and a portable TV set. He set it and played the STAR TREK episode "Space Seed" for the people in line. This was the episode that set up the plot of the movie. When the box office opened, he took the videotape recorder and TV set away while everyone got politely back in line—in their original places! (No one

---

*STAR TREK is seen in Japan, and has a very large fan following in that nation too. Some of the episodes, however, have undergone a rather interesting transformation in the process of translation. "The City on the Edge of Forever" has become "The Dangerous Trip to the Past." "The Devil in the Dark" has become "Horuta: The Underground Monster." "The Doomsday Machine" is called "The Gigantic Monster in Space." "Errand of Mercy" is now "The Invasion of the Klingon Empire." "Journey to Babel" is "The Invasion of the Planet Orion." (I don't understand that one either.) "The Menagerie" is "Phantomatic Mystery Beings on Talos." "The Naked Time" is "The Evil Space Disease." "The Trouble with Tribbles" is called "The New Species" (*Kuwadotoritikeeru*). "Wolf in the Fold" is "The Bloodthirsty Felon of Planet Arugirisu." "The Tholian Web" is "The Crisis of Captain Kirk Entering the Other Dimensional Space." And finally, "Where No Man Has Gone Before" is now "The Glittering Eyes." (Thanks to Bjo Trimble, Megamart #3, and Star Base Kyoto for this information.)

knows who the mysterious stranger was, but he left a silver tribble. . . .)

But the very best waiting-in-line story happened in Los Angeles when *Star Trek II* opened at the (world-famous) Chinese Theatre. Waiting in line were Karen Willson and Chris Weber, two longtime fans of the series, and a group of their friends. Some weeks before, Chris had casually asked Karen how she would like to be proposed to. Karen had told him she wanted it to be romantic with a capital "R": candles, roses, the seashore, soft waves, and music.

At the proper moment, Karen was presented with a single red rose, and everybody in the group lit the candles they were holding. The music? Everyone in the group began to play the *Star Wars* theme song on kazoos. Chris started to get to his knees, but Karen stopped him. "Where's the ocean view?"

Precisely on cue, one of the group whipped out an extra large picture postcard of the seashore and began moving it back and forth for realistic wave action, and making swooshing wave noises. Another fan held a glass of water and flicked drops of water at Karen and Chris as he proposed. "I had to ask," said Karen.

By now, of course, they had the undivided attention of just about everybody in the line, waiting to see what she would say. Karen could not resist a proposal with that much creativity. She accepted—and the entire line broke into applause and cheering.

PART FOUR

STAR TREK—
The Unfulfilled Potential

Science fiction demands, above everything else, *believability*.

Without it, the writer is only telling a fantasy. With believability comes immediacy, and an increased concern for the fate of the story's characters. But science fiction extracts a high price for believability.

The format requires visual production values—usually these are expensive. The format requires a high level of technology—and familiarity with same. The format requires characters that can understand and move through their environment easily—and that demands a high level of competency from the writer.

In a sense, the writer has to be a god. He has to create a whole world and all of its peoples. He has to know all of its physical laws and all of its geography. He has to play all the roles, answer all the questions, confront all the crises, and in the end be responsible for the solutions to all the problems he has created for himself.

And if he doesn't do a good job of it—then the reader or viewer is going to feel unsatisfied and cheated.

This is especially true in television. Gene L. Coon, line producer for STAR TREK, and the only man other than Roddenberry who could make the show work on a regular basis, has said, "All of your production problems can be solved best *in the typewriter*. They can be solved a lot cheaper and faster than they can on the set."

Corollary to this is the fact that television's best producers often start out as writers. Both Gene Coon and Gene Roddenberry began their television careers as writers. In a sense, STAR TREK owes its success to the fact that it has good Genes.

Star Trek's first season was generally regarded as its best. About this, Gene Roddenberry says, "When I do a concept for a show, if four or five or six stories don't come to me pretty fast, I know that somewhere I'm in trouble on that concept and I put it aside and start looking at it again.

"One of the interesting things about Star Trek, talking about stories, is that I came up with—in the final premise—about twenty-two story ideas, and we recently made a count and I believe fifteen of them were actually used in the series. I did not take screen credit for all of those stories because it was just stated in a paragraph, and the development came from someone else. During the first two years many of the scripts you saw came out of those stories.

"I think one of the mistakes of many I made on the show was that I probably should have continued that system. In between every year, I should have sat down in the show's hiatus and come up with twenty or more stories, of which maybe ten or twelve would have set the stage for the next season. It would have saved us a great deal of time because it means instead of a writer coming and you talk a story with him and he goes home and thinks and in three or four days you talk it some more and maybe waste two or three weeks getting a story ready, he could have come in and said, 'Yes, I dig this one. There's some changes I see and so on, but wow, thematically, I think it's great,' and I say, 'Go on, we're off to work.' "

The very nature of television production puts incredible pressure on the people involved. On Star Trek a director had to shoot ten minutes of usable film per working day. He had only six days in which to make a one hour episode. (Actually fifty-six minutes after commercials and credits are subtracted; today that total is down to forty-eight. More commercials, longer credits, a news update, and previews of the next episode have eaten up the time.)

Budgets are limited too—far more than the layman would think. On Star Trek, a significant part of each budget went for special effects—sets and actors were expensive too. There aren't many stores in Hollywood that sell authentic Rigelian furniture, it all has to be built. And every actor has to be costumed. On any other show, say a Western or a private eye series, much of this kind of background detail could be drawn from stock, or if necessary, purchased. But with Star Trek, it all had to be designed and built.

As Gene Roddenberry says, "We were creating a whole new world every week. But, with the limited budget we had to work with, we could only afford to show a very small part of that world." Everything shown in every episode had to be *built*. If it was part of the *Enterprise,* then it could be used again in future episodes, and so every dollar spent for in-ship improvements was an investment in the overall look of the show.

As a result, the *Enterprise* gradually became more and more detailed. For instance, the engine room as portrayed by the end of the second season was quite a bit more complex and detailed than it had been the first time it was shown. In "Mirror, Mirror," for example, a small set on stilts was built. It was called the "Emergency Manual Monitor." It had a window in its rear wall through which the original engine room set could be seen. The effect was as if the actors were in an additional control room overlooking the main floor. It was a particularly well thought out set device and the result was quite convincing. It opened up the engine room by increasing its apparent depth.

If STAR TREK had been telling only shipboard stories, quite a detailed spaceship could have been constructed and shown. But unfortunately, the network wanted lots of "planet" stories. Hence, most of STAR TREK'S expenses were *not* for reusable items. The *Enterprise* had already been built. The phasers, tricorders, and communicators had already been designed. The costumes were established. Aside from the occasional piece of detail work required by a specific script, most of the money had to be spent for development of items that could not be used again—and there was never enough time or money to do the job as thoroughly as it should have been done.

The average script allowed for the construction of three sets and some corridors, very little more. It allowed no more than five or six speaking parts—and rarely were more than three of them *major* parts. (The limitation of how much story you could tell in forty-eight minutes was a factor here too.) If there was any particularly difficult special effects or costume work—such as an alien Gorn, or a crew of Romulans—all the other budgets had to be cut accordingly.* (Fortunately, things like corridors, jungles, and cave walls can easily be redressed to look like an additional set.) The show rarely used more than twenty extras to suggest a crowd—or even a whole population.

While this restriction was a seriously limiting one—it was not a fatal one. There were many successful episodes that managed to work within these

---

*Klingons were easy aliens to do. All they needed were costumes, mustaches and swarthy makeup. Romulans were more expensive because they had pointed ears and fancy helmets that had to be built. Andorians and Tellarites were very expensive because of the amount of makeup time required. Andorians with their blue skin and Tellarites with all their facial appliances presented problems of time and money. Any makeup problem can be solved eventually—but in television, it has to be solved this week. That STAR TREK'S aliens were so often so "unbelievable" is tribute to Fred Phillips, the show's makeup man.

restrictions. In some cases, these restrictions even worked to strengthen a particular show—by forcing the writer to concentrate on the immediate story and not waste time on extraneous material.

Examples:

"The Doomsday Machine" (by Norman Spinrad): A retelling of Ahab and the whale. The only guest star was William Windom, and most of the action took place aboard the *Enterprise* or on a ship identical to her.

"Amok Time" (by Theodore Sturgeon): Once every seven years, Spock has to swim upstream to spawn. This script involved an arena on the planet Vulcan, four additional speaking parts, and a handful of extras.

"Journey to Babel" (by Dorothy Fontana): The *Enterprise* is ferrying a group of interstellar ambassadors, including Spock's parents. Although this story takes place entirely aboard the starship, there were a considerable number of aliens portrayed, requiring a good deal of costume and makeup work.

The typical STAR TREK script was never really a fully fleshed drama, per se. There are few television series that are. Rather, it was a story told in visual shorthand. Only the basic fragments are presented, details are merely suggested, and the viewer is left to fill in the gaps for himself.

Most television dramas depend on this kind of shorthand for their success. It has been called "the willing suspension of disbelief," but there is more to it than that.

Film as a storytelling medium has been in existence for more than sixty years—ever since Edwin Porter filmed *The Great Train Robbery*. Four generations have grown up with visual communication an ever-increasing part of their lives. Film is the primary means of storytelling in the world today. With increased film viewing comes increased sophistication in film techniques. The original *King Kong* had women fainting in the aisles in its premiere engagement—today it's shown on television and rated suitable for children. In just a few decades, it has gone from horror story to fairy tale. And the animation techniques that were so startling in 1935 are merely routine today.

Filmic devices and conventions quickly become easily recognized by a sophisticated audience. "Yes, we know all that already," they are saying. "Let's go on with the story." Hence, movies become faster and faster paced, packing ever more story into shorter and shorter bits of time. Long involved explanations aren't necessary any more. The audience doesn't care how you have set up the situation—they want to see what you are going to do with it after you've got it.

The motion picture *Destination: Moon* was made in 1951. Fully half of it was spent in detailing and justifying the construction of an atomic rocket with which to journey into space. Only the last half of the film portrayed the actual trip.

Sixteen years later, *2001: A Space Odyssey* compressed all the same information into the space between one frame of film and the next. An ape learns to use a bone as a tool. He tosses it into the air—and the bone becomes a Pan Am spaceship carrying Dr. Heywood Floyd to Clavius crater and Tycho Moon Anomaly One. That picture *starts* with a trip to the moon.

In George Pal's *Destination: Moon* (and also his later film, *Conquest of Space*) there were long involved explanations of the condition of weightlessness and why it involved a need for magnetic boots. In Stanley Kubrick's *2001: A Space Odyssey,* there were none—in fact, all the dialogue in that picture was kept to a minimum, with a corresponding lack of explanations. None were needed anyway. Far more than any other film, *2001* depended on its incredible imagery to tell its story. The visually startling centrifuge set, around which Keir Dulea ran interminable wind-sprints was never explained as being necessary to provide a simulated gravity environment. Sophisticated audiences were able to accept it without the explanation.

Television works on a more limited scale than the motion picture. A *much* more limited scale. It is impossible to accomplish ten million dollars worth of amazement for a mere two hundred thousand* (per episode)—but the same principles of storytelling hold true for both media.

Thus television must concentrate on the more immediate and personal story. What can't be shown must be suggested, and the audience will simply have to imagine the details that the producer can't afford to portray.

A motion picture depends on the same kind of suggestion on a much larger scale—but on that scale, enough is shown so that the audience is *helped* in their imagining. In television, the skimpiness of the suggestion is more obvious.

Therefore, television is at its best in telling the immediate and personal story. What this means is that the kind of conflict that would be an epic on a motion picture screen must be stripped to its bare essentials in order to fit on the twenty-one-inch TV screen.

Cecil B. DeMille or David Wark Griffith might have been able to use two

---

*In 1966, the average episode of STAR TREK cost approximately two hundred thousand dollars. Give or take a few. "The Trouble with Tribbles," for instance, came in around $187,000, while "The City on the Edge of Forever" cost $262,000. By 1978, the cost of an hour of science fiction television had almost tripled. The TV series "Buck Rogers" was originally budgeted at a half million dollars per episode, and "Battlestar Galactica" is reported to have cost more than a million per hour. To do STAR TREK again today as a TV series would probably cost at least as much. If it was an expensive show in 1966, it has become even more so in 1984.

mighty armies of ten thousand men each to portray a decisive battle of the
American Civil War on screen. Joe Pevney or Marc Daniels (two of STAR
TREK's directors) had to content themselves with one soldier from each side
in a face to face meeting—but that could be a much more *intense* kind of
story. And a better one for television.

STAR TREK's best stories were those that were about *people;* one or two
individuals caught in a trying situation.

Examples:

"Charlie X" (by Dorothy Fontana, from a story by Gene Roddenberry):
Charlie has been raised by aliens, now he has to learn how to be a mature
human being—unfortunately the aliens have given him superpowers in order
to help him survive, thus depriving him of the *need* to mature. His whole
problem, thus, is how to relate to humans. He can't of course—for Charlie
it's too late.

"The Corbomite Maneuver" (by Jerry Sohl): The *Enterprise* encounters
an immense alien vessel. Kirk must save his ship and prove that Terrans *are*
friendly. He bluffs that the "corbomite" in the *Enterprise*'s hull will explode
and destroy both ships. After he makes the bluff work—basically a duel of
personalities—Kirk returns to aid the disabled alien.

"The Devil in the Dark" (by Gene Coon): That rock-monster lurking down
in the mines is only a mother Horta trying to protect her eggs. Spock discovers this through the Vulcan mind-meld. McCoy is able to patch up her inju-
ries with a glob of silicon cement. ("I'm a doctor, not a plasterer.") You
can get more personal than mother-love, but not much.

"Balance of Terror" (by Paul Schneider): A thinly disguised retelling of
The Enemy Below, a submarine-vs.-destroyer duel. Here, it was the *Enterprise*
vs. the Romulans. But it worked because of the intensity of the subconflicts
aboard the *Enterprise*.

"The Squire of Gothos" (by Paul Schneider): Trelane, a very playful fellow of extraordinary power, has captured Kirk, Spock, McCoy, Sulu, and
Uhura. He teases them until his parents show up and tell him it's time to
come in now.

All of the above mentioned stories are from STAR TREK's first—and generally most successful—season. All of them are quite good as individual episodes,
but they are also representative of the overall "feel" of that first season.

In general, most of the scripts written involved highly personal conflicts
for members of the *Enterprise* crew. Thus the stories were kept to a manageable scale.

"It all had to be designed and built": a city for
"A Taste of Armageddon"...

...and a phaser pack for "The Menagerie"

Extra expenses: a Gorn captain...

...an Andorian...

...the *Enterprise*'s shuttlecraft...

...and an alien population.

Kirk with an alien diplomat: "Journey to Babel"

"The Corbomite Maneuver"

"The Devil in the Dark"

A transporter beam: "Friday's Child"

The transporter room

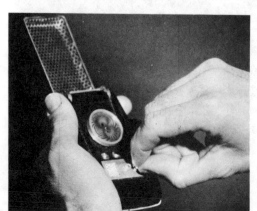

A communicator

A portal to the past: The Guardian of Forever

Kirk and Spock in 1930s America

Edith Keeler

"Operation—Annihilate!"

McCoy and Spock: "Court-Martial"

Kirk and tidbits: "I, Mudd"

A shipboard wedding:
"Balance of Terror"

If the show could have kept to that same kind of personal story, its high level of quality could have been maintained throughout the succeeding seasons. Unfortunately, there were several things that tended to work against STAR TREK as time progressed. These elements of decay can happen to any TV show. Format becomes Formula via *Hardening of the Arteries* and *Erosion*.

Consider what a format is.

When a producer says, "Hey, I'm going to make a show about Captain Hornblower in outer space!" the studio wants to know, "Yes, but what is your format?" Meaning: Tell us the details. *How* are you going to do it.

At this point the producer has to sit down and figure out how he is going to tell his stories—what set of situations, characters, equipment, background, and physical laws of the universe will give him the broadest possible base for the stories he wants to tell?

"Well, I need a Captain and a spaceship and a crew. The spaceship should be able to travel faster than light so it can visit other planets, but it takes too much time and money to show it landing on a new planet every week, I need—yes, a transporter beam . . . and let's see, we'll need a big crew so we can tell stories about individuals aboard the ship . . . oh, now who sent him out? We ought to know what his orders are . . ." And so on.

A format is a guide for whatever is to come later. It's a flight plan for a series. But just like any other kind of flight plan, the slightest error will magnify itself over a period of time if it isn't corrected or compensated for. The errors in a show's original format will repeat themselves until they become so noticeable as to be annoying. Twenty-six repetitions a season make a mistake very hard to live with.

Actually, *mistake* isn't quite the right word. Let's say miscalculation instead. That is, something that seems quite workable in the first two or three stories may turn out to be a very rigorous trap by the thirteenth or fourteenth episode.

The transporter room is a good example. It was one of STAR TREK's best ideas—a teleportation device so that the Captain and crew of the starship could "beam down" to a planet whenever they chose. Thus, the special-effects crew was relieved of the responsibility of having to show either the starship or its shuttlecraft landing on a new planet each week. A golden flicker mixed with a dissolve and an over-dubbed reverberated whine is not only cheaper—it's more versatile and impressive.

Unfortunately the use of the transporter set up conditions of its own that were not foreseen in the initial postulation.

For the transporter to work, the individual had to have a "communicator"—a gold-and-black clamshell device that served as an all-purpose walkie-talkie. The transporter would "lock on" the human being holding the device and "beam" him up.

And that was the miscalculation. If the transporter had been designed for the express purpose (pun intended) of getting our heroes into the story faster, then it also allowed them to get *out* of it just as quickly.

Any time Captain Kirk got himself into real trouble, all he needed to do was call the *Enterprise* and holler, "Scotty! Save my ass!" and Scotty would beam him up so fast the air would crackle. Knowing that, then there certainly would be no suspense whenever Kirk was captured by the giant Yangyangs or the Creeping Blorch. Both he and we knew that it wasn't permanent.

Therefore, one of three things had to happen to keep Kirk in a story where he was personally menaced:

He would run into aliens of such superior ability that they could nullify his transporter beam. Thus he got captured.

He would run into aliens of such inferior ability that they would knock him over the head and take his communicator away from him without knowing what it was. Again, he got captured.

Or—contact between the Captain and the *Enterprise* would be cut off by some arbitrary force created by the writer for this specific purpose, thus *trapping* Kirk in the story until contact could be restored—usually not until just before the last commercial.

Individually, any one of these alternatives might have been part of a good story—indeed, they all were, as witness "The Squire of Gothos," "Tomorrow Is Yesterday," and "Errand of Mercy," respectively.

However, by the time we get to the fifth or sixth repetition—"The Apple," "Bread and Circuses," "A Private Little War," "The Gamesters of Triskelion," "A Piece of the Action," "The Omega Glory," "Spectre of the Gun," "The Paradise Syndrome," and "Plato's Stepchildren"—the cumulative effect is the focusing of attention on the mechanism used to prevent Kirk from being rescued. We become aware of the format's degeneration into formula. We begin to realize that "Plato's Stepchildren" is the same story as "The Gamesters of Triskelion"; the only difference is in the details. We've become too familiar with the device for it to be effective as a dramatic tool any more—now it's a cliché.

The extreme use of any device will wear it out (literary or otherwise). The rapid degeneration of this particular element of the STAR TREK format only points up which writers were (at that point in their scripts) creatively bankrupt. Rather than looking for another way to solve the problem, they fell back on old tricks. Pretty soon, that same old trick got boring.

The real answer, of course, was simply to *avoid* situations or stories that required Kirk to be overpowered. Gene Roddenberry says about writing in general: "*Every* story starts with a need. A need for something to happen or something not to happen. That need must be closely and deeply associated with the main character. Perhaps he needs a thousand dollars to pay off a gambling debt to keep the mob from killing him. Or perhaps he needs *not* to have himself placed in the electric chair tonight at 12:01 A.M. and the switch pulled which will execute him for a murder he never committed. Whatever need you propound for the character in your story, it is absolutely necessary that that need get more and more pressing, also more and more difficult to fulfil, as the story progresses. In a good story, you finally get the reader or viewer clawing at the pages or the screen in his anxiety to get fulfillment since he has become the hero and feels all the jeopardy, frustration, and agony which is building and building toward the story climax. When the need is resolved in the story climax, the reader or viewer feels fulfillment."

Now, returning to the contention that the real answer was not to let Captain Kirk be placed in positions where he would be overpowered. To do so *once* is a valid story. To do so *twice* might even be valid. To do it more than that, you begin to undermine the character of Captain Kirk—what kind of a Captain is this anyway? He keeps letting himself get clonked on the head and captured. You'd think he'd learn.

The writers that let Captain Kirk continue to be trapped this way were creating an *artificial* need. Remember the artificial excitement of having the actors fall out of their chairs while the camera was shaken?—this is the same kind of thing, but a little more sophisticated. Oh, it's adventure all right, but it isn't real drama.

Gene said that the need must be "closely and deeply associated with the main character." Trapping a character into a situation and asking him to solve it does *not* fulfil this requirement—being in a situation does not mean that the character will automatically care about it "closely and deeply." In such a situation, the hero's *primary* need is to escape, not to solve the problems of anyone else. But a hasty writer will "solve" this problem by arbitrarily constructing a white rat's puzzle box test: Captain Kirk must solve the problem posed in order to win his reward, i.e., escape.

These white-rat puzzle-box stories are the illegitimate offspring of the forced marriage of two extremely different forms: the hero-in-danger story and the "Mary Worth" story.

You see, as it's set up, the *Enterprise* IS a cosmic "Mary Worth," meddling her way across the galaxy, solving problems as she goes. But drama—*real* drama—requires that the hero be forced to make a decision, an *important* decision. Unfortunately, to many writers that means that the hero must be *placed in danger*. Period. Thus, in the typical story, the hero is trapped into somebody else's problem (on STAR TREK, a cultural one) and must solve it to escape.

The result is a series of puzzle-box episodes. Unfortunately, these kind of stories are generally unimportant ones. We don't really care about them. We know the hero will escape—that's why he's the hero. Thus our only reason for watching the show is to see *how* he does it. Ho-hum. Unless the situation is particularly good, or the escape is particularly imaginative (*à la* "Mission: Impossible") it's just so much chocolate pudding for the mind. Instead of "The End," the film might just as well say, "So what?"

One of STAR TREK's episodes that *worked* was "The City on the Edge of Forever." It was written by Harlan Ellison (with some rewriting by Gene Roddenberry) and won the Hugo award for the best science fiction drama of 1967. The story involved a portal to the past; Dr. McCoy, accidentally under the influence of an overdose of cordrazine (a very strange drug) jumps into the portal and is transported into Earth's history, specifically 1930 America. Kirk and Spock must follow him in order to keep him from changing the past and all the events that stem from it—including the establishment of Starfleet Command and the construction of the *Enterprise*.

But, once in the past, Kirk meets and falls in love with Edith Keeler—a woman who is also strangely out of her time; although native to the era, her ideas and dreams are those of a later age. She talks of peace and worldwide wealth, and even of ships to the stars. But Kirk soon discovers to his horror that the event in the past that must not be changed or altered in any way is Edith Keeler's impending death. If she should be allowed to live, she would form a pacifist movement that would eventually result in America losing World War II to Hitler's Germany. This is the problem that Kirk must solve in order to escape the trap of this story.

Essentially, this *is* a puzzle-box kind of story. The time portal is only a device to trap Kirk into the situation. He must solve it to escape. But this story works—and if we examine *why* it works, we'll see why most puzzle-box stories don't. This one is the exception that tests the rule.

First of all, in the writing of this story, both Harlan Ellison and Gene Roddenberry recognized that the problem as it is set up is basically unsolvable. Captain Kirk cannot save both. He must lose either his ship or his woman. Of course, his decision must be to save the *Enterprise*. Edith Keeler must die and James Kirk must lose her.

The situation that Kirk is trapped into is not an arbitrary one—it is *his* situation. He is not solving someone else's problem to escape, he is solving his own. Thus, the important decision that he must make at the climax of the story is one that will affect him *deeply*.

—And that's the second reason for the success of this story. The *need* in it is "closely and deeply associated with the main character." Captain Kirk is truly affected by these events. In a puzzle-box story, his need to escape would have been primary. But in "The City On the Edge of Forever" that need becomes secondary to a much stronger conflict.

Which leads into the third reason. The time portal, as it is used in this episode, is more than a trap. Although it does function to separate Kirk from any kind of support from his ship, its primary purpose is to propel Kirk into a *more important* conflict. Rather than a trap, it is a vehicle to get the Captain into the real story: the decision between Edith Keeler and the *Enterprise*.

In the hands of a lesser writer, this would have been a lesser story. The conflict would have been arbitrary, it would have been one that did not affect Kirk (or any other crew member) deeply, and the time portal would have been merely a trap.

Contrast "The City on the Edge of Forever" with "All Our Yesterdays," in which Kirk, Spock, and McCoy are once again trapped in the past—only this time, the past is not Earth's, but some other planet's. And it's not Kirk that falls in love, it's Spock. (Ho-hum.) There's no further decision to make. It is foregone that Mr. Spock will return; he is giving up nothing more than a chance encounter. The story deals with an arbitrary trap and an arbitrary solution. No matter who they meet, their primary need remains one of escape.

Thus, in the puzzle-box story, *real* drama is defeated before it ever has a chance to get started—all of the relationships are secondary. Neither Kirk nor anyone else has any real need to explore the relationships that might develop with any of the people they will meet in the process of escaping. For all the personal involvement that is required, they might just as well be hacking their way with machetes through a jungle.

Referring back to the original format of the show, Gene Roddenberry felt that STAR TREK would be stronger if there were a high degree of personal involvement by one or more characters aboard the ship in every story told. Personal involvement was a very basic part of STAR TREK's original format. Unfortunately it was also one of the most misused.

Personal involvement—*if it is superimposed onto the primary conflict of the story*—is little more than a dramatic device. Like the last device we considered, it can be worn out too.

The involvement of a familiar character in a conflict heightens the tension we will feel as the story approaches its climax. There is a stronger identification with the story, thus there is more involvement on the part of the viewer with the crisis to be confronted.

But when a device is superimposed on a weak story—and when it is done continually—the cumulative effect is to focus the viewer's attention on the device and not the story. Again, the overuse of this device is a symptom of creative bankruptcy.

Given a weak story, how do you make it stronger?

James Blish, a noted science fiction author in his own right and author of nine STAR TREK books, once said quite simply: "Analyze the basic conflict. Ask yourself, 'Who does it hurt?' That's your story."

A weak writer, however, takes the easy way out. "Well, you see, Kirk falls in love with this girl . . ." Or, "Well, you see, Spock falls in love with this girl . . ." Or, "Well, Scotty falls in love with this girl . . ." Or, "Well, McCoy falls in love with this girl . . ." Or, "Chekov falls in love with this girl . . ." Or, "Well, you see, Uhura . . ." Never mind.

Once, or even twice, this story might be interesting. "The City on the Edge of Forever" was Kirk's love story. "This Side of Paradise" was Spock's adventure of the heart. They should have stopped there. Kirk shouldn't have been allowed to fall in love again for at least thirty episodes. Same for Spock. And the other characters should have had other kinds of stories told about them—not love stories. The cumulative effect is that the ship is crewed by 432 incurable cases of satyriasis. (Or nymphomania, as the case may be.)

But not only is a love story the easiest story to tell—just show a man and woman talking meaningless dialogue and smiling at each other—it also seems to be the only story that some writers can tell (I have no quibble there, but they tell it so *badly*.)

There are other kinds of personal involvement that are every bit as strong. In "Operation—Annihilate!" Kirk finds that his brother has been killed in part of a planet-wide plague of insanity. In "The Conscience of the King" Kirk is one of the last two survivors who can identify an interplanetary war criminal. Kirk had lost many friends to the man twenty years before, and one of the members of his crew had lost his family. In "Court-Martial" Kirk's whole career as Captain of the *Enterprise* is at stake. In none of these stories is there the kind of love interest that would work against the believability of the series as a whole. And that's important.

We can't ever fade out on a happy ending of Kirk with his arms around the girl; nor can any other character in a series fall in love, for that matter. Not without changing the format; *because* the following week, we'll want to know what happened to the girl. Where is she? What happened to her? Why isn't she back? The fact that she *isn't* back just proves that there wasn't that high a degree of personal involvement after all. She was just a one-night stand. That's why she has to either die or go away—then we can believe the hero really loved her, and we're not in any danger of having to change the format.

The need for a heroine in every story is a leftover convention from the era of romanticism. There, the hero killed the dragon, slew the giant, conquered the trolls, defeated the goblins, and saved the kingdom—and his reward was the beautiful princess who immediately agreed to be his wife. (Love was never a consideration. Of course she loved him—that was her job!)

Frankly, it's a stupid convention—it reduces women to objects. The subliminal message is that a woman is merely a reward for a job well done. Superimposed on a science fiction series—especially STAR TREK—the effect is unreal. No, surreal.

We are continually shown that women are responsible members of the *Enterprise* crew. Lieutenant Uhura, for instance, is fourth in command, right after Mr. Scott.* Obviously, in the STAR TREK universe, equality between men and women is a reality—except for Captain Kirk. More often than not, when he solves a particularly difficult problem, he is rewarded with a particularly luscious tidbit whose function in the story is just that—to be Kirk's reward.

There are a lot of variations on the theme, but eventually it begins to grate like Johnny one-note on the kazoo. A story does not *need* a heroine. It needs a problem for the hero to solve. His reward is the solving of the problem. To then give him objects (a chest of gold, a medal, a woman) reduces the magnitude of his bravery and places the emphasis of the story on the object to be gained, not the problem to be solved.

Kirk should be a starship Captain, not a cosmic womanizer. Certainly he will have love affairs, but for goodness sake, couldn't they be mature affairs between two real live human beings? That means they should be kept in proportion to the rest of his life—as a Captain, he's going to have more problems than women. And the same should apply to every other member of the crew.

(As a sidelight here, one of the subplots in "Balance of Terror" involved Kirk officiating at a wedding between two of his crew members. This seemed a particularly fascinating development. We should have been seeing more of

---

*My source on this is D.C. Fontana, STAR TREK's story editor. Nichelle Nichols also confirms this.

the in-ship relationships. Weren't there any man-wife teams of scientists aboard? There should have been—certainly all those people didn't remain celibate for five years. . . .)

The love story kind of involvement was particularly overworked during the third season—during that set of shows, *everybody* had a chance to fall in love at least once, and all the major leads got two or three chances.

During the second season of STAR TTREK a different kind of involvement was experimented with—"Well, who are we going to *almost* kill this week?"

In "Amok Time" Kirk gets killed—no, he doesn't; we just think he is for a while. In "The Changling" Scotty gets killed—no, he doesn't; he gets brought back to life. In "The Apple" Spock keels over after being shot by a poisonous plant—no, he's immune to its effects.

And in the third season: Kirk gets killed in "The *Enterprise* Incident"—no he doesn't; it's just a trick on the Romulans. In "For the World Is Hollow and I Have Touched the Sky" McCoy gets clobbered by a computer—no, not quite. And in "The Tholian Web" Kirk is missing and presumed dead for half the episode. Ho-hum.

Again just as with the others, once is valid, even twice—but more than that and the device becomes recognizable, repetitious, and worn-out. We know that these characters are not going to be killed; they're the heroes. So stop cheating us and start telling us some real stories.

The almost-death is a fantasy, a fairy tale. We kill the hero and then double-talk him back to life. A *real* drama would work within the conventions of the format, exploring the relationships that are created thereby and confronting the conflicts that develop.

Examples:

Two of STAR TREK's very best episodes were "Amok Time" and "Journey to Babel." Both of these stories presented a good deal of Spock's background as well as the history and customs of the planet Vulcan. Both of these episodes were true dramas. All of the conflicts and relationships were honest, they were developed out of what we already knew. They were expansions and explorations.

Episodes that didn't expand the universe or explore the characters only served to diminish the series. For instance: an alien or group of aliens takes over the ship for their own purposes until Captain Kirk tricks them into defeat. It was titled "Who Mourns for Adonais?" and "Plato's Stepchildren" and "Catspaw" and "Spectre of the Gun" and "And the Children Shall Lead" and "By Any Other Name" and so on.

These were all variations on the same theme. The only time it worked, however, was in "The Squire of Gothos." In that episode, the alien was shown to be a super-powered child—which is the only reasonable explanation for that kind of a power trip anyway. After all, if your aliens have that much power, why do they want the *Enterprise* anyway? The only possible reason could be as a plaything—in which case, your alien is only a super-child: Trelane, the Squire of Gothos.

In general, the story of the aliens taking over the *Enterprise* is a phony. It's an artificial menace—it doesn't truly explore the real drama of meeting an alien race face to face. The sense of wonder, the *awe,* have been traded off for the easier story of Kirk versus one more super-villain. It's an interesting story once, perhaps even twice. More than that and it begins to look like one more slice off the same old baloney.

Dorothy Fontana once remarked that one of the biggest problems in telling some of the stories was the size of the ship's crew. What could you do with all those extra people when you didn't need them?

In "I, Mudd" for instance, we're told that Harry Mudd's five hundred identical beautiful girl androids beamed up to the ship, grabbed everybody and beamed them down. But we've never shown any of this. It was too expensive to show. So, as it was written, the script was about Kirk, Spock, McCoy, Uhura, Scotty, and Chekov. The rest of the crew was out of sight and out of mind.

In "By Any Other Name" we're shown that the alien Kelvans have the power to reduce human beings to plaster dodecahedrons. What happened was that neither Dorothy Fontana not Jerry Bixby nor Gene Coon could figure out a way to get all the extra crewpersons out of the way, so Dorothy and Gene went in to see Gene Roddenberry and as they explained the problem to him, he was toying with a Mexican onyx dodecahedron which he had on his desk as an ornament. (To save you a trip to the dictionary, a dodecahedron is a twelve-sided solid with equal and regular sides, each side a perfect pentagon.) Gene began to muse aloud, "Suppose the aliens could freeze the pattern of each person into a solid block like this . . ."

Dorothy Fontana admits that the solution is basically an unsatisfactory one—it's arbitrary—but at the time, nobody could come up with a better idea and they did have to get the script to the sound stage on schedule. . . .

A large part of STAR TREK's story problems stemmed from a misperception of the format and its potential. STAR TREK looked like an action-adventure series, when in fact, it was structured to be—and was at its best as—a *dramatic* series.

If a writer thinks of STAR TREK as only (or merely) an action-adventure series, then he has already defeated himself—because the only story he can tell in that format is a variation of "Kirk in danger." (If not Kirk in danger, then someone he loves is in danger, or someone he's responsible for—but always, *someone in danger*. Helluva way to run a starship.)

Some of the writers rose above this: Theodore Sturgeon with his delightful "Shore Leave" script; Harlan Ellison and his award-winning "The City on the Edge of Forever"; Gene Coon's clever "Devil in the Dark." These stories demonstrated that STAR TREK was at its best as a *dramatic* series.

Look, it's too easy to create dramatic tension by putting someone in danger, then throwing obstacles in the path of his rescuers. The viewer *knows* he's going to be rescued, so essentially it's a phony device—unless it is used to open up a bigger, more important story.

It wouldn't happen in a twenty-third century starship with the annoying regularity that it did on STAR TREK. Considering a real-life example: out of the ten Apollo space missions, there has only been *one* space disaster; the rest of the missions have come off pretty much as planned. Considering the total Apollo lunar program, only three astronauts have died—and that was while they were still on the launch pad in a preflight check-out. If it only happens once—or even twice—out of every nine missions in real life, then it certainly shouldn't happen any more often in a series that depends so much on scientific accuracy for its believability. And considering the way that technology continues to advance, it shouldn't happen *at all* by the twenty-third century. If it does, it would be a major story by itself, not a lesser part of some other one.

But putting someone in danger is the *easy* story to tell. To a hack writer, that's what action-adventure means.

Of course, it's impossible to have a real adventure without *some* danger. But danger need not always be physical. There are a lot of different kinds of danger.

If STAR TREK had been produced as a dramatic series, then the essential STAR TREK story would not have had to have been "Kirk in Danger," but "Kirk Has a Decision to Make." The decision is the core of every dramatic episode. It is why an audience will stay tuned for forty-eight minutes of story.

So. If we reconsider all those devices inherent in the original format, or developed as the series progressed, we'll see that many of them were little more than ways to portray Captain James T. Kirk, or some other member of the crew of the *Enterprise,* in danger. They are devices to create artificial excitement.

THE WORLD OF STAR TREK

The "formula" story is the pat story, the easy story, the one that gets written by the book. It's a compilation of all the tried and true tricks. It's six devices in search of a plot. It's a hero-vs.-villain story. It's generally a waste of time.

With STAR TREK, it might work something like this: The *Enterprise* approaches a planet. Something happens. Anything. Kirk, Spock, and McCoy get captured by six-foot green women in steel brassieres. They take away the spacemen's communicators because they offend the computer-god that these women worship.

Meanwhile, Scotty discovers that he's having trouble with the doubletalk generator, and he can't fix it—the *Enterprise* will shrivel into a prune in two hours unless something is done immediately. But Scotty can't get in touch with the Captain—

Of course, he can't—Kirk, Spock, and McCoy have been brought before the high priest of the cosmic computer, who decides that they are unfit to live. All except the Vulcan, who has interesting ears. She puts Spock into a mind-zapping machine which leaves him quoting poetry (seventeen-syllable Japanese haiku verses) for the next two acts. McCoy can't do a damn thing for him, "I'm a doctor, not a critic!" Meanwhile, it's been more than seven hours since Kirk's last love affair and he starts getting twitchy. McCoy can't do anything for him either. So Kirk seduces the cute priestess—there always is at least one.

On the ship, sparks fly from Chekov's control panel and everybody falls out of their chairs. Uhura tries opening the hailing frequencies, and when she can't, admits to being frightened. Scotty figures only fifteen minutes are left. Already the crew members are starting to get wrinkled as the starship begins "prunifying."

Down on the planet, Kirk, Spock, and McCoy are being held in the dungeon—why is it always a dungeon?—until the girl he has seduced decides that she has never had it so good in her life and discards all of her years-long training and lifetime-held beliefs to rescue him, conveniently remembering to bring him his communicator and phaser. Abruptly, Spock reveals how hard he has been working to hide his emotions and then snaps back to normal. Thinking logically, he and Kirk then drive the cosmic computer crazy with illogic—naturally, it can't cope; its designers never having been as smart as our Earthmen—and it shorts out all its fuses and releases the *Enterprise,* just in time for the last commercial. For a tag, the seduced priestess promises Kirk that she will work to build a new civilization on her planet—just for Kirk—one where steel brassieres will be illegal.

Sound familiar?

It should. It's a compendium of all the bad plot devices that ever wore out their welcome on too many STAR TREK episodes. Probably, a competent script could be built on this formula plot—eliminating some of the facetiousness, of course. But it wouldn't be a very good STAR TREK episode. Because there's nothing really new or interesting about it. Kirk doesn't have much of a decision to make; it's all excitement and very little story.

If it were a real drama, it could be described in one sentence. The sentence begins with: "Kirk has to decide between . . ."

And ends with:

". . . saving the woman he loves or allowing the past to be changed."

". . . risking his ship or saving Spock's life."

". . . being a diplomat or being a soldier."

Those three sentences were the basis of three good STAR TREK stories. But "Green Priestesses of the Cosmic Computer" has no such internal conflict. It's all formula.

Formula occurs when format starts to repeat itself. Formula occurs when format does not challenge writers—or when writers are giving less than their best. Formula occurs when a show becomes creatively bankrupt. Flashy devices can conceal the lack for a while, but ultimately the lack of any real meat in the story will leave the viewers hungry and unsatisfied.

Formula occurs primarily when a show has been trapped in a format which does not allow full exploration of the given situation. Thus, the producers and writers are condemned to repeat only that which the format does allow. And action-adventure is nowhere near as broad as drama.

There are two ways by which Format turns into Formula.

One is *Hardening of the Arteries*, the other is *Erosion*.

Considering the first process of decay as it applies to a television series, every time something is postulated or established in a continuing series, from that episode on, every writer who works with the format must be aware of that condition. If it is shown in the STAR TREK universe that the galaxy has an edge which blasts spaceships to smithereens, then you cannot write any episode about the *Enterprise* going into intergalactic space unless you explain how the starship gets around the galaxy's energy barrier.*

---

*Frankly, I think the idea of a definable "edge" to the galaxy is a load of peanut butter. It's like tying to bisect a sneeze. And the idea of an "energy barrier" around the galaxy—Hoo! It is to boggle the mind.

However, Sam Peeples, who wrote the second pilot script, "Where No Man Has Gone Before,"

"Amok time": T'Pring, Spock's betrothed, as a child...

...and as an adult.

A Vulcan wedding procession

Ritual combat

Harry Mudd

"Six-foot green women in steel brassieres"

"Why is it always a dungeon?"—"Catspaw"

"Patterns of Force"

"A Piece of the Action"

The infamous airbrushed picture

Amanda and Sarek, Spock's parents:
"Journey to Babel"

"For the World is Hollow, and I Have
Touched the Sky"

The "Salt Vampire"

Spock and the Romulan Commander:
"The *Enterprise* Incident"

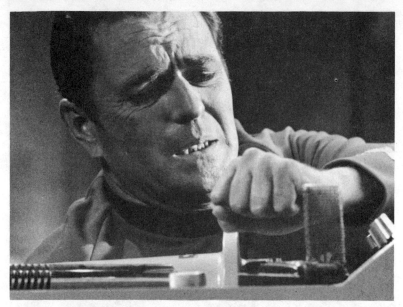

"If Scotty can't fix it, it can't be fixed."

"The Return of the Archons"

"This Side of Paradise"

"The Apple"

The alternate Spock: "Mirror, Mirror"

"The Way to Eden"

Thus, hardening of the arteries is the process by which a television show gradually limits itself by setting up conditions which will affect all episodes that will come after. Producers are always a little bit wary about expanding on their formats because of the danger of this happening—the happening—they might inadvertently set something up that could backfire and severely limit them in the future.

A few examples from STAR TREK:

The Prime Directive—also known as General Order Number One. This, according to the STAR TREK Writers' Guide, third revision, is "a wise, but often troublesome rule which prohibits starship interference with the normal development of alien life and societies." It was first postulated in an episode entitled, "The Apple" in which Kirk and crew must violate the directive and destroy an Eden. The justification was that this Eden was an artificial condition which was already interfering with the normal development of this particular culture. It rapidly became clear that the Prime Directive was to be more honored in the breach than otherwise.

In fact, the *only* times we ever heard about the Prime Directive was just before Kirk broke it. There never was a story told where he obeyed the rule.

The Prime Directive was broken in "A Private Little War," "Patterns of Force," "A Piece of the Action," "Bread and Circuses," and quite a few other episodes. This is why it was such a troublesome rule—it was troublesome to the writers who had to work their stories around it. In all of these episodes, Kirk eventually *had to* interfere with the so-called normal development of the alien society. Sometimes he was putting it back on its proper course after someone else had tampered with it, "Bread and Circuses," "Patterns of Force," for example.

The STAR TREK Writers' Guide summarizes the rule like this: "It can be disregarded when absolutely vital to the interests of the entire Earth Federation, but the Captain who does violate it had better be ready to present a sound defense of his actions."

Which means, translated into English: The Prime Directive is a great idea, but it's also a bloody nuisance. Let's forget about the whole thing.

The Prime Directive gets in the way of telling "Mary Worth" stories. It keeps the *Enterprise* from being a cosmic meddler. And that's too much of a limitation on the format. It keeps Kirk from being a moralist because he can

---

verified the *possibility* of such concepts before he wrote the script. Sam is a member of First Fandom, a long time SF buff and a recognized contributor to the field. He does not make stupid mistakes and he even forced down Isaac Asimov on this particular question. So, it could be possible.

no longer say, "This is right and this is wrong" to the people of Eminiar VII and Vendikar in "A Taste of Armageddon." In fact, he can't even blow up the computer that controls their simulated war if he subscribes to General Order Number One.

Nor can he destroy the Landru computer on Beta III in "Return of the Archons." Nor is he allowed to upset the status quo on Triskelion in "The Gamesters of Triskelion."*

The Prime Directive is a very idealistic rule—but it keeps getting in the way of the story. Therefore, it has to be disregarded. Regularly.

In the third season, it was totally ignored. Forgotten. They had problems enough without it.

By far the most serious hardening of STAR TREK's arteries, however, was on a much more subtle level. The relationships between the characters sometimes solidified to the point where occasionally they could not break out of a set pattern of responses. The result was that relationships began to dictate the shape of some of the stories. Conflicts would be distorted so as to create specific but tangential scenes for individual characters. One character in particular—Spock.

Spock was one of the great strengths of the show—but he was also one of the biggest crosses it had to bear. His popularity tended to overshadow that of the rest of the show.

(An interesting note here. The network had had qualms about Mr. Spock's alienness long before the show went on the air. At one point, they even put out an advance publicity brochure with his ears and eyebrows airbrushed back to normal. But later on, after the show became a hit, not a single network executive would cop to being wrong. Harlan Ellison tried to track the order down for an article he had been planning to write, and was present as the order was traced all the way down the line, and each time the buck was passed a little farther. Finally, they tried to pin the blame on a guy they caught in the art department holding an airbrush. They wanted to fire the poor fellow on the spot! And all he had done was follow orders that no one would admit to giving!)

Because of Spock's importance as a drawing card, more and more stories began to focus on him. Many of these were valid stories to tell, "Journey to Babel" and "Amok Time," for instance. But sometimes—

---

*Originally, this episode was called "The Gamesters of Pentathlon." It must have been too expensive that way, so they knocked two points off the symbol and changed the name to "Triskelion."

Although the character was almost always kept in dramatic proportion to the overall story, he began to play pivotal parts in *too many* episodes—at the expense of other characters in the series. The cumulative effect was that Lieutenant Uhura was only good for opening hailing frequencies, and Sulu could only sit at the helm and occasionally fall out of his chair. Chekov was little more than a Captain Kirk in training, but with a Russian accent. And Christine Chapel was the ideal woman—silent and dutiful.

In the course of a season, it should be possible to focus on every regular character at least once. This episode will be Uhura's story, that one will be Chekov's, this one is Sulu's, that one is Chapel's.

But in the course of three seasons there was never an episode which dealt in depth with Mr. Sulu. Chekov fared a little better, but there never was a script that was specifically about Lieutenant Uhura. Nurse Chapel was lucky, she was important in two or three episodes.

There was only one episode especially about Dr. McCoy ("For the World Is Hollow and I Have Touched the Sky") and only one or two about Scotty ("Wolf in the Fold" and "The Lights of Zetar"). While there were episodes where any or all of these characters did play pivotal parts, the episode that was particularly an individual's own was the rare occurrence.*

In general, it all went to Kirk and Spock.

It had to go to Kirk, he was the lead. Besides, the Captain is the man with the ultimate responsibility; he would be the focus of any conflict. And the Kirk-Spock relationship was basically a good one, Kirk's adventurousness and sense of humor contrasted nicely with Spock's cool aloofness. They were a good team. But far too many of the stories used Spock when any other character might have functioned just as well. The overuse of Mr. Spock enlarged him out of all proportion to everything else on the *Enterprise.*

The working format of the show, as we have seen, was "Kirk in Danger." This meant that Kirk—and whoever he worked best with—had to solve a problem. It was natural to write the story about Kirk and Spock.

If the format had been a dramatic one, "Kirk Makes a Decision," the stories could have focused on any individual crew member. Kirk would not have *always* had to place himself in dangerous situations—the danger could

---

*There was supposed to be an episode called "Joanna," about Dr. McCoy's daughter, but the third season producer felt that McCoy was Kirk's peer, and therefore not old enough to have a grown daughter, so the episode was changed to "The Way to Eden," and the focus became Chekov's Russian girl friend. Dorothy Fontana had written the first version of "Joanna," but quit when it became "The Way to Eden." That episode was written by Michael Richards and Arthur Heinemann with teleplay by the latter.

have been to someone else, but still Kirk's responsibility. As long as the climactic decision remains the Captain's, he's still the most important character and he's still the star of the show.

But the format *wasn't* dramatic. It was action-adventure. The story was "Kirk in Danger"—and this led to the further petrification of the STAR TREK format into formula.

—And this is the most deadly of all the criticisms that have ever been leveled against STAR TREK:

A Captain, whether he be the Captain of a starship or an aircraft carrier, simply does not place himself in danger. Ever.

A Captain is too important an officer, his training is too expensive, his skills are too vital to the running of the ship to be risked. A good Captain is like a good general, he stays in his command and control center *and delegates authority.* He tells other people what to do—it isn't necessary for him to do it himself.

An aircraft carrier captain doesn't fly the planes himself. An army general doesn't hit the beaches until they've been secured. And a spaceship Captain won't do it either. The first time he tries it—well, maybe that's a special case. The second time he goes beaming down into the thick of things, he's going to be hauled up before a review board. The third time, he's going to be relieved of command and a more responsible man will replace him.

And to take Mr. Spock, *his second in command,* with him, is a compounding of the offense!

Should anything happen to them, the *Enterprise* would be deprived of her two top officers. It simply doesn't make sense that these are the two individuals who would risk their lives regularly.

And yet, as pictured on STAR TREK, not a week went by that Captain Kirk and Mr. Spock didn't end up in front of the business end of a gun, club, phaser, or other tool of destruction at least once.

The real reason for this, of course, is that these are the two top stars of the show. They're getting paid to be the stars. Therefore, the stories have to be about them. It doesn't make sense to pay top money to William Shatner and Leonard Nimoy and then have to hire someone else to be the stars of the stories. If you're going to do your stories about someone else, then you might as well make them the stars in the first place. No, your stories have to be about Kirk and Spock.

This is the *essential* problem in the STAR TREK format, the one difficulty that forces the show into a set of formula situations week after week—the focusing of attention on two characters who should not logically be placing themselves in physical danger, *but must do so regularly.*

This is the real pity of hardened arteries—the show ends up telling and retelling only variations of the same story because it has so limited itself it can't tell any other kind of story.

There is a solution for STAR TREK—but it involves a major change in the show's format. Considering it, however, it would be a logical extrapolation of the starship's use of its manpower:

In addition to all the other members of the *Enterprise* crew, there should be a "Contact Team," a specially trained crew of men and women whose sole purpose is to deal with alien cultures and civilizations. Kirk and Spock would stay on the bridge—as their jobs should require them to do—and monitor the duties of the team. Kirk would make his decisions by remote control, after being carefully advised by his medical, science, and engineering officers.

The Contact Team would risk their lives—but that would be part of their jobs and they would be aware of the risks involved. They would not be allowed to beam hastily back up from the surface of a strange planet because of the possibility of biological contamination of the ship. One of their members would have to be a medical expert, constantly monitoring the alien environment that these individuals are exploring—not until he gave the okay, would they be allowed to return to the *Enterprise*. And even then, an in-ship quarantine would be necessary. This team would be frankly expendable, there would be a high turn-over in its members—so the show *could* use mostly guest players instead of having to hire new regulars. Kirk and Spock could become directly involved *only* after the contact team had failed. Then, it would be a problem worthy of their personal attention.

Probably, the best place from which to draw this Contact Team would be the *Enterprise*'s own Security Forces. These are men who are trained in combat anyway and should be alert to the slightest possibility of danger. That's probably why they were aboard in the first place—but because they weren't used as such, but rather functioned as an inboard police force, they gave the ship a kind of totalitarian feeling.

A good man to place in charge of the Contact Team would have been Ensign Chekov. As originally postulated, he was meant to be a brilliant young officer of great potential. This would give him a chance to show off some of that potential, a chance he was rarely given otherwise.

All this is theoretical, of course. STAR TREK is no longer being produced—and any analyses of the show at this point can be only be Monday morning quarterbacking. Almost everybody has twenty-twenty hindsight. But still, it's nice to think about.

And besides, maybe the guy who produces the *next* outer space series will read this book. . . .

*   *   *

The last process of STAR TREK's decay to consider is Erosion.

Erosion in a TV series is the wearing down of the original concept, the destruction of it piece by piece as various elements chip and crack it away: carelessness in production, lack of pride in what one is doing, network restrictions, writer apathy, front-office feuds, and so on.

For instance, in the very first episode telecast, "The Man Trap" (by George Clayton Johnson) black crewmen, as well as Orientals, were very much in evidence aboard the *Enterprise,* and in a variety of costumes to indicate the wide range of jobs and skills represented aboard the ship. One of the most subtly startling and *correct* moments of the whole season came during that episode. The "Salt Vampire" could make itself appear to be an attractive member of the opposite sex to whomever it had selected as its victim. McCoy saw it as a lost lover, Janice Rand saw it as a handsome crewman, but Lieutenant Uhura saw the creature as a tall and virile black man. There was something very *right* about that scene—probably the implication that Lieutenant Uhura is more than a token Black, she is a real woman. (Yeah . . . !)

Blacks and Orientals were important in other episodes. And other minorities as well. This was more than just progressive thinking on the part of Gene Roddenberry—it was a necessary part of the STAR TREK concept. The ship *had* to be interracial because it represented *all* of mankind. How can the human race ever hope to achieve friendship with alien races if it can't even make friends with itself?

However, as the series progressed, especially in the last half of the second season and most of the third, this concept began to erode away. With the exception of the regular characters, the rest of the crew of the *Enterprise* began to erode from their multiracial makeup into a White Anglo-Saxon Protestant (WASP) regime.

It was probably not a conscious decision on anyone's part—it was more likely just carelessness. In the rush of production (in an industry dominated by white actors) the use of blacks and other minorities was forgotten. Yet there are few roles in STAR TREK's seventy-nine scripts that specifically call for either a white-skinned or black-skinned man. Any of the parts written could have been played by an actor of any race, provided he was human— and extra-terrestrials were probably welcome to audition too.

This kind of erosion must have happened in the casting sessions—and it is a kind of thoughtlessness. To break out of one's preconceived ideas always requires a conscious effort. As an aside here, let me point out that the proportion of blacks and Asians on STAR TREK was not a fair or accurate representation, at least not of the human race in general. The white race is in the minority—less than a third of the world's population. Most of the rest are black and yellow. It's a probable assumption that this proportion will not change significantly in the next two hundred years. We should have seen some of that reflected in STAR TREK's casting. (The network, however, specifically forbade the use of any Chinese crew members . . .)

What we did see *was* progressive—it was far more than most other television shows of that time were attempting. But STAR TREK should have begun to use more members of other ethnic groups, not less. Despite the fact that most of the world's technology is presently dominated by white-skinned human beings, it will not always remain so. The stars and the planets will not be colonized by the Ku Klux Klan.

Another kind of erosion, a more serious kind, came in the quality of the scripts. The decline could almost have been charted on a curve. We've already seen how the stories began to petrify into formula efforts and the relationships of the characters as well, but at the same time, individual characterizations were being eroded. Characters were being taken out of context and superficial or dishonest motivations were being superimposed on them.

For instance, in "The *Enterprise* Incident," Mr. Spock plays a love scene with a Romulan female. In the first draft of this, Spock never touches her—his most tender line is, "I admire your mind." The Romulan woman, understanding the Vulcan mind, understands this as the compliment that Spock intended. By the time the scene was rewritten, however, it was no different from anyone else's love scenes. And all of the charm of Spock's Vulcan attitudes was lost. Only Leonard Nimoy's skillful handling of the scene kept it from being totally out of context.*

---

*Dorothy Fontana, who wrote the script had protested the revision mightily. In a memo to the producer, she said.

"Gentlemen:
"These are not the outcries of a wounded writer, but of an ex-story editor with four years of service stripes for STAR TREK. The points I mention here appear in the yellow cover copy (first approved draft) of my script and I feel need correction.

"Sc. 93—seduction scene—Spock and Commander. Vulcans and Romulans have been firmly established as cool, unemotional creatures. True, Spock is half human—but only under the most extreme circumstances will he behave in any manner other than Vulcan. We have established Vulcans do not nuzzle, kiss, hug or display any other form of *human* affection. The Vulcan outward sign of affection is expressed in a certain touching of hands as demonstrated in "Journey to Babel." If Spock behaves in such outlandishly embarrassing human manner as is indicated in this scene, he violates the character we have established for him, and the culture he comes from. And the Commander had jolly well better be suspicious if Spock starts slobbering all over her. Their seduction scene should be cool, suggesting an alien sexuality—but *not* human passion.

". . . Please consider making these changes especially in regard to the seduction scene between

Other characters had chances to fall in love during the third season, Chekov, Scotty, and McCoy, for instance—and each time they did, they stepped out of character to play puerile love scenes. In "The Lights of Zetar," for example, Scotty falls in love. Fine, okay—Scotty is a normal healthy Scotsman, he should have an interest in women.

But remember, Mr. Scott, as postulated in the original STAR TREK concept, loves his machines first. ("If Scotty can't fix it, it can't be fixed.") To him, relaxation is a stack of technical journals. And shore leave is an unpleasant duty, he doesn't want to go.

Yet, in "The Lights of Zetar" Mr. Scott is shown falling head over heels in love with a woman who seems to have nothing more going for her than a short skirt and a good bust measurement. Scotty is portrayed as a pre-pubescent, terminal acne case casting lovesick, moony glances at the mother-object. It's out of character.

Sure, Scotty has the right to fall in love—but couldn't he do so as Mr. Scott?

Just as Mr. Spock should have been allowed to play a love scene as Mr. Spock, so should Scotty have been allowed to fall in love as Scotty. What an opportunity to expand on his character!

In "For the World Is Hollow and I Have Touched the Sky" McCoy gets his chance to fall in love. In it, he has an incurable disease and falls in love with the high priestess of a doomed planetoid. (He gets to fall in love and almost die in the same episode—a plethora of devices!) That he does not want to go back to a Starfleet base to die and instead falls for one of the green priestesses of the cosmic computer seems ridiculous. In this episode, he's so

---

Spock and the Commander. Frankly, our fans—especially the vocal ones who write a lot of letters to networks—are very hip to what is and what isn't 'Vulcan.' They write whole treatises and fanzines (for a large circle of fan subscribers) based on Vulcan psychology, psysiology, emotions, mores, and what Spock eats for breakfast. And they will tune us out if the 'business' in this seduction scene goes unchanged.

"Respectfully,"

—D.C. Fontana

The changes weren't made, and when she found out about it, she went to the set and apologized to Leonard Nimoy. "Leonard, I didn't write the scene."

And she was right about the fans, too. Within a few weeks after "The *Enterprise* Incident" was telecast, articles started appearing in fanzines. One of them began, "Curse you, Dorothy Fontana . . . Vulcans are cool, logical, unemotional . . ." And focused on that love scene as the prime example of what was wrong with the script.

Even though she was not responsible for that scene, still it was her name on the screen, so she had to take the blame for someone else's mistake.

out of character, he really isn't Dr. McCoy at all. He's someone else with
the same name.

The STAR TREK concept was carefully delineated in The STAR TREK Writers'
Guide. But the process of erosion wore away that concept bit by bit until
the point where the writers were no longer using the guide as a referral—and
with that, there was no more STAR TREK concept at all.

There is one last aspect of STAR TREK's unfulfilled potential to consider. It
may be the most telling criticism of all.

It's partly an error of format, partly a piece of formula. It's a little bit of
hardening of the arteries and a little bit of erosion. It's the "American Way"
syndrome.

I said earlier that STAR TREK is not *pure* science fiction, and never was
intended to be. It was designed as a set of contemporary morality fables against
a science fiction background. The stories are about twentieth century man's
attitudes in a future universe. The stories are about us.

And I said that this was probably the most flexible format that had ever
been designed for a television series; the format was broad enough for an
almost unlimited potential.

It is my contention that it was this aspect of STAR TREK's format that made
it such a special show. If our heroes represented the American attitudes, then
as such, they could be thrust into a variety of situations which would test
those attitudes.

And once in a while, those attitudes would be wrong. Once in a while
they would come up against a culture that might be just a little more
compassionate, or a little more aware, or a little more *alive*.

—And when that happened, the crew of the *Enterprise* would be students,
not masters.

Once in a while, the American attitudes might be tested and found wanting.

It is precisely this potential that was STAR TREK's greatest strength. Imagine a story where the hero does everything that he believes to be correct—
and the audience identifies with him totally in his actions because they believe
them to be correct too. Imagine that he is ultimately *wrong* in some of his
decisions—when (and if) he learns better, then so will the audience.

The self-examination of the human condition is what drama is all about—
but if you are going to test yourself, then you must be prepared to be found
wanting in any respect. Self-awareness includes one's faults, otherwise it becomes narcissistic onanism.

But STAR TREK rarely went that far. Too many of the stories were facile,
and required not much more than a mind that was easily gulled by flashy

technical effects. All that valuable background work, the props, the sets, the costumes, is a waste of time unless the story justifies it.

In 1966, when STAR TREK first came on the air, Lyndon Baines Johnson was President; it was a time when the Viet Nam "adventure" was at the core of the American dilemma—were we supposed to be the world's policeman or not?

As far as STAR TREK was concerned, we were—because STAR TREK was the galaxy's policeman. By implication, that ratified and justified the American presence in everybody else's culture. The *Enterprise* was a cosmic meddler. Her attitudes were those of twentieth-century America—and so her mission was (seemingly) to spread truth, justice, *and the American Way* to the far corners of the universe.

STAR TREK missed the opportunity to question this attitude. While Kirk was occasionally in error, never was there a script in which the *Enterprise*'s mission or goals were questioned. Never did they run into a situation that might have been better off without their intervention. (In "Errand of Mercy" they ran into the Organian culture, which didn't *need* their intervention, but that's not the same thing.)

There were too many stories where Kirk upset a local planet's status quo—in effect, saying, "Your culture isn't as good as mine, therefore I have the right to effect whatever changes I feel necessary. I want to make you into a carbon copy of me because I'm so good . . ."

On the surface, most of these intervention stories were intended to make very dramatic points. They had been designed as situations specifically for the making of these points.

In "A Taste of Armageddon" two planets are shown involved in a computer-controlled war—this war has provided social stability for centuries through the controlled waste of material and human life. Captain Kirk restores the horror of war by destroying the war computer.

The point of this story was that death had been made "clean." Invisible. Somehow, it isn't really there. The analogy with Viet Nam is strong—oh, those damnable body counts. These people were obediently and cheerfully doing their duty and trotting into the disintegrators when they were told to—never questioning why, or whether their war could be turned into a useful peace. Kirk changed the situation so that death was no longer so clean—if people were going to die, they were also going to have to see the blood and broken bodies. The point here was to force the two combatants to recognize the horror of their waste-based society—like ours.

The situation had been set up specifically to make the above point—and in order to make it, Kirk had to intervene.

In "The Return of the Archons" Kirk destroys another culture-controlling computer. (How IBM must hate that man!) This one has stabilized its culture by a more direct control of its people's lives. The life-style is totalitarian, except for occasional "festivals" when the computer releases the populace from its control for short periods of time. Here too, we are told that this culture has endured for hundreds of years.

The situation was set up to say that totalitarianism—of any kind—is wrong. In order to escape, Kirk had to destroy the Landru computer, thus making the point that human beings were meant to be their own masters.

In "This Side of Paradise" a colony has found peace and contentment—and stagnation—living in symbiosis with a kind of spore. In fact, it is only the presence of the spores which allows humans to survive on this planet; the spores nullify a certain type of radiation, and also keep the colonists in excellent health. The point to be questioned was whether humans could exist in total stagnation with no creativity, no growth, no exercise of mind or talent of any kind.

Kirk's answer was to nullify the effect of the spores and remove the colonists—but he had to do so in order to escape personally. His decision was between his mission and the symbiosis.

In "Who Mourns for Adonais" Kirk decides that it is time for the human race to give up its old myths, and an ancient Greek God is destroyed. Although Kirk indicates some remorse at the end, his answer is still the same.

In "The Apple" (one of the worst offenders) Kirk destroys a garden of Eden. Vaal, the Godzilla-head rock god, controls the weather, and hence, the ecology of the planet. He provides a pastoral situation for his servants. This story, like most of STAR TREK's moral statements is oddly anti-machine.* Vaal must be destroyed—no attempt is made to tame him.

In "Mirror, Mirror" an alternate *Enterprise*, one dedicated to violence, is portrayed. Kirk convinces the alternate world Spock to rebel—implying that he will eventually bring peace and justice and the "American Way" to this alternate galaxy.

In "Bread and Circuses" a modernized Roman Empire is encountered. We are shown that they have their local equivalent of Christians too. Hence, the implication is that this culture will eventually evolve into one more suitable to Starfleet's tastes.

---

*STAR TREK was never against technology—obviously, it couldn't be. It used technology as part of the adventure. But the series did make the statement several times over that humanity must be in control of the machines, not the other way around. In fact, this was the single most repeated theme of the show: that even as individuals, we must be in control of the machinery of our lives.

In "The Gamesters of Triskelion" Kirk must win his freedom from an arena situation—in the process, he convinces the gamesters that gaming with human and other beings is immoral.

In "A Piece of the Action" Kirk encounters a 1920-mobster civilization. This one was a comedy, so Kirk succeeds simply by out-mobstering everybody else. He simply takes over totally and says, "Dis is de way we're going to do it from now on." But it is in character with everything he's done before.

In "Patterns of Force," a neo-Nazi culture is defeated—even though it had raised an agricultural populace into an industrial one in just one generation. Kirk feels that although the goals are laudable, the methods are wrong.

In "The Cloud-Minders" another form of oppression is encountered—a cultural and social delineation produced by the fact that the elite live in sky cities floating above the harsh surface of their planet, while the worker-class are forced to dig zenite from the mines. The answer is gas-masks to protect them from the zenite gas. (It's the gas that makes them so unhappy.) Now, they can go back and dig in peace! (And the real social problem is left unresolved.)*

—It wasn't just cultures that Kirk had to contend with. It was attitudes in general:

In "The Way to Eden" the *Enterprise* picks up a shipload of cosmic hippies. Naturally, the hippies' attitudes are found to be without value. Apparently, peace and happiness are alien to the commander of the *Enterprise* by now. The kids have to be reeducated that there's no such thing as a free lunch. You pays for what you gets.

In "By Any Other Name" agents of the Kelvan empire grab the *Enterprise* for an intergalactic sojourn. Kirk grabs it right back by teaching them how to be human.

In "Plato's Stepchildren" another group of cosmic gamesters is encountered and defeated. It is not good manners to force things on people—Kirk forces them to appreciate this attitude.

Individually, any one of the above episodes was designed to make a specific point. Slavery is wrong. Exploitation is wrong. Racism is wrong. And so on.

Cumulatively, the effect is quite different.

---

*The script of this episode is based on an outline of mine called "Castles in the Sky." The original conception of this story was far more disquieting, because there was no easy answer to the situation—only an uneasy beginning. (Just like in real life.) I do not pretend objectivity here. I cared about that story, I wanted it to be important. I think that the episode as ultimately presented was a cheat to the audience. To me, it represented all that was wrong with STAR TREK's third season. Gas-masks indeed!

Cumulatively, the effect is that each situation has been constructed for Kirk to make that point. And cumulatively, the effect is of a set of straw men—or straw cultures, actually—for Kirk to knock down.

While each of the individual stories may have been valid, in the context of the series as a whole there is an implication of Starfleet's attitudes that reflects seriously on the attitudes of American television, as well as the American culture.

The subtext of the series, the subvocal message, is that if a local culture is tested and found wanting in the eyes of a starship Captain, he may make such changes as he feels necessary.

Granted, Kirk never touched a culture that didn't *need* it in the context of the given story. But, in point of fact, each of those stories and cultures had been set up to make a specific point. Looking past the individual points, to the implied power of the Captain, he was functioning not so much as Starfleet's ambassador—but as Starfleet's *judge*.

Every culture he encountered was weighed and tested. Rarely was Captain Kirk tested.

If STAR TREK was to be about contemporary man against a science fiction background, then it is not just that background we are exploring—it is the nature of contemporary man as well.

Every time Kirk knocked down a straw-man culture, he was reinforcing the message that "In the name of *my* morality, this is the proper action."

The worst offender was an episode entitled "The *Enterprise* Incident." In this episode, Kirk (seemingly) goes crazy and orders the *Enterprise* into Romulan space. The *Enterprise* is captured, Kirk is killed (we think), Spock allows himself to be seduced by a Romulan captain. Kirk puts on a Romulan disguise and—aha! Now we find out that it has all been an espionage plot— sneaks aboard the Romulan ship to steal their Cloak of Invisibility device. Never mind the holes in the story big enough to drive a starship through— the episode came about as a result of the Pueblo Incident. Remember the American spy ship that the North Koreans captured? Well, the way STAR TREK told it, we won.

In fact, the way STAR TREK told it, we were *justified* in spying because our side was right and theirs wasn't.

(Oh, Organia—where are you when we really need you?)

The story was as dishonest as anything ever presented on American television, and representative of STAR TREK's worst failures. Instead of test- ing Kirk—and by implication, contemporary man—it said that the ends jus- tify the means; because our ends are just, then no matter what means we choose, our means will be just too. It ignored the fact that the means *shape* the ends; if a culture uses espionage and trickery and force, then no matter what is written in its laws and Constitution, it is not an honorable culture. As presented in "The *Enterprise* Incident" Starfleet was no better than the "evil" Romulans.

STAR TREK could have told a far better story if they had really retold the Pueblo Incident. And in point of fact, this is exactly what Dorothy Fontana had intended. But when she presented the idea, NBC flinched. "Too dangerous. It has to be something else."

Had the show retold the Pueblo Incident, Kirk's decision would have been a much more crucial one. He can save his honor and refuse to sign the confession that he was spying—or he can save his ship and the 431 human beings (and one Vulcan) whose lives he is responsible for. And suppose he really *had* been on a spying mission—!

The kind of human being he was presented as, Kirk would sacrifice his honor rather than one single life. Had he been forced to do so, he would have then returned to base and confronted the Starfleet authority that had ordered him on such a mission. Supposedly a shamed and defeated Captain, he would confront the Admiral who had ordered him into such a situation and he would say, "We had no right to be there, that was Romulan territory! I didn't embarrass us—you did by ordering me to undertake such a mission."

And the Admiral might reply, "You're right, Kirk—but we needed that information that you gathered in order to maintain the balance of power. I didn't like having to give you those orders, but they were necessary. And if it's necessary to repeat them in the future, I'll give those orders again. And you'll follow them too."

And Kirk might look at him and reply, "I don't know . . . I don't know . . ."

And we would leave it at that.

There is no satisfactory resolution to such a situation—only a gained awareness of the reasons for its occurrence. STAR TREK had the opportunity to comment on one of the most shameful American adventures—as it had the opportunity to comment on all of them—and muffed it thoroughly.

STAR TREK had the greatest potential of any television series ever created—but its potential was only rarely fulfilled because too often the decisions that Kirk was called upon to make were facile ones. A facile decision doesn't test Kirk. And it doesn't test the contemporary man who is the unwritten hero of every STAR TREK episode.

There is no question that television is the most powerful medium of communication ever invented. That power carries with it an awesome responsibility.

It is becoming more and more apparent that television can no longer claim to be only a reflection of the American culture; television is one of the primary influences on that culture.

An awareness of this simple fact mandates that those who use the medium be responsible for the message they send. If those who write for TV use it only as a stage on which to demonstrate how right we are in our attitudes, opinions—and prejudices—then they will perform no service to us at all. We learn nothing from being right. We don't have to.

The truly courageous shows are windows into the human soul. They are mirrors in which we can see the traps we have made for ourselves. These are the stories in which the hero might—just *might*—discover that he has been wrong.

The moment at which the hero finally confronts the problem head on is the single most important moment in the story. It is called the climax. The hero's survival—or the survival of something important to him—is at stake. It could be something as intangible as his honor, or as big as a world—what counts is that it is important to the hero. It is in the moment that he faces its loss that the hero actually learns something about himself and his relationship to that thing he holds dear. The story is about the realization, not the circumstance. The circumstance is only the context, the frame for the moment.

We have seen that moment occur in more than a few episodes of STAR TREK. We have seen it in "The City on the Edge of Forever" and "Errand of Mercy" and "A Taste of Armageddon." We have seen the moment in "Amok Time" and "Journey to Babel," "The Naked Time," "Shore Leave," and "This Side of Paradise." And other episodes too. Perhaps not as often as we would have wished—STAR TREK's interesting failures still outnumber its successes—but often enough to inspire us.

And yet—even in STAR TREK's weakest episodes the show was still about the best that human beings can be; in that respect STAR TREK has served us extraordinarily well.

Taken as a whole, the STAR TREK TV series makes a profound statement: There *will* be a future. Yes, we will have problems—*but* we will be big enough to handle them. As individuals, *and as a species,* we are big enough to meet ourselves face to face. That is the vision of STAR TREK.

PART FIVE

The Return of
STAR TREK—

S TAR T REK's fans never quit hoping.

They knew the show would *have* to come back. In fact, there was a seven-year letter campaign directed at Paramount, asking them to bring the show back either as a movie or a TV series—but please bring it back.

Finally, in 1977, Paramount studios announced plans to create a fourth TV network. S TAR T REK would be their key attraction. It sounded almost too good to be true—but it was actually, *finally* happening!

Gene Roddenberry returned to his old offices, hired Harold Livingston as a line producer, arranged to bring back most of the original cast, and began interviewing writers.* The S TAR T REK sets were redesigned. Soundstages were reserved and construction was begun. New costumes were created and new special effects were planned. The new *Enterprise* was going to look bigger and better than ever.

The Writers' Guide for *Star Trek II* (dated August 12, 1977) explained that the new episodes would portray the *second* five-year mission of the U.S.S. *Enterprise*. It was extrapolated that following its first mission, the starship had returned home and entered orbital drydocks in the naval yards high over San Francisco, where the vessel was completely refit. While its basic contours, both interior and exterior would remain generally the same, the details of the

---

*I was told I had a definite assignment, but on the morning we were to block out the story, I was offered a position as story editor on the still-in-planning ''Buck Rogers'' TV series over at Universal. It was a rare opportunity and I accepted the job. (It was the only time in my life I ever had to turn down a S TAR T REK assignment.) The ''Buck Rogers'' operation was shut down by Universal a few months later, to be later resurrected in a different format by a different producer.

165

ship (such as instrumentation, readout systems and controls) would be vastly more sophisticated than the original.

James T. Kirk would still be the Captain of the *Enterprise*—having refused an Admiral's star to do so. According to the guide, Kirk has managed to recruit many members of the original crew. "An exception to this," said the guide, "is Mr. Spock, who has returned to high honor to Vulcan to head the Science Academy there."

The starship's mission, of course, would remain the same—to patrol a section of the galaxy, representing Earth and the Federation, assisting colonists, aiding scientific exploration, helping those in distress, and engaging in diplomatic missions with other planets and peoples.

The new Writers' Guide listed several interesting changes. While the character of Spock would no longer be a regular, it was hoped that he would frequently return as a guest star. In the meantime, a young Vulcan named Xon would be the new science officer. Xon (pronounced Zahn) is described as a twenty-two-year-old Vulcan on his first space voyage. Despite his youth, he is a genius even by Vulcan standards. He is also a full-blooded Vulcan (unlike Spock who had a human mother) and lacks firsthand experience with human beings.

According to the guide, Xon recognizes that if he is to perform as well as Spock, he has to eliminate his Vulcan revulsion to human displays of emotion and will instead have to reach down within himself to find the emotions that his society has repressed for thousands of years in order to have a basis for understanding. "What this means," said the Guide, "is this: whereas Spock was engaged in a constant battle within himself to repress his emotions in order to be more Vulcanlike, Xon will be engaged in a constant struggle within himself to release his buried emotions to be more humanlike for the sake of doing a good job. This will be at least as difficult for him as it was for Spock to maintain his stoic pose."

In other words, Xon would be more open and vulnerable to his own emotions. He would be cautiously curious and even willing to explore his own feelings, as opposed to Spock who felt he had to keep them hidden.

Furthermore, as a full-blooded Vulcan, Xon would be even stronger than Spock, able to endure greater physical hardships and more adept at the Vulcan mind-meld.

Another major change in the format of *Star Trek II* was the addition of Commander Will Decker as First Officer, second-in-command under Kirk. His father and grandfather were also Starfleet officers of flag rank. (While the Guide does not specify this, it's safe to assume that Will Decker is the son of Commodore Decker of the *Constellation*, last seen entering "The

Doomsday Machine.'') Also aboard, at the navigator's station will be Lieutenant Ilia, a strangely beautiful native of Delta V. The Guide describes her as completely hairless, except for her eyes. The Deltan race is much older than humans, with brains much more finely evolved in areas of art and mathematics. Furthermore, the Deltans are a *very* sexual species. Sex is a part of every Deltan friendship, social engagement, and profession. Because constant sex is *not* the pattern of humans and others aboard the *Enterprise*,** Ilia must totally repress this part of herself.

Mr. Chekov was to be promoted to a full lieutenant, now commanding the starship's security division. Dr. McCoy, Chief Engineer Scott, Lieutenant Uhura, and Mr. Sulu would be seen again at their familiar stations. Yeoman Janice Rand would return to the *Enterprise,* and Nurse Chapel will now be *Dr.* Chapel.

Except for these character changes, the essential format of the show would remain the same: a magnificent starship, a highly qualified crew, a noble mission to seek out new life and new worlds.

The new STAR TREK promised to be even better than the first.

Unfortunately, Paramount could not get enough TV stations to affiliate with their projected network for it to be profitable. Only a few months before they were supposed to go on the air, the whole idea was scrapped. No episode of the new STAR TREK was ever filmed.

But the effort wasn't going to be wasted.

Paramount had a better idea. They would make a STAR TREK movie instead.

Where did they get this idea? Perhaps they had seen it in the newspapers. A movie called *Star Wars*—a *science fiction* picture—had just become the most successful motion picture in history, easily outgrossing *Jaws,* the previous box-office champion. Or perhaps they realized that all those letters, all those years, represented people who would line up at the box office with five-dollar bills clutched in their hot little hands.

The sets were standing and waiting, the costumes were built, the cast was signed, there were plenty of scripts in the works—perhaps they could scale one of them up and make a modest little movie out of it—and perhaps make enough money to recoup the investment. It seemed a logical thing to do.

The project was announced at a lavish press conference early in 1978. The modest little movie had been scaled up to gargantuan proportions. *Star Trek: The Movie* would be Paramount's *big* picture for 1979.

The studio promised an uncompromising commitment to the effort. After

---

**Except perhaps for James T. Kirk.

much speculation about his return, even Leonard Nimoy was signed aboard the project, once more to play Mr. Spock. The rest of the original cast would also return: William Shatner as James T. Kirk, DeForest Kelley as Dr. McCoy, James Doohan as Scotty, Walter Koenig as Mr. Chekov, Nichelle Nichols as Lt. Uhura, George Takei as Sulu, Majel Barrett as Dr. Chapel, and Grace Lee Whitney as Yeoman Janice Rand. Robert Wise (*The Day the Earth Stood Still, The Andromeda Strain, The Sound of Music*) was signed to direct, and Jerry Goldsmith was signed to compose an original score.

In the months of production that followed, other plans became known. A brand new *Enterprise* was being designed and built, inside and out. The beautiful new sets that had been built for the abortive fourth-network TV series were being torn down to be rebuilt larger and more detailed than ever. Extravagant special-effects sequences were being prepared. New costumes were being designed—again. And new props: phasers, communicators, feinbergers—everything!

Star Trek: The Motion Picture began shooting in August 1978.

The first time the cast was assembled together on the new bridge set was for publicity stills.

"Walking back onto the bridge of the *Enteprise*," said Shatner (in an interview in *Starlog* magazine), "was eerie. It was *déjà vu*. And yet at the same time there was a feeling that time had not passed at all. Most of the old crew members were there, and in the first couple of moments, before filming started, all I was aware of was that all these laughing and talking people were the laughers and talkers of old. It was as though ten years hadn't passed; quite strange and bizarre."

Other cast members noticed the feeling too. Walter Koenig noted it in his own book, *Chekov's Enterprise*. (He wrote that the phrase *déjà vu* would probably replace the words, "My character isn't being written right," as the most common phrase aboard the bridge.)

Leonard Nimoy said the magic began for him when the cast got together for the press conference announcing the production of the picture. "That day was the first time since the end of the series that we had all been assembled together in one room. I felt that the chemistry that day was very exciting, and from that day I looked forward to doing it."

Shatner continues: "For the cast, it was as though we'd never stopped acting together once the initial ice had been broken. Our timing, our manner of interacting, the way we reacted to each other, it could have been as though we'd gone off for a summer hiatus . . . rather than almost ten years. It was a source of astonishment to a lot of people, and for Bob [Wise], it must have been a little alarming. There he was, the director, suddenly faced with a cohesive whole, and he'd only really just begun to grasp STAR TREK. But he's wonderful to work with, he really is. A very gentle and wise man.''

At one rehearsal, the following exchange took place:
Spock: "There is an object in the center of the cloud."
Bonnie Pendergast (script supervisor): "There is an object in the *heart* of the cloud."
Spock (turning to Kirk): "There is an object in the liver of the cloud."
Kirk (to Spock): "You have the guts to tell me that?"
Some things never change.
On another occasion, as Kirk and Spock leave the bridge, Kirk tells Decker that he has the conn. Stephen Collins, playing Decker, drops to his knees and wraps the captain's chair in a big bear hug, blubbering, "At last, it's mine, it's mine!''
Kirk turns around and stamps his foot petulantly. "I change my mind! I change my mind!''
It must have been a long day.

STAR TREK's fans speculated endlessly about every little detail of the production. The STAR TREK grapevine *buzzed*. Of course, the greatest goal of many of the fans was to actually *be* in the STAR TREK movie. That wish actually came true for a lucky few.
In one of the grandest gestures in STAR TREK's history, Gene Roddenberry acknowledged the contribution of STAR TREK's fans to the show by casting more than a hundred and fifty of them as the crew of the *Enterprise*.*
The sequence occurs near the beginning of the movie, when Captain Kirk assembles the entire crew of the ship on the recreation deck to tell them of a sinister alien force headed toward the Earth. The lucky fans who appeared in the scene were not only delighted at the opportunity—they were even more delighted to discover that they were going to be given a free lunch and paid for a day's work as well. As one thrilled fan said, "I'd have paid *them*!''
Director Robert Wise carefully explained the scene to the extras. The large panel at the front of the set is a viewscreen. On it, in the movie (but not here on the set, it will be matted in later), the crew of the *Enterprise* will see the destruction of a distant space station by a vast unknown object. The crew must react with horror and apprehension.

---

*Yes, I was there too. I'm the fellow standing next to the director's wife. Also in the scene were Bjo Trimble and Susan Sackett (Gene Roddenberry's secretary), though not as easily visible.

Then, Kirk will enter and give them their orders.

A few moments later, William Shatner walked onto the set, followed by the other bridge officers in that scene—and the soundstage erupted into *thunderous* applause.

In that moment, William Shatner transformed once again into Captain James T. Kirk of the starship *Enterprise*—and these people before him were his proud and dedicated crew. It was a reunion of friends—in real life as well as on film. Reality and dreams had become indistinguishable. For all who were there, it was an extraordinary moment.

The sequence had actually been scheduled for two days of production—but the fans were so cooperative and professional in their work that all of the major crowd scenes were finished the first afternoon. The production crew was pleasantly surprised by the professionalism of STAR TREK'S fans.

Unfortunately, not all of STAR TREK'S production problems ran as smoothly.

Many of those who worked on the film are quite candid about its problems. Robert Wise felt one of the biggest mistakes was starting production of the picture without the script being finished. There were too many rewrites! In fact, on some days, Gene Roddenberry, Robert Wise, William Shatner, and Leonard Nimoy would retire into Gene's office for a rewrite conference before the day's shooting began.

Because of that, the production of the film was very much a mad caucus race, with scenes being written and rewritten and rewritten, sometimes only hours before they were to be shot. Two-thirds of the film was actually in the can before the climatic scenes were finalized, and even they were still subject to daily rewrites. The tag-ending of the picture was rewritten several times in the week before it was finally shot. Leonard Nimoy wanted Spock's final line to be (instead of, "I have no business on Vulcan."), "If Dr. McCoy is going to remain aboard, my presence here is essential." Even though it was shot both ways, the original line was kept.

The film was also plagued with a series of minor accidents. The gigantic V'GER set used at the climax of the film was made out of lights, panels, and plastic forms. A board was put up to keep score which department had the most people falling through it.

The company hired to produce STAR TREK'S special effects was running up huge expenses and still had not turned in a foot of usable film. Doug Trumbull, special-effects wizard for *2001: A Space Odyssey* and director of *Silent Running*, eventually had to take over. It was becoming more and more apparent that *Star Trek: The Motion Picture* was not only going to be very big—it was also going to be very expensive.

Eventually, the movie would cost more than $44,000,000—almost enough to pay for two Apollo missions to the moon. (In 1969, an Apollo lunar landing cost $24 million.) To be fair, not all of that money was actually spent on the production—but Hollywood has a peculiar way of bookkeeping and all of the production costs of STAR TREK II: The TV Series also had to be charged against the production of the movie. In addition, there were several million dollars literally *wasted* by the first special effects company hired for the film that also had to be charged against the movie's budget.

Indeed, the complexity of the film's special effects were the source of a number of problems. Paramount executives felt that director Robert Wise's first cut of the film had too much emphasis on the people and not enough on the effects. They ordered the film recut to use more of the effects shots— and less of the actual story. (A source who prefers to remain unidentified described the attitude as: "We paid for these effects, we want to see them.") The only place that Robert Wise's version of the film was ever publicly shown was on airplanes. (Those who have seen it said it was far better paced.)

But not all the delays were painful ones.

One day, five months into the shooting, they were shooting a scene on the bridge. Uhura's line was: "Captain, the alien has ejected a large object."

When Nichelle Nichols said the line, William Shatner replied, "A large turd, obviously."

When everybody stopped laughing—five minutes later—they tried again. This time, they got as far as Uhura's second line: "Captain, the alien has ejected *another*—"

After another ten minutes of hysterical giggling, the line was changed to: "Captain, the alien has *released* a large object."

Every production problem used up time.

Indeed, as the day of release grew closer and closer, there was considerable worry the film might not be ready, and as a matter of fact, the prints of the film were ultimately shipped "wet"—that is, when they came out of the processing tanks, they were put immediately into film cans and shipped to the theatres. The prints would complete their drying out process while being projected.

Star Trek: The Motion Picture officially premiered at a gala held at the MacArthur Theatre in Washington, D.C., on the evening of December 6, 1979.

It opened for the fans on the morning of December 7. In Hollywood, the lines began forming at Mann's Chinese Theatre at eight o'clock in the morning.

That evening, the film was also screened for STAR TREK'S friends in the film industry at the prestigious Sam Goldwyn theatre on Wilshire Boulevard.

The immediate reaction was . . . mixed. The fans were glad to see the film, but they were troubled too. The reactions from the industry professionals were also mixed.

The movie didn't exactly sparkle.

Star Trek: The Motion Picture was a curious mixture of success and failure—it was so eagerly anticipated, it could not possibly have lived up to the expectations of the audience. It was so big, it could not help but be perceived as ponderous and overdone. And yet—despite an avalanche of speculations, hype, and hoopla—the STAR TREK movie still *touched* its audience.

The first hour of it is the strongest one. Perhaps a large part of this is the emotional effect of seeing the original cast reassembled once more. Now— Admiral Kirk reassumes command of the *Enterprise* to confront a new threat to the solar system; he is as quickly decisive as ever—but it is equally obvious that he needs his top two advisors, Spock and McCoy. The picture wastes little time in bringing them aboard.

Spock is colder than ever. He has been undergoing the Vulcan process of *Kolinahr*—the final purging of all emotions. When he arrives on the bridge of the refitted *Enterprise,* he seems almost a zombie. He is greeted with enthusiasm; he does not even raise an eyebrow in response.

Dr. McCoy, on the other hand, is even more boisterous, emotional, and outspoken than ever before. DeForest Kelly's performance sparkles; it is the stuff of magic.

The finest moment in the movie, of course, occurs when the new *Enterprise* begins to move majestically out of its orbiting drydock. It is a moment to bring a lump to the throat and a tear to the eye of even the most jaded science fiction fan. It is nothing short of wonderful.

Unfortunately, it is in the second hour that the picture begins to bog down—as the *Enterprise* finally confronts the mysterious alien force. The picture takes too long to get to the ending, and the resolution isn't strong enough to justify the trip. One is left wanting something more from the story.

As a result, *Star Trek: The Motion Picture* was received by the fans with a mixture of delight and disappointment. They were glad to see the refurbished *Enterprise* and all their favorite characters back on the job again; but they were disappointed with the script, which played like a pastiche of three of the episodes of the original TV series: "The Immunity Syndrome" (in which the *Enterprise* must penetrate to the center of a mysterious energy cloud in space), "The Doomsday Machine" (in which the *Enterprise* confronts an immense device that chews up planets and spits out asteroids), and "The Changeling" (in which the *Enterprise* encounters an alien-rebuilt space probe, Nomad, which now possesses strange new powers and has come back to look for its creator). The fans recognized the familiar situations and quickly dubbed the picture, "Where Nomad Has Gone Before."*

The critics were also unhappy with *Star Trek: The Motion Picture,* in particular its ending in which an Earthman, an alien woman, and the machine-spaceship, V'GER, are united into a single new life form which disappears into a high dimension.† Its aspirations toward cosmic importance were sometimes dismissed as confusing, other times as "silly." One of the most telling criticisms was that the story was lost in the special effects. Harlan Ellison, author of the Hugo-winning STAR TREK episode, "The City on the Edge of Forever" noted that, "It's Gene Roddenberry's standard plot. The *Enterprise* meets God. And it's either a child or a computer. Or both."

Star Trek: The Motion Picture is actually a much better picture than most of its detractors gave it credit for. Among its virtues are those of careful production and loving attention to detail. Very few other science fiction pictures have achieved such a high level of technical accuracy, either in their science or in their portrayal of the procedural details of its use. The notable exceptions include *The Andromeda Strain* and *2001: A Space Odyssey.* (It's worth noting that STAR TREK'S director, Robert Wise, also directed *The Andromeda Strain,* and Doug Trumbull, the special effects wizard, performed the same duties on both *The Andromeda Strain* and *2001.*)

Most important—unlike so many other entries in the high-stakes science fiction derby—STAR TREK is about something. This is no mere galactic shoot-em-up; this is a film of gigantic ideas. The weakness of the film is not from any failure of nerve on the part of the filmmakers; it is clear that this was not an easy movie to make. The film bogs down in good part because the ideas it wants to discuss simply cannot be portrayed as special effects: sparkling lights and auras are pretty to look at, but they hardly create the experience of a new dimension of consciousness.

Curiously, the *real* strength of the film was ultimately demonstrated when it showed up on television as a Sunday night movie on ABC. The network, wanting to broadcast the movie as a three-hour spectacular, asked Paramount to restore the lost footage: the scenes that had been cut from the original theatri-

---

*Also "Spockalypse Now" and "STAR TREK: The Motionless Picture."

†In the original conception of STAR TREK I, it was Spock who had had the affair with Ilia, during his days at Starfleet Academy, and it was Spock who united with her at the end of the picture to become a higher life form. His excursion into the heart-liver-bowels of V'GER and his subsequent transformation were preparation for that moment—but it never happened. The ending of the picture was not finalized until more than half of it had already been shot.

cal release of the film. There were about fifteen minutes of the movie that had never been seen in motion picture theatres—including some of the most important parts of the story.*

While most of the missing pieces were barely more than curious little snips or interesting discoveries about this character or that, several of the scenes turned out to be crucial ones—particularly those concerning the character of Mr. Spock. Indeed, the whole emphasis of the picture is shifted by the inclusion of the lost footage.

Now, it is much clearer that the story is not simply about the *Enterprise*'s confrontation with V'GER; it is also (and more importantly) about what Mr. Spock learns in that confrontation. Indeed, this story may be the most important of all STAR TREK stories because it is about the most important event in Mr. Spock's life—his recognition of his own humanity. The essential problem for Mr. Spock has always been his inevitable confrontations—both large and small—with the undeniable existence of his own feelings.

As originally conceived, the character had no emotions. However, this conception of the Vulcan experience quickly evolved into one in which the Vulcans had such *powerful* emotional states that they had to train themselves to keep their emotions permanently suppressed. (In *Star Trek: The Motion Picture,* we see that the highest (?) level of this training is *Kolinahr,* in which the trainee finally purges the last emotional feelings from his/her being. Spock stops himself from completing the training to return to the *Enterprise.* There is an answer he seeks and he senses a vast and powerful consciousness *somewhere out there. . . .*)

By Earth standards, therefore, Vulcans are an emotionally *retarded* race. The Vulcan conception of emotions is that they are a burden, that they cause the being to function as if it, he, or she is out of control. Emotions, according to Vulcan philosophy, get in the way of producing results. Therefore, eliminate the emotions, become entirely logical, and you can be much more *efficient.*

This is a terrific philosophy. For a machine.

It doesn't work too well for human beings. And the evidence is that it doesn't work too well for Vulcans either.

It is clear that Gene Roddenberry (and very probably, Leonard Nimoy as well) was very much aware that this was Spock's essential problem—the one thing he needed most to resolve for his life to be complete—because this is

---

*Paramount Pictures has since released *Star Trek: The Motion Picture,* The Special Edition, on videotape. Hard core STAR TREK fans now regard it as the *official* version of the movie.

the subplot of *Star Trek: The Motion Picture* that gives meaning to every-thing else in the film.

Up until this point, the character of Spock functioned very much like a temperamental chess master—a genius at the chessboard, but prone to wild breakdowns in situations where his emotional buttons are pushed. Despite his claims that logical consideration of the universe is the highest function of intelligence, Spock seems never to have turned the attention of his logic to the state of his own emotions. Had he done so, surely he would have had to ask the question, "*Why* are there emotions? Is there a logical reason for them?"*

Having never pondered that question (at least not in any episode of the TV series), Spock was essentially an unhappy character. Happiness for Spock was the rare exception, not the rule. The character was clearly a very strong personality desperately trying to make himself into a machine and being con-tinually reminded by his own feelings that he was not and never could be *entirely* logical. In that world view, Spock cannot help but see his emotions as afflictions, momentary losses of control, and the enemy of logic.

It is in *Star Trek: The Motion Picture* that Spock finally discovers/confronts the truth about his own emotional state. V'GER, the powerful alien menace, is actually a living machine—a machine that grew so complex that it devel-oped consciousness.

In the movie, Spock enters the heart of V'GER to mind-meld with its consciousness. Clearly, Spock is demonstrating his willingness to die to dis-cover the answer. The truth is more important to him than survival; this is a moment of transformation for him—because in discovering the truth about V'GER, the old Spock dies and a new one is born.

Recovering in the sick bay, Spock reports ". . . with all its pure logic, V'GER is barren, cold." It is a profound irony to him—because the same description could apply to Mr. Spock. Indeed, we see him laugh gently at the joke*ness* of it all. He recognizes the kinship. In his own machinelike pursuit of logic, he had turned himself *into* a "living machine" too. What else can you do when you get the joke, but laugh?

Spock reports that V'GER is asking questions: "Is this all that I am? Is there nothing more?" He has been asking those same questions himself. Spock

---

*Yes, there is. Emotions are the evolutionary result of primate survival mechanisms. In cir-cumstances where survival is not an issue, therefore, the expression of emotion would be an inefficient and inappropriate behavior. However, the Vulcan answer, at least as much as we've seen it expressed in Spock, still seems . . . ah, something of an over-reaction.

takes the hand of James T. Kirk and says, "This simple *feeling*—is beyond V'GER's comprehension."

The moment is profound. It is the acknowledgment of emotion. The action is both human *and* Vulcan. What Spocks says is logical, what he *expresses* is joyous. This is the most important moment in Mr. Spock's life—because it is in this moment that Mr. Spock finally accepts the experience of his own emotions. This is the instant in which he finally integrates *both* his halves into one mature being.

Later in the same film, in the most extraordinary of the restored scenes, the camera pans around the bridge, showing the face of each of the ship's officers, ending finally on Spock—whose back is to the camera. Kirk turns to him; sensing that something is wrong, he asks, "Spock?" When Spock turns around, there is a tear rolling down his cheek. The mere act of allowing James T. Kirk to see his vulnerability is evidence of the profound transformation that Spock has experienced.

Kirk asks him, "That's not for us, is it?"

And Spock explains, "I weep for V'GER as I would for a brother. As I was when I came aboard, so is V'GER now: empty, incomplete, and searching. *Logic and knowledge are not enough.*"

From Mr. Spock, this is a startling admission.

It is also a demonstration. For Spock to have recognized the emptiness of a machine existence, he has to have moved beyond it. McCoy, of course, is the one to recognize it. He asks, "Are you saying that you found what you needed?"

Spock replies, "Each of us, at some time in our lives, asks, 'Why am I here? Why was I meant to be?' " Spock has recognized that V'GER's search for its creator is like his own search for meaning. Has Spock found his meaning? At the end of the picture, he says that he has finished with his task on Vulcan. He is back aboard the *Enterprise*.

Star Trek: The Motion Picture ends with: "The human adventure is just beginning."

For Mr. Spock, that is clearly true.

To the fans—and indeed, even to Gene Roddenberry himself—*Star Trek: The Motion Picture* had been envisioned as the first of a series of STAR TREK movies, to be produced at the rate of one every two or three years. Even while the first movie was still working its way through its theatrical release, the speculation was already beginning—will there be a second STAR TREK picture?

The answer was primarily a matter of economics.

Would a second STAR TREK picture be profitable?

In fact, it was even more immediate than that. To the studio, the question was: "Will the *first* STAR TREK picture be profitable?

By Paramount's bookkeeping, *Star Trek: The Motion Picture* cost $44,000,000 to make. (Remember, the picture also had to pay for the development of a TV series that was never filmed and $5,000,000 of unusable special effects.) Just to break even, a movie has to earn three dollars at the box office for every dollar spent in production. (The theatre owner and the distributor get to keep about sixty percent—it varies with the picture—of a film's earnings.)

What this meant was that *Star Trek: The Motion Picture* would have to earn $132,000,000 just to break even!

This was truly an all-or-nothing situation. The picture would have to be one of the all-time box-office champions or it would be a disaster.

The film's early reviews were not promising. Neither was the word of mouth. Many industry observers were speculating that the picture would have two or three good weeks—while all the hard-core Trekkies binged out—and then would quickly fade away. The feeling was that the picture wasn't good enough to justify a lot of repeat business and there probably weren't enough dedicated Trekkies to keep it alive for long.

Translation: "The picture's a dog. Once the real movie-going public finds this out, it'll die."

Right.

Star Trek: The Motion Picture earned over $175,000,000 worldwide.

Either there are a few *very very* rich (and very very dedicated) Trekkies, or there are simply a lot of people around who want to see more STAR TREK. During the spring and summer of 1980, the film continued to attract audiences of all ages, reaching across the demographic boundaries so dear to the hearts of statisticians, and generated a healthy repeat business.

Additionally, ABC television paid another $10,000,000 for the right to broadcast the movie twice on commercial television. High prices were paid for the cable TV rights, and the videotape and videodisk versions of the film have also sold briskly. As a matter of fact, the videotape of *Star Trek: The Motion Picture,* The Special Edition has already established itself as a steady bestseller.

So, the issue of STAR TREK's profitablity as a property was finally resolved. The earnings of the first film demonstrated that STAR TREK truly could reach a large and enthusiastic audience.

But that still didn't guarantee a second STAR TREK movie.

The issue was still *profitability*.

Despite their public optimism and confidence in the film, the executives at Paramount had experienced more than a few moments of very real concern that they might take a disastrous loss on *Star Trek: The Motion Picture*. This made them very hesitant about doing a second STAR TREK movie.

On the other hand . . .

The sets were still standing. All the props and costumes had already been built. The miniatures could be used again—so could many of the same special effects shots. A second picture wouldn't have to carry the costs of initial development, nor would it have to pay for an unmade TV series and unused special effects. A second STAR TREK picture *could* be made at a much lower cost, and if it earned as much as the first picture (or *more* if it was a better picture), the studio would show a correspondingly *larger* profit.

It would be the accounting that determined the scale of the second STAR TREK picture. The executives at Paramount were willing to make another STAR TREK movie *only* if its production costs could be kept manageable. (In fact, *Star Trek: The Wrath of Khan* was actually produced by Paramount's television division. It was conceived as a TV movie—with the option of theatrical release only if it was judged *good* enough. This was their escape hatch. Midway through production, the studio brass were so pleased with what they were seeing, they finalized the decision.)

The studio offered Gene Roddenberry the producership of the picture—but *without* creative control. Roddenberry declined, and instead became an "executive consultant." For the first time in STAR TREK's history, his name would not appear in its familiar position on the credit roll. Another man would be taking over the responsibility of producing STAR TREK.*

It was a difficult decision for *everyone* involved. STAR TREK was Gene Roddenberry's baby. It had always been so. He was as completely identified with the series as any of its cast members. Now, to ask him to *not* produce the second picture was exactly the kind of "heartless" action that gives studio executives a bad name.

Furthermore, finding the *right* man to follow in Gene Roddenberry's footsteps would not be easy either. For one thing, STAR TREK was known to be one of the hardest shows to produce. For another, whoever accepted the job would very likely be looked upon as a "hired gun" by many of those he would have to work with. How would the STAR TREK cast feel about another

---

*The studio executives blamed Gene Roddenberry for letting the budget of *Star Trek: The Motion Picture* get out of control. This was probably an unfair judgment as several of the worst decisions about the picture were over Roddenberry's objections (including the decision to recut Robert Wise's version of the picture).

man in Gene Roddenberry's chair. (Indeed, how would the fans feel? This might not normally be a consideration, but STAR TREK fans—perhaps because of the success of the letter campaigns—tend to feel that they have a vote on the matter. More than that, the fans feel a sense of *ownership* in STAR TREK, so any change at all in the show becomes a public issue—as was proved again, when the fans found out what was in the script for *Star Trek II*.)

And finally, how would the new producer feel about jumping in to this can of worms? It was clear that this could be a golden opportunity for disaster. Should he fail, he would be blamed for killing STAR TREK, and should he succeed—STAR TREK would still be known as Gene Roddenberry's baby.

In any case, you don't just put an ad in *Daily Variety* that says: "Wanted: Producer for one of Hollywood's most notoriously difficult properties. Must have the vision of Arthur C. Clarke, the poetry of Ray Bradbury, the cinematic skills of D. W. Griffith, the storytelling ability of Charles Dickens, the miserliness of Ebenezer Scrooge, the charisma of John F. Kennedy and the enlightenment of Ghandi."

Certainly whoever might answer such an ad would not win points for modesty either.

Harve Bennett had produced a number of successful television series, including "Rich Man, Poor Man"; "Mod Squad"; "The Six-Million-Dollar Man"; and "The Bionic Woman." Now he was on the Paramount lot to make the TV-movie, *A Woman Called Golda*. (It turned out to be Ingrid Bergman's last picture. It was Harve Bennett's great success that he was able to cast her.)

Despite the fact that he had never produced a feature film before, the studio executives asked him if he would also take on the production chores of *Star Trek II*. The reasoning here was that STAR TREK had begun as a TV series. Perhaps a STAR TREK movie would be best if it were made by someone who understood its television roots.

Translation: Harve Bennett had the one skill that Paramount was most looking for in a STAR TREK producer. He could tell a story *and* stay in budget.

Harve Bennett had not been a long-time STAR TREK fan, but he had seen many episodes (the lady he lived with was a devoted Trekkie, he'd been exposed despite himself) and was aware of the show's unique history—and he was intrigued by the challenge. "Besides—" he admits, "—if I didn't take the job, my kids would have divorced me." He accepted the job.

It turned out be a very *right* choice.

Harve Bennett proved to be exactly the kind of producer that a difficult show like STAR TREK needed—a man willing to take interesting risks. As a result, he was able to continually create novel solutions to impossible problems.

Perhaps the biggest problem of all was the Vulcan one.

Although every other member of the cast had indicated his or her willingness to return for another film, Leonard Nimoy had already made it known that he did not want to play the character of Mr. Spock again.

Of course, the rumors had already begun to circulate that this was a ploy—that Nimoy was holding out for a million dollars. ("No, he's already gotten a million dollars for the first picture. Now he's asking for three.") And there were fans who believed that Nimoy had turned against STAR TREK altogether.

This was not the case either. The truth was far more personal. Nimoy didn't want to get bored with Spock. He didn't see what else the character could do that he hadn't already done. Besides, there were other projects that he wanted to tackle, and he didn't see the challenge in doing Spock again.

But Harve Bennett wouldn't take no for an answer, and finally Nimoy agreed to appear in the picture—but asked if Spock could be written out of the series. Bennett said to him, "Why not end it once and for all. Let's kill the character off."

Nimoy was intrigued.

What actor could resist the challenge? It was something Spock hadn't done yet. Nimoy not only agreed to be in the picture, he also wrote the first version of Spock's farewell speech to Kirk.

One of the ways Harve Bennett prepared for the job was to screen as many episodes of the TV series as he could, sometimes two, three, or four episodes a day. He was looking for two things—the first was that almost indefinable *essence* of STAR TREK. What were the qualities of STAR TREK'S success that he most needed to capture in *Star Trek II*?

To Bennett, it wasn't the special effects. Although STAR TREK'S special effects had been quite sophisticated for television at the time, they were still quite limited. STAR TREK had never been able to visualize its stories on a large scale; the show had always had to tell stories that were small and immediate and centered on an individual's personal crisis. In fact, fifteen years of advanced technology applied to fantastic filmmaking had already begun to make STAR TREK'S best effects look quaint by comparison. No, it wasn't the effects.

Nor was it the stories. Even hardcore fans of the series admit that the show had more weak stories than effective ones. No, it had to be something else.

Bennett was quick to realize that the one element that held true in *all* STAR TREK episodes, weak as well as effective—including *Star Trek: The Motion Picture*—was the unique relationship of Kirk, Spock, and McCoy. This was the key to STAR TREK. *Star Trek II* would have to be about that relationship.

The second thing that Bennett looked for in all those episodes was a *catalyst*—something that would trigger a story idea. One of the episodes, "Space Seed," made a particular impression on him. Part of it was the theatricality of Ricardo Montalban's performance. Part of it was a line at the ending.

In this episode, Richardo Montalban played Khan Noonian Singh, the leader of a group of genetically superior human beings, refugees from the Eugenics Wars of the late twentieth century.* Kirk discovers their "sleeper ship," the *Botany Bay,* between the stars, boards it, and finds that the inhabitants are in hibernation for the duration of the journey. Once awakened, Khan and his tribe attempt to take over the *Enterprise.* They are thwarted (of course), but instead of punishing them, Kirk deposits them on Ceti Alpha V, a rugged but not inhospitable planet. At the end of the episode, Kirk wonders aloud, "I wonder what will happen twenty years from now?"

That line stuck in Harve Bennett's mind. That was the seed of the idea. Although, he had never intended to do a sequel, Kirk's final question was just too inviting to pass up. Bennett wrote an outline for the picture, had it approved by the executives at Paramount, and turned it over to Jack Sowards, a very capable scriptwriter—but not a STAR TREK writer.

When the script came back, Bennett recognized that it was not yet what it needed to be. It was close, but there were problems. (This is true of all first drafts; it is expected.) Gene Roddenberry, of course, gave Bennett a long memo listing those things that he felt needed to be fixed. William Shatner also contributed considerable input to the story, as did Walter Koenig. But Harve Bennett also wanted to get a different perspective as well. He secretly showed the script to Bjo Trimble, Theodore Strugeon, and one other STAR TREK writer.† (Later noted in the film program book as special consultants.)

In that first draft, the *Kobeyashi Maru* simulation did not occur as the opening sequence. Instead, it happened well into the story, and was shown to be only a simulation, so there was no surprise of discovery.

Also in that draft, Spock's death occurred in the middle of the story, as a result of the *Enterprise*'s first encounter with the Khan-commanded *Reliant*. Much of the rest of the story is about the relationship between Kirk and Saavik (then conceived as a male Vulcan). Kirk is shown to have an intense grief for Spock, dramatized by a montage of scenes from the original TV series

---

*Something to look forward to . . .

†Modesty forbids me from naming names.

and the first movie. Although Saavik never utters the line, "I am not Spock," that is what Kirk needs to realize before the picture is over.* There were a great many strong story elements in that first draft, but they were still too disorganized; the thrust of the story wasn't clear yet.

Eventually all of the memos, notes, and comments on the first draft made a document thicker than the original script itself. There was a lot of good advice there. It was at this point that Harve Bennett made one of the most important decisions in the production of *Star Trek II*. He recognized that the future of STAR TREK was in his hands. Right or wrong, it was time to do the job he was hired for—so he sequestered himself away with a typewriter and wrote the final draft of the script himself.

In one sense, this decision represents the entire production of *Star Trek II*. Follow:

Only a few of the behind-the-scenes people had worked on STAR TREK before. As experienced as they were as filmmakers, most of the production crew for this picture were aboard the *Enterprise* for only the first or second time. They could not draw upon their years of experience on how to make a STAR TREK movie, because they didn't have it.

What many of them did have, however, was years of experience on how to *love* STAR TREK. And that was what they had to bring to the project that was most important. It wouldn't be sufficient to just get the details right. That would be imitation—even self-parody. At some point, on some level, Harve Bennett recognized what really needed to happen here. He had to *recreate* the *spirit* of STAR TREK.

So—as important as all that good advice from all those well-intended advisors may have been—ultimately, the only place he had to look for the spirit of STAR TREK was inside his own feeling for the show. (And as Dorothy said in her return from Oz, "If it's not there, you never really had it to begin with.")

Star Trek II was budgeted at $10,000,000.

In keeping with a long-standing tradition, the *Enterprise* sets were rebuilt, new costumes, and props were designed, and new miniatures were made.

Part of this occurred because of vandalism and theft. The bridge set, for instance, had been an incredibly complicated machine to run. Now, when the soundstage was reopened, it was found that the monitors were gone from

---

*Leonard Nimoy, of course, once wrote a book with that title. In the introduction, he said, "I am not Spock, but if I could be Spock, I would be Spock." Nichelle Nichols once joked that she was writing a book too. It would be called, "I am not Spock *either*."

the console stations, and the Captain's chair had been stolen—or at worst, misplaced. Nobody could find it, and a new one had to be built. A four-foot $50,000 model of the *Enterprise* from *Star Trek I* had disappeared from its crate. And so on.

But this was also an opportunity to simplify the bridge set and other parts of STAR TREK that had gotten too complex for the more rigorous film schedule that Harve Bennett envisioned.

Indeed, in one of his earliest assessments of the challenge, Bennett recognized that he could obtain great economies by adapting television production methods to a motion picture scale. A TV show has to film at least eight or ten minutes a day. A movie is budgeted to a film at a slower pace, usually about three minutes a day. Bennett planned to schedule *Star Trek II* at about six minutes per day.

One of the greatest economies in the production of *Star Trek II* was achieved by minimizing the number of sets actually used. Most of the action of the picture takes place aboard the bridge of the *Enterprise* or the bridge of the *Reliant,* so only one bridge set was really needed. The *Enterprise* bridge was redressed by designer Joe Jennings to also represent the *Reliant.*

The sick bay of the *Enterprise* and the engine room sets already existed, so did the corridors. These three existing sets accounted for two-thirds of the movie. The only other sets that needed to be built were Kirk's apartment, the space station at Regula I, the Genesis cave, and the wreck of the *Botany Bay* (located in the garden spot of Ceti Alpha V).

Mike Minor, the film's other designer, detailed the specifics: "During the first picture, all the sets were buttoned up. The bridge was built as one solid structure. It could never be opened up to get a camera into it for a better angle. That camera was going to be inside a *real* ship and we were going to wander around the vessel with it in a very slow, stately manner. That situation forced the filmmakers into a corner. They had to use very dim lighting on the sets. They couldn't get the proper amount of lights onto them because everything was so cramped.

"Plus, they had to dim the lighting even further in order to record all the console screen designs. In the first movie, the screens were 8 mm. and 16 mm. film loops being projected onto monitors. The dull lighting gave the whole ship a rather gloomy, dull atmosphere. In this film, everything is lively, bright.

"We made the bridge set totally wild. All eleven sections of the bridge, as originally designed by Joe Jennings back in 1977 [for the TV series that didn't happen], were unbuttoned, disconnected. We could pull sections out like you pull out slices of a pie and get that camera in there on a twelve-foot crane. We could get that camera to swoop and dive and dolly and truck. There's a lot more action aboard the ship this time out. You race down the corridors. You have the image of the *Enterprise* whizzing right past you.

"Nick Meyer and Gayne Rescher plotted out ways to make that tiny bridge seem very impressive. The camerawork is very fluid. It's always doing something. The ship is a lot brighter looking, snappier.''

This time around the film loops were replaced by real video monitors, a custom-built system. The readouts from the first film were transferred onto videotape, and new material was synthesized at the Jet Propulsion Laboratory by graphics designer, Lee Cole.

Kirk's quarters were revamped to give them a more homey feel, including pieces of personal paraphernalia and equipment scattered around his quarters. The same set was later redressed to function as Spock's much more monastic room.

For the difficult job of director, Harve Bennett chose Nicholas Meyer, who had previously done *Time After Time* with Malcolm McDowell and Mary Steenbergen. (After *Star Trek II*, Meyer went on to direct the extraordinary TV-movie, *The Day After;* that film, depicting the nuclear devastation of Kansas City and neighboring Lawrence was the most viewed TV-movie in history.) Meyer was known to be young, talented, and efficient. He had also demonstrated not only a love for science fiction in his own work, but a healthy respect for it as well. Clearly, he was an appropriate choice.

About Meyer, Bennett says, "Nick is one of the most stimulating men I've ever met. He has the capacity for being 100 percent irritating and 100 percent flexible at the same time. It's quite a gift. He is so filled with ideas that it's like attaching yourself to a comet. . . . he's a rocket and it's wonderful.''

Meyer says this about working on *Star Trek II:* "What I wanted to do was take the STAR TREK characters very seriously. The phrase I used a lot was 'make it real.' I wanted these familiar characters to come across as *real* people. I wanted them to do *real* things, even if they were really mundane things. I started out by saying 'Why don't we ever see Kirk read a book?' All these people seem so disembodied out there in space. Let's give them some real presence.

"I've never had any desire to do a film about spaceships. I did have the desire to make a movie about the people aboard them, however.''

Meyer also says, "What struck me as engaging about the original series is that it wasn't really a science fiction show. It was a show about certain moral and ethical dilemmas that were placed before our STAR TREK characters. Ques-

Bjo Trimble, William Shatner, and David Gerrold on the set of
Star Trek: The Motion Picture

The V'GER set

Spock arrives aboard the *Enterprise*

Spock prepares for the final test of *Kolinahr*

Ricardo Montalban in "Space Seed"

Kirk's apartment in San Francisco

Spock's solution to the *Kobeyashi Maru* test

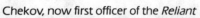

Chekov, now first officer of the *Reliant*

Khan Noonian Singh

Carol and David Marcus

"Remember…"

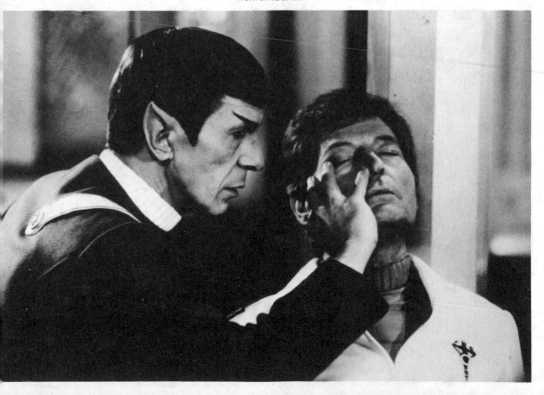

The *Enterprise*'s new engine room

Saavik with her mentor, Spock

tions concerning life, death, meaning, honor, and friendship were brought up in every episode. This movie tries to echo that concept, with greater sophistication and depth.''

The special effects for *Star Trek II* were assigned to Industrial Light and Magic. ILM came into being for *Star Wars*. Since then, the company has not only established the new standards for motion picture special effects, they have raised the standards every year. Even more impressive (by Hollywood standards), they deliver their work consistently on time and within one percent of the estimated budget.

Production on *Star Trek II* officially began on Monday, November 9, 1981.

Security was extraordinarily tight.

All production personnel were required to wear identification badges—with photographs. No visitors were allowed on the set, and the copies of the script were to be treated like a top secret document.

So, of course, the word got out.

As soon as one fan knew, they *all* seemed to know.

Paramount was planning to kill Spock!

The word spread through the STAR TREK rumor mill at warp speed. (The speed of light just wasn't fast enough for this communication.)

The fans were horrified. Aghast. Angry. Upset. Unbelieving.

They were everything but speechless.

Of course, a "Save Spock" letter campaign was begun immediately.

After all, a letter campaign had saved the series for a third season. A letter campaign had convinced President Ford to name the prototype space shuttle the *Enterprise*. A letter campaign had helped convince Paramount to bring back STAR TREK. Of course, a letter campaign would save Spock's life. Or so the reasoning went.

At one point, a committee of concerned fans even took out an ad in *Daily Variety*, Hollywood's trade paper, urging Paramount to save the life of their favorite Vulcan. Because—said the ad—if they didn't, STAR TREK fans would boycott the picture and the studio would lose about $28,000,000.*

---

*It isn't clear how this committee of concerned fans arrived at this figure. Perhaps they assumed that 5,600,000 people would not see the film at all, or that 1,120,000 hard-core STAR TREK fans would each skip seeing the film five times—or some other formula perhaps computed by Klingon math. The only evidence of an actual boycott I ever saw was a lady who went to see *Star Trek II* three times in the first week of release, each time getting up and leaving the theatre at the moment Spock gets up and leaves the bridge for his appointment with destiny in the engine room. This particular method of boycott still earned Paramount Pictures their share of three full admissions. You figure it out—who was she punishing?

Another group of fans declared their intention to wait in line for the *second* screening of the movie—and if exiting theatre-goers told them that Spock did indeed die in this film, they would tear up their tickets in protest and loudly quit the line.

All sorts of bizarre rumors and speculations began to circulate. One of the best had it that Paramount was chickening out. They had filmed two separate endings to the movie, one in which Spock lives and another in which he dies, and would only decide which would be the real ending after sneak-previewing both versions. Another story had it that the whole thing was just a publicity stunt to generate interest—and box-office revenue—for the movie.

Because they hadn't seen the movie yet, and couldn't know what was planned, all the fans had to operate on was rumor and misinformation. Many of them wanted someone to blame. Some of them blamed Nimoy. Others blamed Harve Bennett. Still others said it was Roddenberry's fault. And when in doubt, the studio itself was always a convenient villain. (NBC was off the hook this time around.)

Understand. For ten years, the fans had had to generate STAR TREK by themselves. For ten years, they'd been the keepers of the dream. Consequently, they felt a deep sense of connection to the series—even a sense of ownership. For Paramount to tamper with the substance of their dreams was tantamount to betrayal! It was a heresy.

Ultimately, the uproar reached such a point that Paramount Pictures, Leonard Nimoy, Gene Roddenberry, and Harve Bennett all felt it necessary to issue statements explaining their respective positions. But without giving away any plot points either.

It was a difficult time for all.

But making STAR TREK had *always* been as easy as making love in a fishbowl, so by now the studio had learned to live with the attention of the fans. It was clearly a sign of their enthusiasm for the show. The time to worry would be when the fans *stopped* writing letters. . . .

On the subject of Spock's death, Nimoy has said (in an exclusive interview in *Starlog* magazine): "The audience, who we dearly love and need, must understand what their role and function is as well. And [it's not] to create an aura of censorship and say such and such must never happen in STAR TREK. . . . I almost did it myself and learned a very big lesson. During the first season, the show had been on the air only a short time, Dorothy Fontana came to me and said, 'I have an idea for a love story for Spock.' How can you do that? That's a terrible mistake! I don't see it, I'm playing this very cold distant reserved character and just beginning to get a real handle on that. Here comes a writer saying to me we want him to fall in love. I don't . think it'll work to deny so quickly what we've stated about the character. She wrote a lovely thing called 'This Side of Paradise.' Lovely, and I thought she pulled it off and it worked very well. And what it did was enhance the character because it showed us what Spock suppresses—terribly important. Now, with that in mind, I say to myself, I will never again say, 'This won't work in advance about a character.'

"You've got to try and experiment with it. And maybe what you've been afraid of, what you want to deny as a possibility, is really a tremendous breakthrough: an opening of a whole new process of thinking, a whole new way of looking at things, and certainly if one wants to consider oneself an artist involved in an art form, then you have to be open to those possibilities."

When the time came to actually play Spock's death scene, Nimoy began to experience terrible tension: "I really came within a hair's breadth of walking off the lot rather than playing the scene. The day we were going to shoot it, I was very edgy about it and scared of it—scared of playing it, almost looking for an excuse not to. . . . It was a very tense time. And I *still* feel that way, seeing it.

"There's a moment, a very interesting moment to me in terms of audience reaction, when you see Spock on the floor through the glass in the distance and Kirk at the glass saying, 'Spock! Spock!' and cut back to see Spock rising. And after hearing McCoy say he's already dead, now you see him rise. I'm sure you start to wonder if maybe he's going to be okay.

"Then, when he gets up and straightens his jacket, I've heard people laugh. I've also heard some sharp intakes of breath. And there are two very interesting things happening on that straightening of the jacket, it's a pretty strange and wonderful moment. I think there are some in the audience who think that he's getting himself together again and is going to be okay, that we'll have some strange magical kind of explanation as to how he survived this thing. And then there are others in the audience who are very moved by it because they see it as Spock kind of recovering his dignity for his last moments with his superior officer. It's a very moving thing."

Nimoy adds, "The way it's perceived by an individual in the audience depends on whether or not the individual is willing to accept the fact that Spock has died. There are people who are not going to accept it. It has been denied by many. It's the strangest thing. I had an experience where I was coming back from the east coast and I went to the airline to check in and the lady behind the counter said, 'Mr. Nimoy, did you die in the movie?' I said, 'You're going to have to see the picture.' She said, 'I did.' Now *there's* a case of denial. Absolute denial. I mean, she does not want to come to grips

with the fact that Spock is dead. Even temporarily dead. She's just so un-
comfortable with the idea. Loved the picture, but she's dealing with it in her
own way. And the point is that everybody will do just exactly that.''

Indeed, there's a whole school of interpretation based on the fact that it is
Nimoy who does the final narration, not Shatner. "It could be Spock's final
good-bye," says Nimoy. "Or it could be Spock on the other side speaking
to us. And the words, as I spoke them, for me took on a new and possibly
very interesting connotation, when he [Spock] said, '. . . to boldly go where
no man has gone before.' He could be talking about some other kind of
life. . . .''

The music for *Star Trek II* was written by a young composer named James
Horner, who had previously scored *Wolfen* and *Battle Beyond the Stars*.

Horner knew the film needed a powerful score. In fact, director Nicholas
Meyer had already told him that he wanted to give the film a Captain Horatio
Hornblower mood. (Where have we heard that before?)

Although Horner was instructed not to use any of the Goldsmith score
from *Star Trek I,* he was free to use the STAR TREK theme from the TV series.
About that, Horner has said, "I didn't think there would be any place for it
in the film. I said I'd think about it. I worked out a way to use the STAR TREK
fanfare, which I used about four or five times, and it works very well. I
always had wanted to use that fanfare. Unlike the first film, I wanted right
from the start, from where the curtain first opened to grip the audience, to
tell them that they were going to see STAR TREK. And there are only two
things that can do that. Either the *Enterprise* or the fanfare. The fanfare draws
you in immediately.''

Horner was working under unusual conditions with the music. Usually a
composer has twelve to fourteen weeks on a major picture. On *Star Trek II*,
Horner had only four and a half. It was a very rushed schedule throughout.
(In fact, director Nicholas Meyer was shooting the film during the day and
editing at night.) Horner worked twelve to fourteen hours a day, doing the
orchestrations. He composed separate themes for Kirk and the *Enterprise,*
and then intertwined the two themes throughout the film. There was also a
strange ethereal theme for Spock, which is also heard when the *Enterprise*
leaves drydock.

To the fans, the most controversial part of the score for *Star Trek II* was
the use of "Amazing Grace" at Spock's funeral. Horner had begged Harve
Bennett, "Please don't make me use 'Amazing Grace.' '' But Harve Bennett was firm on this point.

Bennett had a very real personal reason for the inclusion of the music—

and Scotty's bagpipes: "I lost a very dear friend who was the Counsel General of Great Britain here in L.A. He was a remarkable man who, among his achievements, had been one of the few Royal Air Force pilots in World War II.

"A memorial service, attended by a thousand people, was held at St. James Cathedral. It was a High Episcopal service with a choir and distinguished speakers. And at the end of the service, a lone bagpiper walked down the aisle to the nave, turned and played 'Amazing Grace'—and seven hundred people wept." Bennett adds, "I have never recovered from that.

"Afterward, I walked back and asked, 'Is this something he requested?' And his wife said, 'Oh no, this is standard burial procedure, if you wish it, in the entire United Kingdom.' So I just extrapolated that and since that time I've heard of hundreds of times where bagpipes played 'Amazing Grace.' It's a traditional Scot's theme.

"So here I am writing this funeral, and I wondered, how do I get this into *Star Trek II*? How do I get the same experience shared with other people? And the answer is standing right there and his name is Montgomery Scott! And when everyone says, 'Well, a Vulcan wouldn't have that!' I just say, 'It's not Vulcan! It's Scotty's tribute to his friend.' That's what it is, and it comes down through five centuries from the Scottish army to its descendants."

By the time Horner came aboard, the scene had already been shot and he had to match it. "Then I had the additional problem: Would I continue the bagpipe music outside the ship or would I switch to orchestral music? My feeling was to do something ethereal." Horner still feels the bagpipes were a mistake—and many STAR TREK fans seem to agree with him on that point. Other STAR TREK fans, however, like the bagpipes a lot.

During most of its production, *Star Trek II* was subtitled *The Vengeance of Khan*—but just a few short weeks before its release, the studio hastily changed the name to *The Wrath of Khan*. What happened was that Lucasfilm had expressed some concern about conflict with the title of their own upcoming film, *Revenge of the Jedi*. (The message of concern may have been delivered by Jedi lawyers with light-sabers. However, no film entitled *Revenge of the Jedi* was ever released, and so the whole point was moot.)

Star Trek II: The Wrath of Khan was released to the theatres in June 1982. It was an instant hit. It was the summer's big success story.

The picture is fast-paced, clever, and crisp; clearly a STAR TREK episode, but one that has been scaled up to motion picture dimensions. The story is a classic STAR TREK confrontation, but with a very real personal involvement for James T. Kirk. Best of all, the main characters are shown in greater depth than We've ever seen them before—courageous and brave, yet refreshingly honest and vulnerable too. And the villain? Khan Noonian Singh has always been one of the most formidable. Here, he is obsessed to the point of insanity; his passion for vengeance is even more important than his own life.

Star Trek II is a razzle-dazzle adventure that careens across the galaxy, like a pinball bouncing from plot-twist to plot-twist to reversal to surprise. The picture has enough clever twists and turns to fill three ordinary STAR TREK episodes.

This was the movie the fans had been waiting for.

Unlike the first picture, which had gotten so big it had become ponderous, this film was light on its feet.

It was as big and gaudy as a Christmas tree, chock full of pretty lights and flashing gimcracks. It had all kinds of delicious technical readouts and intriguingly baroque hardware. It was tacky and overpainted and totally wonderful.

It was STAR TREK at its best—with all of its virtues (and all of its flaws as well, but who cares?) all rolled up into one great big Christmas present, delivered six months early.

The movie was fun. But it also touched the heart.

Clearly, it was Captain Kirk's picture—and William Shatner had never been better as Kirk. Kirk had always been a man grappling with his own mortality. In this script, he is allowed to finally come to grips with himself. Shatner brought wisdom and self-awareness to the role, and a welcome dimension of maturity.

Likewise, the script gave Leonard Nimoy ample opportunity to show his range as a performer. Spock has become sensitive here to an extraordinary degree. No longer disdainful of human beings, Spock has become *understanding*. This is an incredible shift in his character from where he was fifteen years ago, when he seemed perpetually puzzled (and annoyed) by humanity's illogical emotions. Spock is clearly operating at an advanced state of consciousness in this picture. He is still calm, cool, and rational—yet he has added to that a capacity to accept the emotional quality of life. It's a very *subtle* thing—but nowhere in this script does he derogate human emotions as he used to. Instead, he actually admits to friendship—a feeling of affection. (Is this a result of his encounter with V'GER and the transformation he experienced? No indication is given in the script. Perhaps it's implied. If there's a connection, we have to assume it. The fact is, this picture pretty much *ignores* the existence of *Star Trek I*. What else could they do?)

DeForest Kelley has always been the best damn galactic quack this side of the Clouds of Magellan. Once again, De Kelley brought his own warmth, humor, and grace to the role of Dr. McCoy. Indeed, he gets off several of the best lines in the picture.

Jimmy Doohan had had a slight heart attack a year before the production of the picture, a fact referred to in an oblique line when Kirk first inspects the *Enterprise* engine room. Scotty admits, "I had a wee bout, but Dr. McCoy pulled me through." To Kirk's questioning glance, McCoy explains, "Shore leave." But he looks good here, and it's great to see Scotty back among his favorite toys—the engines of the *Enterprise*. His character also is given the opportunity to demonstrate an increased sensitivity to the people around him, and it wears well.

If any of the regular characters are slighted, it's Uhura and Sulu. They're here—but they don't really have much to do. Uhura is still opening hailing frequencies and Sulu is still manning the helm. It's a disappointment that we don't get to see more of them, because both Nichelle Nichols and George Takei look terrific.

When the picture opens, Mr. Chekov is missing from the bridge of the *Enterprise*. It turns out that he is now First Officer on the *Reliant*. It's a suitable promotion for the character. (And long overdue.) Chekov gets to have a lot of fun in this picture, and it's good to see Walter Koenig stretch himself in the role. Walter Koenig turns in his usual enthusiastic performance.*

And finally, Ricardo Montalban, as Khan, is nothing less than superb. He brings a dynamic theatrical quality to Khan that provides just the right touch of flowery nastiness. All that's missing is a mustache for him to twirl. Khan's obsession with vengeance against Kirk is the primary motivating force of the picture.

Also worth noticing—in fact, damned hard to ignore—are the strong performances of Kirstie Alley as Mr. (yes, *Mr.*) Saavik, half Vulcan, half Romulan; Merritt Butrick as David Marcus, Kirk's son (no mention of a marriage here, by the way), a perfect bastard—until he learns better; Bibi Besch as his mother, Dr. Carol Marcus (a *smooth* lady!); and Paul Winfield as Captain Terrell. In fact, all of the performances in this picture display that crisp military quality that we've come to expect from STAR TREK. Director Nicholas Meyer brings out the best in his people.

The picture is also true to another grand old STAR TREK tradition.

It's view of the workings of the universe is only slightly more advanced

---

*Ever notice how when someone has to be put in the agonizer or attacked by a creature or frightened out of his wits, it's always Chekov? Maybe it's because he has the best scream in the business since Fay Wray.

than the flat-Earth theory. It is about as scientifically accurate as the 1803 edition of the Farmer's Almanac. Those who go to a science fiction movie to demonstrate how much more they know about science than the filmmakers can have a field day with *Star Trek II*.

For example: the battles between the *Enterprise* and the *Reliant*.

The two ships are shown lumbering around each other like arthritic dinosaurs—as if they were World War I battleships cruising for the best firing position. In space, the difference in respective velocities would make the approaches pictured here almost impossible. What is much more probable is that the two ships—unless they are specifically matching *parallel* vectors— would zip by each other so fast that each would be out of visual range of the other even before the viewscreen could be focused. The best view either could have of the other would be as a radar(?) blip.

Furthermore, the weapons capabilities of both the ships (as previously established in the STAR TREK universe) make such approaches unnecessary. What's the range of a high-powered phaser bank? What's the range of a photon torpedo? Why are such close approaches necessary here?

Probably because they look good on the movie screen.

STAR TREK has a history of sacrificing scientific accuracy in favor of a startling image or a good plot point. In this picture, the payoff is the scene where the *Reliant*'s phasers carve great gaping holes into the engine decks of the *Enterprise*. It is a gut-wrenching image. It is the most shattering vision we have ever had of the mortality of the *Enterprise* itself.

And that's what this film is really about: mortality.

It's a parable about the way we approach living and the way we approach dying. The picture begins with the *Kobeyashi Maru* simulation, a test of character—how does a command officer deal with a life or death situation? This sets the theme for everything that follows.

James T. Kirk never truly confronted the *Kobeyashi Maru* simulation. (He cheated it.) This picture is about James T. Kirk finally completing his own *Kobeyashi Maru* test. He says it himself: "I've never really faced death before. I've always cheated it." This is the one time he doesn't get to cheat.

The picture is also about Spock's *Kobeyashi Maru* test. As he is dying in the *Enterprise* engine room, Spock says to Kirk, "I never took the *Kobeyashi Maru* test. How would you judge my solution?" Spock's solution is both logical *and* emotional. One should die so that many can survive.

Spock dies to save the *Enterprise*. It's not clear exactly what he's doing—it looks like he's unscrewing the top of a gigantic thermos bottle, and then mixing the matter and anti-matter with his bare hands—but it's clearly dangerous.

Spock's death is not a terrible moment. It is actually a joyous one. In the face of the worst possible circumstance, Kirk, Spock, and McCoy are finally able to acknowledge the depth of their affection for each other.

The ending of *Star Trek II* is an affirmation. It is a completion. And as such, it is a celebration—not of death, but of the quality that we as individuals can bring to life.

It is one of the proudest moments in STAR TREK.*

Star Trek III: The Search for Spock is probably the most difficult of all the STAR TREK movies to assess—because it comprises the very best of STAR TREK'S virtues and the very worst of its weaknesses. This can't help but produce a schizophrenic reaction in the viewer. It's quite possible to sit through *Star Trek III* and have a wonderful time, enjoying all of its best moments— and yet still come out of the theatre somehow dissatisfied with the tale it has told.

The story is simple. It picks up exactly where *Star Trek II* leaves off. Spock has died and his body has been left on the Genesis planet. The *Enterprise* is heading back to Earth. Shortly before docking, security reports an intruder in Spock's cabin. Kirk investigates and finds a deeply disturbed McCoy. "Take me home," he tells Kirk.

"We are home," Kirk replies.

The docking scene that follows is one of the most moving sequences in the picture. The great hull of the *Enterprise* has been scarred and ripped by the weapons of the *Reliant*. As she slides majestically into place, we see the stunned reactions of the men and women in a nearby observation lounge— including former *Enterprise* crewperson, Janice Rand (in a surprise cameo). The scene strikes chords—it is the sailors watching the return to port of a proud battlecruiser, damaged but unbowed after a great battle with an uncompromising enemy.

It is here that we discover that the *Enterprise* will not be refitted. The ship is twenty years old. She will be decommissioned and her crew will be assigned to new duty stations. Scotty, for instance, is immediately reassigned

---

*After Spock's casket is ejected into space, we see it nestled among the green of the Edenlike world created by the Genesis Project. We are left with the hint, the suggestion, that someday Kirk will return here, and someday, perhaps—just maybe, we're not saying for certain, of course, but we're leaving the possibility open, it could happen—that Spock could be brought back to life.

The theory among STAR TREK fans was that Spock would return, glowing in the dark, somewhat like Obi-Wan Kenobi.

Apparently in the movies, death is only a phase you pass through on your way to enlightenment. . . .

as Captain of Engineering for the new pride of Starfleet, the *Excelsior,* the first ship with trans-warp drive. (Whatever that is.)

Ambassador Sarek, Spock's father, comes to visit Kirk in his apartment overlooking San Francisco. He accuses Kirk of betraying Spock, of not bringing him home to Vulcan. Kirk is confused, he doesn't understand. Sarek mind-melds with Kirk and discovers that Kirk is not carrying Spock's *katra*—Spock's immortal soul. In playing back the ship's log of Spock's final moments, they discover Spock's last words to McCoy, "Remember. . . ." They see the mind-meld touch. McCoy is carrying Spock's identity. Now, we understand McCoy's erratic behavior.

But Starfleet will not release a ship to James T. Kirk. The galaxy is in an uproar over the military possibilities of the Genesis device and Kirk is advised to forget about returning Spock's soul to Vulcan.

Kirk is left with only one option: (Any long time STAR TREK fan could see it coming, of course) He reunites his key officers, busts McCoy out of the twenty-third-century equivalent of Bedlam, steals the *Enterprise* and heads for the Genesis planet to pick up Spock's body. (Just why he has to collect Spock's body as well is not actually explained, but it works out to be necessary to the ultimate resolution, so. . . .)

The brand-new *Excelsior* attempts to follow, but Scotty has stolen her spark plugs. Her engines grind uselessly, but nothing happens. The ship does not achieve trans-warp speed, and the *Enterprise* escapes.

Meanwhile . . .

A Klingon Bird-of-Prey scoutship has obtained a copy of Kirk's report on the Genesis device. Her commander, a scummy-looking nasty whose only soft spot is for a dog-thing with four extra sets of incisors, orders his craft to investigate the new planet.

The planet is already being explored by the Federation ship *Grissom.* (A very good name for a spaceship.) Kirk's son, David Marcus, and Mr. Saavik, are down on the surface of the planet investigating a peculiar life form reading. They discover Spock's casket—but it is *empty*.

As they continue to explore, it starts to snow. The planet is very unstable. They find a set of footprints and follow them to—a very young male Vulcan child, shivering in the cold. They wrap the boy in Spock's robe (which they just happen to be carrying)—but before they can beam back up to the *Grissom* that ship is destroyed by the Klingon Bird-of-Prey.

By the time the *Enterprise* arrives, Saavik, Marcus, and Spock-boy have been captured by a Klingon scouting party. It is here that we discover that David Marcus has made a fatal mistake with Genesis. The planet is in the process of shuddering itself to destruction. In a way that is never precisely explained, the planet is aging rapidly—and so is the Vulcan child. He and the planet are somehow locked together.

The *Enterprise* and the Bird-of-Prey fight a brief but devastating space battle. The *Enterprise,* still carrying the wounds from her last battle, is unable to destroy the Klingon scout. The Klingon Captain threatens to kill his hostages unless Kirk surrenders. He orders one of the hostages killed just to prove he means business. David Marcus attacks his Klingon guard—and is killed. Kirk is so grief-stricken, he collapses to the floor in tears. He agrees to the surrender, and tells the Klingon to beam his boarding party over.

And then, he, Scotty, and Chekov trigger the *Enterprise's* self-destruct command and beam down to the planet. The Klingon crew beam over to the *Enterprise* and are destroyed *when the ship disintegrates in a ball of orange flame.*

Kirk, McCoy, Sulu, Chekov, and Scotty, silently watch the fireball streak across the sky of the Genesis planet. The sense of loss is profound. That ship was *home.* It was more than that—it was their whole purpose for being. It was the vehicle for their mission. (The scene brings screams of horror in the theatre.) Make no mistake, this is the end of an era.

As Kirk wonders what he has done, McCoy puts the moment in perspective. "Once again, you've turned defeat into a fighting chance for life."

Quickly, they meet up with Saavik and Spock—who is now just the right age. But he is still mindless.

The Klingon Captain is willing to beam up all of the survivors on the surface of the planet—except Spock. As the planet shudders itself to its final destruction, Kirk and the Captain are engaged in a final hand-to-hand combat. At the last moment, the Klingon Captain ends up hanging by his fingernails from a ledge. Kirk offers him a hand—instead, he grabs Kirk's leg and tries to pull him off the ledge too. Kirk says, "I've had enough of you," and kicks the Klingon off.

Kirk picks up the Klingon communicator and imitating the Klingon command, orders himself and Spock beamed up. Of course, he captures the Klingon Bird-of-Prey and they head toward the planet Vulcan where Spock's soul (in McCoy's head) can be reunited with Spock's new (but still mindless) body.

The picture ends with dawn on Vulcan. A resurrected Spock looks curiously at Admiral James T. Kirk and says, "I know you—"

It is his first step on the long road back.

Despite its action and its fast pace, the movie is essentially a picture of character. The characters have always been STAR TREK'S greatest strength. To succeed as a TV series, the show *had* to develop its heroes as strong believable individuals that the viewer would enjoy spending an hour with every week, no matter what story is told. STAR TREK's success ever since has equally been a matter of its characters triumphing over some very weak science and some very silly stories. *Star Trek III* continues this tradition. Once again, it is the conviction of its characters—especially Kirk—that carries us through some very hard-to-believe scientific doubletalk.

To be sure, the characters are at their very best in *Star Trek III*. Two of the best sequences in the film belong to Sulu ("Don't call me Tiny,") and Uhura ("This is adventure!") as they help Kirk rescue McCoy. This is the first time we've really seen these two acting as members of the team in a STAR TREK movie. It's too bad we didn't get to see this kind of strength from these characters before. They're terrific.

McCoy, of course, is his usual growly, good-natured self; but his best scene is the quiet moment he spends with the mindless body of Spock, in which he privately acknowledges his own affection for his Vulcan friend. "I miss you," he admits. We see that he too cares deeply for Spock.

And finally, this time around, we get to see deeper into Kirk's feelings than ever before. We get to see the depth of his love for Spock, for his ship, and for his son—as well as the grief he feels for all three. This picture adds significant depth to a character who has previously been seen to be rather stiff-necked and singularly obsessed with commanding the *Enterprise*.

In this picture, the *Enterprise* is characterized as a battered, barely working, twenty-year-old hulk, destined to be scrapped. (This is an odd position for *Starfleet* to take, by the way. In both *Star Trek I* and *Star Trek II*, we see that the ship has been rebuilt with the very latest technology; *Star Trek II* even begins with the training of a new crew for the ship. Starfleet's decision to scrap the *Enterprise* seems a little . . . capricious considered in this context.)

But Admiral James Tiberius Kirk loves this ship—(we all do, it's been part of our lives for the better part of two decades)—and it's been established in the past two pictures that he will do almost anything to regain control of her. In this story, he finally has to let go. It is a *profound* moment. He'd rather see his ship destroyed in battle than let her be ignominiously scrapped. This decision to destroy the *Enterprise* rather than surrender is consistent with what has been established as Starfleet procedure—but on a personal level, it may also be seen as a spiritual breakthrough for the man, a transformation as profound as that experienced by Spock in the heart-liver-bowels of V'GER.

In this story, James T. Kirk finally lets go of the starship *Enterprise*. It must be the hardest decision of his life. Yet, it's clear that Kirk knows where his duty is. Even in death, the *Enterprise* still serves the Federation.

But somehow, the moment is not a proud one.

The grief and horror of the ship's destruction are not quite mitigated by the circumstances. And all of us have too much history with the *Enterprise,* too many fond associations with that great vessel, to take her death with anything but dismay. The destruction of the *Enterprise* casts a pall over the picture that even the resurrection of Spock cannot completely dissipate.

Indeed, the picture almost seems to suggest that Kirk will sacrifice *anything* to save Spock—even his ship and his son.*

Finally, when the lights come back up again, there is the disquieting feeling that too many questions have been left unanswered. *Star Trek III* seems to have left the STAR TREK universe in dreadful disarray.

Witness:

Kirk's son has been killed—seemingly without purpose, so any continuity he might have represented for future stories has now been lost.

Spock is alive again, but still not quite his former self.

Kirk has kept his debt to his friend, but at the cost of his good-standing in Starfleet.

The crew of the *Enterprise* have become co-conspirators in Kirk's crime— and even if not, there are more than a few suggestions that Starfleet wants to break up this team once and for all.

And finally, the *Enterprise* has been destroyed.

Always before, the thrust has been that, "these are the voyages of the starship *Enterprise*. . . ." but *Star Trek III* is the *last* voyage of the *Enterprise*. It is a most *atypical* STAR TREK episode. It is the only one that is not specifically a mission of the *Enterprise*—it is about Kirk and Spock.

This is due to the fact that this picture, more than any of the others, had to be written to accommodate a unique situation.

Throughout the production of *Star Trek II,* it was assumed that this would be Leonard Nimoy's last outing as Spock. Indeed, the whole point of Spock's death was to have the character exit the series once and for all.

At some point in the production, however, Nimoy realized he didn't want to leave STAR TREK. He was having too much fun. (A usually reliable witness says, "You should have seen the look on Harve Bennett's face at the wrap party, when Leonard announced, 'I'm looking forward to *Star Trek III*.' ")

---

*Lord knows what the K/S ladies will make of that. . . .

Suddenly, a character who had been written *out* of the series now had to be written back in.

Spock was dead—well, almost. After Nicholas Meyer had turned in his final cut of *Star Trek II,* Paramount Pictures added two shots showing Spock's coffin nestled in the greenery of the Genesis planet to specifically suggest that maybe Spock didn't have to be *permanently* dead. The intent was to mitigate the fans' reactions. (Many critics, however, felt that those two shots actually weakened the picture.)

In any case, the primary problem for *Star Trek III* had to be the resurrection of Spock.

Harve Bennett realized very early that if Leonard Nimoy wanted to remain an active part of the series, then the only story he could tell would be about that resurrection.

Unfortunately, science fiction is the most disciplined form of the literature of the fantastic. Despite the genre's ability to stretch, it's still hard to make resurrection scientifically plausible. (Some religious leaders have trouble with the concept too; the problem isn't limited to science fiction.)

Whatever manner of resurrection Harve Bennett chose for Spock, the script was still going to require some very fancy tap-dancing at the typewriter.

To give him credit, he resisted the obvious. Spock did not return with a glittery blue glow matted in around him. The solution that Harve Bennett came up with is consistent with the brand of science practiced in the STAR TREK universe. (It doesn't match the brand of science practiced in this universe, however. One SF writer remarked after seeing the film, "The theological implications alone are staggering.")

But there's a second, more subtle, factor that shaped the scripts of *Star Trek II* and *Star Trek III.* Both William Shatner and Leonard Nimoy have become actors with *clout.*

Clout is a Hollywood term. It means the performer not only gets paid large amounts of money, he also is given a variety of perks and privileges to keep him happy. One of the most valuable of all perks is script approval. Another is a guaranteed number of lines and scenes in the picture.

An actor gets clout by becoming a star, by being an important part of the box-office success of a movie. Leonard Nimoy and William Shatner are both stars.

It is clear that Leonard Nimoy's "clout" was an important factor in his winning the directorial responsibilities of *Star Trek III.* When the decision was first announced, it startled many long-time STAR TREK watchers, and there was some concern that it might have been a risky choice. After all, Leonard

Nimoy had never directed a movie before and this was a very complex multimillion dollar project.

But there were two factors in his favor. No one else has appeared in more episodes of STAR TREK—and only one other actor has spent more time on the set of STAR TREK, William Shatner. The other factor in Leonard Nimoy's favor was that Harve Bennett would be there to backstop him. On *Star Trek II*, Harve Bennett was only able to be on the set a limited amount of time because of his other obligations at the time (*A Woman Called Golda.*) On *Star Trek III*, Bennett was able to be on the set continually.

One STAR TREK cast member privately admitted that he feared there would be terrible tensions on the set with Leonard as director, but when production actually started, it turned out to be the most pleasant picture of the three to make. Nimoy was remarkably sensitive to the feelings of the other actors. In one scene (ultimately dropped from the final cut), Nimoy felt that a particular gesture by one of the cast members was "corny"—but rather than embarrass the person by saying so in front of the entire cast and crew, he took the individual aside for a private conference. Little things like that make a considerable difference in a director's rapport with his cast—and ultimately their performances. The performances in *Star Trek III* are generally strong and competent; it is an auspicious debut for Leonard Nimoy as a director.

The performances are probably the greatest strength of the picture. STAR TREK has always depended on its cast to carry it over story weaknesses, and *Star Trek III* rightfully puts its emphasis on the crew of the *Enterprise* and their relationships.

But this also represents a subtle shift in the concept of the show.

Some background here:

In the early days of STAR TREK, Gene Roddenberry was the *boss*—and STAR TREK was about the voyages of the *Enterprise*. When STAR TREK was simply a TV series—one that was *struggling* for survival—it wasn't about Kirk and Spock; it was about a spaceship and its crew. If necessary, members of that crew could be *and were* written out and new members written in to accommodate the circumstances of network television. Yeoman Janice Rand was only on the first season of STAR TREK. She disappeared without explanation before the second season began. Crewman Kevin Riley came and went. Ensign Chekov joined the show in the second season only as a semi-regular character, but quickly became a regular cast member.

And of course, the first Captain of the *Enterprise* was Captain Pike. And the first Officer was Number One—played by Majel Barrett. (That pilot, "The Cage," later became the core of the two-part episode, "The Menagerie.")

In those early days, there was always an awareness that actors could be shifted in and out of the series as needed. Soap operas frequently change the actors playing lead characters. There have been five Doctors Who. The "Buck Rogers" series seemed to change characters and format the beginning of every season. "Bewitched" went through two Darrins—and there have been three James Bonds. If necessary, STAR TREK could have brought in another Captain or another Vulcan Science Officer or another doctor—as a matter of fact, the first doctor on board the good ship *Enterprise* was played by John Hoyt, the second doctor was played by Paul Fix. Finally Gene Roddenberry selected DeForest Kelley to complete the ensemble of characters he was trying to develop.

STAR TREK fans have always been sensitive to this situation. When the production of *Star Trek I* was announced—and again when the production of *Star Trek II* was announced—and still again when the production of *Star Trek III* was announced (and probably for all future STAR TREKS until the end of time) —the first question that they asked was, "Will *all* the cast members be returning?"

Indeed, there was considerable dismay among many of the fans to discover that Kirstie Alley would not be returning as the stoic Mr. Saavik; she was a very strong presence in *Star Trek II*—so much so that her successor in the role, Robin Curtis, has to compete (not always successfully) with the memory of that presence. The same problem of comparision would probably beset any actor who tried to replace one of STAR TREK's long-time regulars— and to a much greater degree.

As the actors in STAR TREK have become better and better known—especially through the movies—they have become more and more important to the success of the show. The fans have developed very strong feelings about the cast.

On TV, the star of STAR TREK was the *Enterprise*.

In the movies, it has developed that the stars of STAR TREK are William Shatner and Leonard Nimoy.

Here are two very good, very important actors, both of whom are integral parts of the success of the series—and both of whom want scripts that will allow them to show off their strengths as performers.

There's no other story to tell except the one about the relationship between their characters.

As a result—we can see it starting to happen in *Star Trek II,* but it is very obvious in *Star Trek III*—the mission of the *Enterprise* has been diminished in favor of stories about Kirk and Spock.

This is not necessarily a bad thing. The relationship between Kirk and

Spock has always demonstrated a considerable amount of tension based on unspoken affection, and the script for *Star Trek III* directly addresses this "problem" in their relationship. This movie is one more opportunity for both Kirk and Spock to continue the process of their maturation into civilized beings*

But—

To many STAR TREK fans, particularly those who care especially about the starship *Enterprise, Star Trek III: The Search for Spock* feels like a major betrayal. The *Enterprise* has been sacrificed. Even though it is Kirk who makes the decision on the screen, the fans know that it was Harve Bennett who made the decision at the typewriter. To those fans, it looks as if Gene Roddenberry's STAR TREK is being dismantled—and it disturbs them.

Nearly a year before the film was released to the theatres, the rumors about the impending demise of the starship were already circulating. A pirated copy of Harve Bennett's first-draft outline showed up at several science fiction conventions.

And yes—STAR TREK's fans reacted with upset and anger.

Once again, they wrote letters, they phoned the studio (unfortunately, some of the calls were inordinately rude—as a result, STAR TREK-fans are not well thought of by many of the receptionists who work on Paramount's lot), and some fans even threatened to picket the main gate of Paramount Pictures.

One long-time STAR TREK fan summed it up this way, "The *Enterprise* is the soul of STAR TREK. STAR TREK could go on without Kirk or Spock or McCoy, if it had to—but where can you go without the *Enterprise*?"

Bjo Trimble, who has maintained close ties to the show agrees. "When we were handling the fan mail for STAR TREK, we only kept a count on the actors the fans wrote to. If we had also been able to count the letters that were about the *Enterprise* itself, the starship would have had the highest fan-mail count of all."

There are many fans who feel that the destruction of the *Enterprise* is more upsetting than the death of Spock. This one is permanent. To those fans, *Star Trek III* is not just the end of an era in STAR TREK—it is the end of STAR TREK.

Harve Bennett was well aware of the potential for upset among TREK-fans long before the picture was released. He sees *Star Trek III* as a bold step foward, an opportunity to set up a grand new format for the series. When speaking at conventions, he would quietly tell the fans, "Give us a chance. First see the movie before you make up your mind." On another occasion,

---

*Yes, I know what I said. I didn't think too much of Yoda's brand of enlightenment either. . . .

he said, "The only way to keep STAR TREK revitalized is through change and growth. Curiously, through the STAR TREK world appears in disarray because of this film, the opposite is intended. Spock is back and the only thing now missing from the matrix is a ship (and exoneration). That is an easily solvable dilemma. . . . I am sure you can guess the directions for *Star Trek IV*."

Looked at in that light, *Star Trek III* is clearly the middle picture in a trilogy.

The directions for *Star Trek IV*?

One current theory suggests that Kirk will end up in command of that new ship we saw in *Star Trek III*: the *Excelsior*. It's certainly a proud and beautiful vessel.

But, somehow—

—it just doesn't feel right.

"These are the voyages of the starship *Excelsior*. . . ?"

Perhaps the only way to mitigate the loss of the *Enterprise* is for *Star Trek IV* to be about the construction of a brand new *Enterprise*.

The name has too proud a history—both in the United States' Navy and in Starfleet's—for it to be this easily discarded.

Not by Starfleet—and certainly not by Paramount.

SUMMATION

PERHAPS the most-asked question of all is, "Why is STAR TREK so popular?" The very best answer I've ever heard is, "Because people like it a lot."

During the darkest days of the sixties and seventies, it was clear that STAR TREK was an optimistic look into the future. It was perhaps one of the only acceptable ways to be optimistic then. In the summer of 1969, for example, we went from Woodstock to Altamont, from the first lunar landing to the Manson murders, from peaceful love-ins to gay liberation riots in Greenwich Village, from demonstrations against the Vietnam war to mass arrests in front of the White House. It was the old Chinese curse come to full fruition: we were living in interesting times.

In those days, it was easy to explain STAR TREK: "STAR TREK says that there will be a future, and that we can and will solve our problems and learn how to live in peace." It was such a clear opposite to what confronted us every morning on the front page of the newspaper, its appeal was undeniable.

But if that's all that STAR TREK was—a voice of hope in the darkness—then it should have faded away by the end of the seventies. Instead, its popularity only continued to grow; so, obviously, STAR TREK's appeal had to be based on something more profound than being merely an attractive form of escape.

I have to qualify this as a personal observation: it seems to me that STAR TREK's appeal is unique. There is something there that is larger than just the actors or their characters, the stories or the special effects, or even the starship *Enterprise* itself. All of these elements are important, of course, but I see them not as the source of STAR TREK's appeal, but as the expression of it.

I think the appeal lies not in the physical production of STAR TREK, but in its underlying concept: ". . . to explore strange new worlds, to seek out

203

new life and new civilization, to boldly go where no man has gone before.''

The mission of the *Enterprise* is neither military nor commercial. It is exploratory. The *Enterprise* is being sent to the top of the mountain to look and see what's on the other side. If necessary, the *Enterprise* will go to the edge of the galaxy—and beyond.

Star Trek is about challenging ourselves. It is about finding our limits by being willing to go beyond them. It is about knowledge being more important than survival. And finally, it is about the ultimate nobility of the human spirit.

Star Trek is a *noble vision* of humanity in the process of achieving maturity—both as individuals and as a species.

Gene Roddenberry always intended Star Trek to be more than just another TV series.

As I've said elsewhere in this book, the series had more failures than successes—but its successes were magnificent. The real success is not simply that Star Trek continues year after year after year; that's merely the measurement. Gene Roddenberry's true achievement was in the creation and expression of an idea that speaks to the inner spirit of its viewers. It is a vision of ourselves being the best we can be.

On that very personal, very profound level, Star Trek does more than merely create excitement and enthusiasm—it inspires. It leads individuals to pursue larger goals and discover possibilities in themselves that they might not otherwise have realized.*

It represents a future we would like to make real.

I offer this thought:

Whoever has the responsibility of creating Star Trek in the future will find that it is more than just a job, more than just a movie or a TV series. He or she will have been given custody of a living cultural artifact—and the job will be not merely to produce a movie that makes money; the job will also be to produce this year's celebration of the Star Trek vision.

That will be the most important—and the hardest—part of the job.

---

*There's the young lady who used to write her own Star Trek stories for amusement who has now become a very polished and professional novelist; the young fellow who got into computing because he wanted to play Star Trek games; the young woman who pursued her interest in makeup and costuming into a successful acting career; the housewife who discovered her ability to organize large conventions and make them work; the little old lady who discovered a whole new circle of friends through Star Trek fandom; the myriad clubs and organizations who've sponsored blood drives and used their conventions as a way to raise money for local charities— the list is endless. Star Trek is not just about what we do in space, it's also about how we as individuals live our lives on Earth.

As we get farther and farther from the source of it all, the original TV series, we can see that STAR TREK is already beginning to evolve. Some of its evolutions—particularly the growth of its characters—are very very right.

Some of its evolutions may not be.

There have been STAR TREK novels, STAR TREK records, STAR TREK comic books, STAR TREK story collections, *ad infinitum*. Many of the stories told in these forms could not have passed the Dorothy Fontana/Gene L. Coon/Gene Roddenberry test—that is, they wouldn't have been purchased as episodes of the TV series.

Early on, some very hard rules were established: the men and women of the *Enterprise* represent the best talent available to Starfleet. You won't find drug users or mutineers or traitors in this crew, for instance; stories based on those notions were quickly rejected. Nor could the science get *too* fantastic—we want to stay grounded in what is known to be possible, not to leave the mass audience behind. (This guideline wasn't always followed, but it was there.)

Paramount Pictures will probably produce STAR TREK movies as long as there is an audience willing to go see them. As long as STAR TREK movies remain true to the original vision—that we as human beings can be better than we are today—there *will* be an audience, and that audience will be well served.*

So far, the *real* STAR TREK—the one that we see on the screen—has remained true to the original vision of the series. Some of the details may not always match; some of the incidents told may seem disruptive—Spock's death, the destruction of the *Enterprise*, for example—but the essential vision of the STAR TREK movies is still the one that Gene Roddenberry created so many years ago.

The final frontier is not space.

The final frontier is the human soul.

Space is merely the arena in which we shall meet the challenge.

---

*And you'll find me right there at the front of the line.

AUTHOR'S NOTES

I find myself in the position of being STAR TREK'S unofficial (and self-appointed) historian, but I make no claims that this is an unbiased account. It cannot be. I have been too close to the series, it has been too much a part of my own life for me to even pretend at objectivity.

In updating the original material of this book, my primary task was to correct errors and edit out those sections that were no longer relevant. In adding the new material, I felt my task was to create a perspective for the appreciation of STAR TREK as a cultural phenomenon.

I have assumed that most of those who will read this book will be STAR TREK fans familiar with most of the episodes and all three of the movies. I have assumed also that we share a common affection for the series—and have written from that perspective.

At the same time, I've also tried to bring a critical awareness to this work too.

The first edition of this book was used as a source by many of those who worked on "STAR TREK Animated," *Star Trek I* and *Star Trek II*. It is possible that this edition may be of some use to those who work on STAR TREK films in the future, and I have had to keep that thought in mind as well.

Finally, I consider most of the cast and crew of the STAR TREK family to be my friends; I freely acknowledge that it is almost impossible for me to be too critical of people I care about this much. I root for them to succeed every time out—and my attention is focused on their successes more than their failures. (Anyone wanting a critical lambasting of STAR TREK will have to look elsewhere. This is an affectionate book.)

At the beginning of this edition is a long list of people who helped make

207

this book possible, but I want to take an extra couple of pages here to specif-ically thank several people who were especially important to this revised edi-tion of the book.

First, Bjo Trimble—the Queen Mother of STAR TREK fandom—once again provided me with access to all sorts of fascinating information. Bjo is the author of the *STAR TREK Concordance,* the most accurate sourcebook of STAR TREK material ever compiled. All of the references made in this book have been checked against the *Concordance.* (If there are errors, they are mine, not Bjo's.) At the time of this writing, the *Concordance* is out of print, but there are plans to make it available to STAR TREK fans once again. Fans who are interested should send a self-addressed stamped envelope to *Con-cordance,* c/o Trimble, Box 36851, Los Angeles, CA 90036.

I also want to thank Rita Ratcliffe for service above and beyond the call of duty in helping to locate hard to find film clips for the photo section of this book.

Very special thanks, of course, to Howard Zimmerman, David McDonnell, and Kerry O'Quinn, of *Starlog* magazine. You will notice that the byline on this edition says: "Written by David Gerrold, in association with *Starlog* magazine." I could not think of a better way to acknowledge the contribu-tions of the people at O'Quinn studios.

Because of the very short production schedule of this book, it was obvi-ous that I would not be able to conduct the kind of interviews I wanted to. Fortunately, most of the information that I needed had already been gathered and published in the pages of *Starlog*—especially interviews with the cast and crew of all three pictures. Kerry O'Quinn kindly gave me permission to use these interviews as source material. The details provided made it possi-ble to write a much more comprehensive account of the productions of *Star Trek I* and *II.* In fact, there was such a wealth of material available, there was too much to use in this book.

I strongly recommend to anyone who wants to stay up-to-date with STAR TREK that he or she read *Starlog* regularly. (If you can't find it easily in your area, you can subscribe by sending $27.49 for a one-year subscription to STARLOG, DEPT G, 475 Park Avenue South, New York, NY 10016.) The magazine is also a terrific source for information about *Star Wars, Superman,* and other science fiction movies and TV series.

Next, I want to thank Harve Bennett and Leonard Nimoy, who kindly in-vited me to the first screening of the rough cut of *Star Trek III* so I could include a discussion of that film in this book. It was an extraordinarily kind gesture and one that was much appreciated.

I also want to thank Harve Bennett for his continual friendship and availability not just to me, but to all of STAR TREK'S fans—through his appearances at conventions, his willingness to be interviewed, and most of all, his candor.

Finally—and *most* importantly—I want to thank Gene Roddenberry once again, for creating it all in the first place.

Thanks, Gene.

—DAVID GERROLD

ABOUT THE AUTHOR:

David Gerrold began his science fiction career in 1967, as a writer for the original STAR TREK TV series. His first sale was the episode, "The Trouble with Tribbles," one of the most popular episodes in the show's history. Gerrold later wrote two nonfiction books about STAR TREK: *The World of Star Trek*, the first indepth analysis of the show, and *The Trouble With Tribbles*, in which he shared his personal experiences with the series. Gerrold has also written episodes for the STAR TREK animated series ("More Tribbles, More Troubles", "Bem") as well as a STAR TREK novel, *The Galactic Whirlpool*. Gerrold's other TV credits include episodes of "Land of the Lost" and "Logan's Run." He has served as story editor on "Land of the Lost" and "Buck Rogers."

Gerrold is also a well-established science fiction novelist. His best known works are *When Harlie Was One* and *The Man Who Folded Himself*, both of which were nominated for the Hugo and Nebula awards. Gerrold has been nominated for the Hugo three times and the Nebula four. He's published eleven novels, five anthologies, and a short story collection. In 1979, he won the Skylark Award for excellence in imaginative fiction.

David Gerrold is thirty-nine years old and lives in Los Angeles with three peculiar dogs, two and a half cats, a computer with delusions of independence, and a butterscotch convertible. He is a skilled programmer and occasionally contributes to various personal computing magazines. Gerrold also writes a monthly column on science fiction for *Starlog* magazine. Occasionally, he teaches an eight-week workshop course for writers called "Authorship."

Gerrold is currently working on an epic science fiction mega-novel: *The War Against the Chtorr*. The first and second volumes of the series, *A Matter for Men* and *A Day For Damnation*, have already been published by Pocket Books. Book Three, *A Rage For Revenge* is scheduled for early 1985. At the time of this publication, Gerrold is hard at work on Book Four: *A Season for Slaughter*. It will be his twenty-first book.